NIK AND EM,

HOPE you Love -

Love From,

Ric + Denise
xx
x

C000199223

CODES OF MISCONDUCT

CODES OF MISCONDUCT

Adrian Hadley

MILO BOOKS

Milo Books

First published in November 2001 by Milo Books

ISBN 1 903854-07-5

Typeset by Avon DataSet Ltd, Bidford-on-Avon, Warks
www.avondataset.com

Printed and bound in Great Britain by
Creative Print and Design, Ebbw Vale, Gwent

MILO BOOKS
P.O.Box 153
Bury
BL0 9FX
info@milobooks.com

Acknowledgements

The biggest thank you goes to Geoff Green, rugby correspondent of the *Manchester Evening News*, for helping me to get my recollections and opinions down on paper. Geoff may not always have agreed with the opinions expressed but was scrupulously impartial in helping me record them. I would also like to offer my appreciation to Rob Cole, Alan Evans, Widnes RL director Tom Fleet, Raymond Fletcher, John Kennedy of the Westgate news agency in Cardiff and Darrell Platt of Salford for their invaluable assistance. Finally, thanks to my old mate and playing partner Terry Holmes for kindly writing the Foreword.

Contents

Foreword by Terry Holmes   ix

Prologue   xi

CHAPTER ONE   St David's Boy   1

CHAPTER TWO   Black and Blue   17

CHAPTER THREE   Day of the Dragon   31

CHAPTER FOUR   Enhanced Performance   47

CHAPTER FIVE   South Seas Adventure   58

CHAPTER SIX   Wales Take on the World   68

CHAPTER SEVEN   Hello Corrie Street   85

CHAPTER EIGHT   Widnes Woes   114

CHAPTER NINE   Back in the Union   129

CHAPTER TEN   Vote of No Confidence   154

CHAPTER ELEVEN   Double Glazing Salesmen   189

Epilogue   218

Appendix   232

Foreword

by Terry Holmes

LIKE all truly great international players, Adrian Hadley made the game look easy. He always seemed to be in control and had that priceless quality, when in possession, of appearing to have both time and the ability to find another gear in pace if needed.

Adrian and another great friend of ours, Gerald Cordle, were the final pieces in the jigsaw of a Cardiff team that dominated Welsh rugby in the 1980s. Both were large, physical wingers who knew where the try line was.

There was no doubt in my mind that Adrian would go on to represent Wales. And he was comfortable at that level, whether scoring tries against England at Twickenham or a hat-trick of tries against Newport in the 1986 Schweppes Cup Final to win the Lloyd Memorial Trophy as Man of the Match.

Our careers followed similar paths. We are both Cardiff-born Catholics who went on to represent our home city and our country. We then went north and finally into coaching and were good friends off the pitch too as, indeed, all the players in that Cardiff side in the Eighties were. Adie and I also enjoyed the occasional pint (those good old amateur days!).

There was, however, a marked difference in our attitude to training. I thought it was a vital part of the week's build-up to the game on Saturday. Adolf, as Adie was known, thought it was an exercise in qualifying for his expenses.

I remember, in his later years, watching him playing in the second row for Widnes in rugby league. That convinced me that there was no better sight during my career than Adrian Hadley in full flight in wide open spaces on the flank on his way to scoring effortlessly, with a natural swerve, hand-off or change of pace that left opponents for dead.

Adrian is a man I will always respect as a player and a friend. I think it's fair to say that rugby was good to Adrian Hadley and he, in turn, was very good for the game of rugby.

Terry Holmes
(ex-Cardiff, Wales and British Lions).

Prologue

THERE was a joke doing the rounds recently about an Australian, a South African and an Englishman having a beer together in a London pub.

The South African called for another round of drinks, drained his glass, tossed it into the air, pulled out a gun and shot it to pieces. "In South Africa glasses are so cheap that we don't need to drink from the same glass twice," he said.

The Aussie immediately drained his own glass, tossed that into the air, pulled out a gun and shot it to pieces too, saying, "In Australia we have so much sand for making glasses that we don't have to drink from the same one twice either."

On seeing that, the deadpan Englishman drained his glass, also tossed it into the air, pulled out a gun and ... shot dead his two drinking companions, saying, "In England we have so many fucking South Africans and Australians that we don't have to drink with the same ones twice."

Work a New Zealander into the joke (not easy with their sense of humour) and, from a rugby perspective, you discover that many a true word really has been spoken in jest. Rather like the wartime joke about the Yanks, one could say that too many Australian, South African and New Zealand players and coaches have been overpaid, overrated and, worse still, over here since our good old amateur game went open.

I've got nothing against the professionalization of a once amateur sport of almost Corinthian proportions. Nor am I opposed to a degree of cross border activity but I believe we allowed the wool to be pulled over our eyes and placed too much reliance on overseas players during the early days of professionalism. In truth I get pretty brassed off with the way those responsible for the game in these islands have squandered millions of pounds on pensions for our Commonwealth cousins who, with just a few exceptions, have done little to enhance our game. And that, often, at the expense of homespun talent that has had limited chances to shine because owners were keen to get their pound of flesh out of expensive imports.

I feel sorry for the directors of rugby, such as myself when I was at Sale Sharks, who have been forced to buy these players to keep their club in the Premiership and also to hang on to their own jobs.

There is no better time than the present to look at what we have been doing wrong because we are able to do so in the wake of a disappointing British Lions tour to Australia when somebody seemed to push the self-destruct button. The bricks were being hurled out of the pram long before the tour started to fall apart and it was no surprise that Austin Healey and Matt Dawson, talkative little souls who always have plenty to say for themselves, were in the front line of brick throwers. What that pair did was pretty unforgivable because, whatever your private thoughts, you keep things in-house during a tour and reserve your poisoned arrows for later. It reminded me of a similar attack on Sale Sharks by Phil Greening, whose tongue, from my experience, never seemed to be even remotely synchronised with his brain.

Whilst not criticising Graham Henry's abilities as a coach, I find it interesting that the British Lions suffered their first-ever series defeat in Australia when we either overlooked or, because the

Prologue

structure is so hopelessly wrong, couldn't find homespun candidates and gave the all-important coaching job to a New Zealander. That he was ever asked to coach Wales is an indictment of my country's administrators, who seem incapable of encouraging or developing their own top coaches and then compounded the felony by agreeing to provide Henry with a fellow Kiwi as his assistant, much to the angst of the New Zealand authorities. If we believe that Kiwis know best and want to copy them then we should perhaps ask whether or not they would be likely to appoint an Englishman, Welshman, Irishman or Scot as coach to the All Blacks. Not on your Nellie.

Our answer to every rugby problem seems to be to send for a Kiwi, an Aussie or a Springbok. Yet, after several years of professional rugby you can probably count on the fingers of one hand those who have actually taken our game forward. In the vast majority of cases the incumbents have been international hasbeens looking for a pension, or simply players who were never going to make it big in their own countries and couldn't believe it when British mugs came calling. Not that I blame the players and coaches who have spent a few years here and then benefited hugely from generous exchange rates. But I blame those who have wasted their money on bringing them over here when the cash could have been better spent nurturing our own young players and converting our older players into future coaches.

All the evidence of the 2001 British Lions tour seems to be that, at the end of a punishing domestic season, the players were put through the proverbial mincer in training. Having worked with New Zealand coaches, that doesn't surprise me one bit because pain and suffering is all part of their culture but that approach doesn't work long over here. Or at least not at the end of a fixture-packed season that would have had even the toughest All Black moaning about his workload. One day somebody will realise that our culture is different and what works with players of one nationality doesn't necessarily work with those of another.

International rugby would be pretty boring if every country played in exactly the same style. Even so, we have developed the habit in the northern hemisphere of trying to slavishly follow the example of New Zealand, in particular, even though they have had little to shout about recently: they haven't managed to win a World Cup for 14 years. In any case, by the time we have taken on board their lessons in the past, the Kiwis have invariably moved on a stage or two by the time we arrive at where they had been. We seem to have little faith in developing our own peculiar strengths. It is only because the French suddenly played like we know the arrogant bastards can that they put a stop to a near certain all-southern hemisphere final at the last World Cup. The All Blacks didn't know what had hit them when the French suddenly seemed to say "sod it" and began playing with a real touch of *joie de vivre*.

When the Lions last triumphed in New Zealand back in 1971, the match-winning genius was Welsh legend Barry John. Now, he would have loved the head banging, let's crash into each other sort of training that is so popular today ... I don't think. I don't know how he would have coped with today's fitter opponents and more disciplined defences but I am sure he would have conjured up something.

Jason Robinson, in his short time in rugby union, has already demonstrated that, no matter how fit and organised you may be defensively, it is impossible to plan for fast-footed wizardry if the wizard is playing with people who can give him just the half a metre he needs to launch himself onto the offensive.

Our reliance on the southern hemisphere has been created in part by home unions looking for a quick fix. Henry was a god in Wales while the inevitable honeymoon lasted but England demonstrated in Cardiff early in 2001 just how far behind we still are in the Principality. Further reliance on what is produced south of the equator is down to men with big egos who rushed to buy rugby clubs and then imported big names from overseas in the belief they would provide them with major trophies and bring star struck fans surging through the turnstiles. In the majority of cases neither has happened.

Because the rugby authorities over here failed abysmally to get to grips with professionalism, it was left to wealthy enthusiasts to make possible what we have today, in England at least. But being an enthusiast and having played the game at a relatively junior level doesn't qualify businessmen to make decisions on the type of player to sign or on team tactics. Yet that has happened and interfering owners can make life very difficult for directors of rugby and coaches who do understand the game at the highest level having, in most cases, played there.

Most owners don't understand the game as well as they pretend and fall into the trap of throwing money at players from overseas in the belief, often mistaken, that they are better than those at home. A question I will address later in this book is just how many of the never-ending procession of overseas players have actually taken the game forward.

The other aspect of the game that concerns me at present is the frenzy to recruit players from rugby league. After shunning the other code – one that I actually enjoyed playing more than the code I started and finished in – and treating both that sport and its players as though they had just crawled out of some rather stale cheese, those running rugby union suddenly decided that players from league were the best thing since sliced bread. Better even than a pensionable Kiwi, come to that.

England started the ball rolling when they came up with the idea of "buying" rugby league players. Jason Robinson was meant to be the first in a series of signings to go straight into the national squad. That initiative was so badly handled that it led to a revolt by the rest of the Premiership clubs when they discovered that Jason would play at Sale with the Rugby Football Union paying half his salary. There was such a fuss that Sale's owner, Brian Kennedy, had to foot the entire bill himself or lose out on the one talent from RL guaranteed to succeed in the other code.

Few could make the switch as easily as Jason, because he is an exceptional talent, but the mere fact that somebody had played the predominantly northern game was suddenly enough to qualify him for a nice, fat, juicy contract to play union. The growing band of agents, something unheard of in the union world until a few years ago, must have thought it was Christmas. Even junior clubs have been rushing out to buy players from rugby league although, of course, some of those in the industrial areas of Lancashire and Yorkshire have happily been playing RL professionals for years.

The latest trend, and one established by England, is to take on board former RL players as defensive coaches. There is hardly a Zurich Premiership club today that doesn't have at least one on the coaching staff. With my intimate knowledge of both codes that is something else I will talk about later.

Union has, quite simply, gone way over the top in its love affair with players from the southern hemisphere and from the other code. I hope the trend changes and that we will produce a structure that enables countries to rely on homegrown talent. Building a side is far more satisfying than buying one in but the desire for success is so great at club level that directors of rugby, like myself, were placed under far too much pressure to produce instant results. The fear of relegation was also too great and led to quick fix solutions (invariably from overseas) rather than being able to adopt a long-term strategy.

I was shown the door at Sale shortly before the end of the 2000/01 season, a victim of that hunger for success and power politics that has become commonplace behind the scenes at top clubs these days. It was not the most glorious end to what had been a long and entertaining career but, in some ways, it was almost a relief. With so many inexperienced and self-seeking people trying to run the show, my job as director of rugby had become a nightmare.

What I did miss, however, was the "craic" with the players, coaches and backroom boys such as Alan Blease and Robbie Dixon at Sale, unsung heroes who made sure everything ran smoothly for the players on match days. Alan and Robbie did it for love, not money, which was rather refreshing in an era where greed rules the day and too many people either want their inflated egos massaged or their bottoms wiped.

With nowhere to go at the crack of dawn each day I decided the time had come to record my career and experiences for the sake of posterity. I played for Wales in both rugby codes, was a record rugby league signing when I crossed the great divide, played in World Cups in each code, scored my share of tries – some more memorable than others – and kicked a few goals too. It would be easy just to relate the good bits but that's not my style. I decided that, if my story was to be told, then it would have to be told warts and all, even it if put myself, as well as others, in a bad light occasionally.

Let me be the first to hold my hands up and say that I enjoyed my playing career as a totally unforgettable experience and, for my sins, also participated fully in the peripheral world of booze and birds that has always gone hand in hand with top class rugby. It is a "laddish" lifestyle that can wreck marriages, including my own, but professional players often find themselves bursting with testosterone and with time on their hands. To some extent the game also had its own drugs culture and I suppose rugby is no different from any other sport in that respect. You will always find players prepared to take a risk if they think they won't be caught. On one occasion I made a "performance enhanced" appearance for Wales and some fellow internationals, to my knowledge, used them on a regular basis before testing became the norm. I hadn't known what I was taking but that's no excuse. I should have made sure.

I know of players who bulked up using steroids and, also against the ethics of the game, others who, like myself, discovered just how easy it is to make money out of the sale of international tickets. The authorities try to clamp down on that practice but flogging tickets is the only way some junior clubs have been able to survive in recent years and there is an insatiable corporate hospitality market out there. I was one of many helping to feed it.

So, this story of my playing career isn't going to be just a tale of matches played, won and lost. It will, instead, provide an insight to what really goes on in both codes of top class rugby. Of course, those who have played alongside me, toured with me and socialized with me may not want to read on in case skeletons come tumbling out of cupboards. So far as my cupboard is concerned, I have laid it bare anyway. So, for a tour of my own codes of misconduct, read on.

CHAPTER ONE

St David's Boy

AS I WAS destined to be born in the capital of Wales, I couldn't have picked a more propitious date to arrive than St David's Day: March 1, 1963. I don't know whether or not my mother deliberately tried to hang on with one eye on both the calendar and the clock but I suppose I, more than most, can claim to be a true son of Wales.

My parents, Ernest and Margaret, had three boys, with me providing the meat in the sandwich. Anthony preceded me by two years. John followed two years in my wake and, even though we all ended up playing rugby at a reasonably high level, I don't recall that we lived in each others pockets as we were growing up, even though there wasn't a massive difference in our ages. Attempting to look back to my early days it came as something of a shock to discover that not only do I not have total recall but actually had great difficulty remembering anything at all. Thank you mum for providing some of the pieces to the jigsaw!

I suppose I was a little closer to Anthony in childhood because there is a tendency to gravitate towards an elder sibling, even if you don't use them as a role model, and many of my friends were in his year at school. I even went out with a girl in his class at secondary school, so could claim to have been one of life's early

1

toyboys. The three of us tended to develop our own group of friends rather than rely on each other for companionship. I certainly fought more with John but that was probably because we shared a bedroom and having your own space is just as important when you are growing up as it is when you become an adult.

On one occasion I tied John's arms behind his back, I think we were playing cowboys and Indians, and he lost his balance and – I swear I never touched him – fell off the bed, breaking his collarbone in the process. I admit I enjoyed winding John up over the fact that he was born in England. When he arrived on the scene we were living in Caldicot, near Chepstow, which was part of England before the borders changed. Of the three of us, John probably had more of a temper and I was the one regarded as being very laid back. I suppose I still am and rarely lose my temper yet, when I do, it is usually big style. We used to go to St Joseph's Boxing Club, run by an appropriately named Tony Cosh, and one of the other lads upset me so much, I can't remember why, that I ended up holding his head in my hands and repeatedly smacking it against the wall. Hardly Queensberry Rules.

Apart from the occasional sibling scrap, the only time I seriously tried to hurt Anthony was when he was baby sitting for us one evening when mum and dad had gone out. He was in the lounge with his girlfriend and I was annoyed with him for some reason and wouldn't let him out into the hall. Every time he tried to leave the room I kept him pinned back by hurling darts at him from the top of the stairs. The barrage continued until I ran out of darts but a barrage of another kind started when dad got home and saw holes all over the doorframe.

Of the boys I was the animal lover, although I didn't have much success with them. I had a tortoise but I put it on to the roof of the shed only to discover that tortoises can't fly. The poor thing walked to the edge and fell off, cracking its shell and dying. Budgies, however, can fly. But they have weak hearts. I cocked

Anthony's air-rifle – there were no pellets in it – pointed it at the birdcage and pulled the trigger. The gun produced a big bang, even thought there was no pellet in the chamber, and the poor bird simply fell off its perch and died of a heart attack.

We also had guinea pigs that were dying and I was so concerned that I found a pipette and filled it with some of my dad's whisky and started administering it to them in the belief that it would revive them. I'm afraid it didn't but at least they died with a smile on their faces.

At the time we lived in a large, end-terrace Victorian house in Wellfield Place, in the Roath Park area of Cardiff. It was an ideal place in which to grow up because there was a park opposite and Thayers Ice Cream Parlour just across the road. The Globe cinema, at the end of the street, was another childhood haunt, although I was outdoors all the time. I watched my first "18" certificate film there, called *Come Play With Me*, but later watched the old place knocked down, only to be replaced by the Billabong Bar – those fucking Aussies get everywhere!

Family holidays tended to be taken in Tenby or Saundersfoot, and it was apparent even then that I didn't like to lose at anything. Nothing has changed over the years and whether playing against Anthony and John at some boyhood game or turning out against England at Twickenham, there was only one outcome that I would find acceptable. I simply had to win at everything and that led to some interesting battles on holiday because neither Anthony nor John much cared for losing either.

It was during my childhood that I developed an aversion to London that has stayed with me over the years. I find the place just too big, too dirty and too busy. Our enlarged family decided on a pre-Christmas visit there and I succeeded in getting myself lost. I have never liked the English capital since, apart from Twickenham, which was to prove such a happy hunting ground for me in later years. There were quite a few of us on the trip including my parents, brothers, aunts and cousins and we were wandering along Oxford Street when I spotted a policeman booking a motorist. As a youngster I fancied being a policeman and was so keen to witness the outcome that I didn't notice that everyone had crossed the road when the traffic lights changed and the next thing I knew I was on my own. I started crying and the policeman finished booking the motorist and took me off to the police station – a situation that was to be repeated in later life but for a very different reason. I was eventually reunited with my family when my anxious parents reported me missing to the constabulary.

We are Roman Catholics and in our district of Cardiff there were two parishes, St Peter's and St Joseph's. Rivalry between the two primary schools was pretty intense but, although we lived in St Peter's Parish, my mother's family had always been associated with St Joe's. Mum, who ended up as a teacher following a tough start to her working life, managed to wangle things so that I could attend St Joe's even though I had to walk about half a mile to the bus stop and then faced what at the time seemed to be a lengthy bus ride. Fortunately, Mark McLean, who became one of my best mates, lived close by and also went to St Joe's so I had someone to travel with. Mark had three pretty sisters and the eldest two, Denise and Carol, helped stir my first interest in the opposite sex. I used to join my mates at Lady Mary High School in watching them through the window as they had gym lessons. Later, the first Cardiff rugby game I ever watched, when I was about eleven, was with Mark, his dad and his brother Alan. His dad and uncle are members at Cardiff and have been for years so there were regular reunions when I went on to play for the club and for Wales.

My abiding memory of junior school, when I started going there with Mark, was the nuns who taught us. To us they were funny women in black clothes who had men's names, such as Sister Cyril, who was the headmistress. I was sent to her office one day for the cane, having done something I shouldn't, although

I can't remember what it was. She closed the door behind us, got out the cane and just slapped a chair with it. She smiled and said, "Now just disappear and don't say anything."

My favourite was Sister Anthony who was the prettiest but she ended up leaving the sisterhood and getting married.

Dad, who was christened Ernest but was known to all and sundry as "Roy", worked as an engineer with British Steel, mainly on the railroads, and was brought up in the tough Tiger Bay area of Cardiff, where he went to school with the singer Shirley Bassey. Mum, meanwhile, had been forced to leave school early because her father had been ill and somebody in the household needed to earn a living to bring in some money. An intelligent woman, she took a job as a waitress in Cardiff but, as soon as we three boys started to grow up, she went to night school to study for her A levels. It was a proud day when, having attended South Glamorgan Institute as a mature student, she graduated and went back to school teaching English and History.

Not that I was terribly aware of what was going on around me at home. My early life revolved around sport and home was just a place I returned to occasionally to eat and sleep. From an early age sport started to play a major part in my life and became the great excuse for getting out of the house and, when I was at secondary school, homework. Mum says that basically I was the most intelligent of her three sons but that never manifested itself because study didn't figure prominently in my list of priorities at that time. I can remember playing baseball for St Peter's the evening before sitting my O level Maths and English examinations instead of revising. Anthony, who played with Harlequins boss Mark Evans at St Peter's Rugby Club, had his playing career cut short by injury, but went on to become a remedial gymnast and is now doing well on the administrative side of the health service in Norwich. John, meanwhile, followed in my footsteps by playing for Cardiff but now plays his rugby for my first club, St Joseph's.

Surprisingly, I didn't have any ambition to become a top

sportsman and I was well into my teens before I started taking rugby even remotely seriously. If I had any sporting ambition at all it was to become a jockey but, unfortunately so far as that career path was concerned, I grew too much. When we lived near Chepstow I became very interested in horse racing and used to ride occasionally. At the age of eleven I used to stand outside betting shops asking punters to stick bets on for me because I wasn't old enough.

Even when I began playing for Cardiff as a teenager it didn't even cross my mind that I might one day play for Wales. Some boys grow up with a burning ambition to play for their country or for a particular team but it was something that never occurred to me. So playing for Wales wasn't my dream and, anyway, my favourite sport in those days was soccer. I used to watch Cardiff City whenever I could. I also played soccer as a bit of a bustling forward but, again, there was no ambition to emulate my heroes in the way youngsters dream today of following David Beckham into the Manchester United side.

At primary school I probably excelled more at athletics than anything else. I represented St Joseph's in all the city under-12 competitions and, by the time I was in my final year, I was the Catholic Schools Athletic Sprint Champion. The school was very successful that year in all sports and I captained the school rugby team to success in both cup and league competitions. Even earlier than that I had played in the Cardiff Sevens side that ended up as champions of East Wales and made my debut at the National Stadium in an East Wales representative side that played a warm-up game before a Wales v Tonga international — not that the significance of where I was really sank in.

I recall St Joseph's sharing the Cardiff Schools under-11s league with St Cadoc's School. At the prize presentation a photograph was taken of myself and the captain of the other team holding the shield between us. Once the picture had been taken, neither of us wanted to relinquish our hold on the shield and we pulled and tugged until the thing broke in half. I suppose that was one way of resolving the dilemma!

A big influence at St Joseph's was our rugby coach Peter Sullivan. He devoted a lot of his own time to developing the rugby, athletics and baseball teams at the school and was a great guy, although I hope he has now got rid of the old black car he used to drive around in. It was so old that the direction indicators were the type that appeared like arms from the side of the car.

The sporting adventure picked up speed when I moved to Lady Mary High School. It was there that I teamed up with Mark Ring, who was in the same year. I'd first come across him when he played rugby for St Alban's Primary School and we appeared together in the Cardiff Under-11s side. Mark used to run the game with his non-stop chatter to the referee even in those early days. I could see that he was a very good player and it is interesting that we both ended up in the Welsh squad at the first ever World Cup in 1987. At Lady Mary he had a spell as rugby captain and I followed on when he left to work for the Department of Trade at Companies House in Cardiff.

After Ringo (Mark Ring) had left I followed a family tradition by helping out when the school staged plays. I was no thespian but my brother Anthony had helped the teacher with the lighting during his time at the school. He did the job with a lad called Andrew Morris and I took over the same role with Andy's brother Paul. We used to have a big lighting deck backstage and produced light in a variety of colours on stage as and when required.

There was an ulterior motive for our generosity in giving up our evenings to man the lighting deck. A perk of the job was being given cans of lager to drink during plays and musicals that would be interspersed by the sound of cans being opened in the wings. It was back stage that I noted how Ringo had been fairly prophetic, not to say supremely confident. He had scrawled the following message on the wall: "Mark Ring will be the next Wales fly-half."

We had a very good rugby side at school but then the Catholic teams were the best in the Cardiff area at the time. Unfortunately, it was obvious that our great success got under the noses of one or two influential people because our players didn't always get the recognition they deserved. I remember a cup final at Blackweir against St. Illtyd's . . . where the old bias almost certainly played its part. We had already won the league and the sevens so were going for the treble. At the end of normal time we were leading but the referee played 16 minutes of extra time until the opposition got the winning score. By the time he blew the final whistle it was dark and both players and parents were going berserk. The guy had obviously got it into his head that Lady Mary weren't going to win. We were only 13 at the time but still had to stop one of our second rows going up and punching him. I used to get frustrated when I was on a losing side and remember going up to the ref and calling him a "wanker". I know that sort of thing is frowned upon, especially when you are the age I was at the time, but I still get very frustrated when officials affect the outcome of a game by bias or simply making a bad decision. A good few years later, when I was playing for Wales, that same referee came up and tried to talk to me but I didn't want to know. Some of the boys had been in tears that night and I still hold a grudge.

The same jealousy problem emerged at district level. A few of us had played for Cardiff Schools, including Mike Budd, a very good back row who went on to play for Wales "A", Martin Daley, a centre who went on to play for Cardiff, and John Taylor, a very underrated scrum-half. Having played all the way through I was also one of those who didn't get picked at under-15 level even though I had played for that side a year early. A new, non-Catholic teacher, whose name escapes me, had taken charge and, suddenly, Catholic boys were being ignored. I think some of the teachers had been pissed off with the success of our schools.

At the same time I was heavily into the athletics and I probably

8

pissed off people at school too because I tended to win just about everything, including the Victor Ludorum every year. Although it wasn't a sport I took any real interest in, I often reached the finals of the tennis competition too but I put that down to being fairly athletic and having a good eye for the ball. Not that it helped me one year because I played in the finals of the singles, doubles with Paul Morris and mixed doubles with Antonella Comatteo, and ended up losing the lot. We might have won the mixed doubles but Antonella had attributes that demanded too much of my attention, if you know what I mean!

On the running track I represented Cardiff at the Welsh Games at Cwmbran, winning gold in the long jump, silver in the 200 metres and bronze in the 100 metres. I had become a member of Cardiff Athletic Club, where I was coached by Walter Thomas, and represented the club at the finals at Crystal Palace, competing in the 100 metres, 200 metres and the relay. The following year I ended up as the Welsh long jump champion and my record stood for a long time. I had also taken up the high hurdles and had the distinction of beating Nigel Walker who, like myself, went on to play rugby for Wales and also represented Great Britain at the 1984 Olympics where he reached the semi-finals. Nigel also went on to win bronze at the 1987 World and European Indoor Championships.

When I beat him we already knew each other because our school rugby sides played against each other. He was a decent player but, unfortunately for him, he was in a team that wasn't very good and all they could do was give Nigel the ball whenever possible in the hope that he would be able to do something with it. He did a lot of damage to some sides but we had too many good players for him to be able to make much of an impression against us. Around that time I started to concentrate more on my rugby and he went down the athletics route instead, only to return later to win caps for Wales. I certainly didn't think it was a big thing when I beat him. We were just kids and I probably had an advantage because I was involved at the athletic club whereas I don't think Nigel was into specified training at that time and just relied on his natural pace.

While still at school I joined St Joseph's Rugby Club. It was a catholic social club but they ran four senior sides and a youth team that could draw on about 30 youngsters, so there was a good deal of chopping and changing. At school I played either at full-back or centre but was then picked on the left wing, because I was the quickest player in the squad, and that's where I was selected for both the Cardiff District side and Welsh Youth. The first tournament I played in for St Joseph's was the Abingdon Sevens at the age of sixteen. Officials didn't really know me at the club but I played so well in the second team at the event that they apologised for not having done their research and I was in the main team from then on. There had been no conscious switch of position on my part, it just came about and, the way things turned out, I've no regrets on that score.

There were some good players at the club but a lot didn't go any further. One who did was Mike Budd and he helped me to a nice record. We played against Aberavon Green Stars and thrashed them 60-0. I ran in six tries and, as I also had pretensions as a goalkicker, I added seven conversions and two penalties for a haul of 44 points. The last try came courtesy of Mike. He knew six would be a record so made a break and then, instead of going on and scoring himself, he waited for me to come up in support and popped me the try-scoring pass.

Those were very happy days and I still hadn't given a thought to playing the game seriously. St Joe's played on corporation pitches in town but, after games, a gang of us who lived in the St Peter's parish would go back there to drink in a little pub called The Tavistock where you could usually find us on Friday, Saturday and Sunday evenings. The pub was about 100 yards from St Peter's rugby club so there was always some friendly rivalry, especially for the local female talent. It was there that I met my wife Ann. My pal Mark McLean was going out with her friend and that's how we came to be introduced.

After a session in The Tavistock we would head back into town to get absolutely blitzed, even though I wasn't legally old enough to drink. One evening I arrived home, went straight upstairs and collapsed on to the bed. That was on the day our youth game had been called off and we were taken to Pyle to play their second fifteen, I got 'man of the match' and had to down a couple of pints of Strongbow. What I had forgotten was that I had been due to take a girlfriend – not Ann – to a party and she was sitting fuming downstairs in the lounge. My gallant brother John came to my rescue and took her instead and I have a feeling she wasn't for me taking her anywhere after that.

Even in my mid-teen years rugby had got me into the drinking culture. You know the sort of thing: drinking a yard of ale or downing a pint for being man of the match. It was fun and we played the game for the love of it. We didn't get paid and the highlight of the week was Saturday night. I stayed in that culture throughout my career with Cardiff, Wales, Salford, Widnes and Sale Sharks. Sometimes I wonder if I would have been a better player if I had treated my body with greater respect, trained harder and watched the booze intake. But, without a shadow of a doubt, I wouldn't have had half as much fun.

Playing for Wales had still never occurred to me because rugby, to me, was just a game to play with my mates. In truth I wasn't interested in rugby, other than enjoying playing the game. I didn't follow any particular team and never went to international matches, even though they were played in the city. I didn't even watch the game on television and still saw soccer as my sport, even though I knew I wasn't good enough to be a professional. At Lady Mary you weren't allowed to play both rugby and soccer and I was pissed off because the teachers wouldn't let me play soccer, even though I trained with the soccer team. They just wanted to make it difficult for me because they preferred me to play rugby. I suppose the beauty of rugby was that I happened to be good at it, I enjoyed playing it and it kept me out of both home and homework. It also helped that we had a very successful side, which couldn't be said about the soccer team, but that never stopped me wanting to play the round ball game.

By that time I had decided to kick athletics into touch because I was just doing too much. Although I was good at athletics, and held the Welsh age level long jump record for many years, I found it difficult training by myself. Truth is I'm not a good trainer and didn't have the discipline for athletics where you have to do a lot of work by yourself. I found it much easier to be involved in the squad activities that are the norm in team games. Plus the fact that my training colleagues at Cardiff Athletic Club had no interest in socializing after training – and I was developing into a very sociable animal.

I had been training two or three times a week with Cardiff Athletic and the other evenings I would be rugby training at St Joseph's. I would rush home from school, grab my kit and dash straight out again and it became obvious, even to me, that I needed to concentrate on just one sport, otherwise all the cards were in danger of collapsing. It was hard on the body because there was a lot of endurance training in athletics during the winter as preparation for the sprints season. I would be doing cross-country runs and hill running and a lot of the time it was freezing cold and pitch black. By the weekend, when I would play rugby for St Joe's, I would be absolutely knackered and you soon lose the enjoyment of a sport when it starts to become tedious.

The straw that broke the camel's back was the knowledge that I was missing out on what my mates were doing on summer evenings – playing football on the local Rec, having a few beers and then going down to the chippy for a Clarke's pie, something of a local delicacy. So you see what my priorities were in those days, although I did get myself involved in another sport, baseball, which is a big and serious pastime in South Wales. A lot of the rugby clubs in the region play the game in the summer months and I started playing for St Peter's Youth. No, I hadn't become a traitor, it's just that baseball at St Joe's was run by the soccer section and it was all a bit political.

Games were played on Saturdays and one evening during the week. It was very competitive and Mark Ring and David Bishop, later to become scrum-half for Wales, both went on to represent Wales at the sport. "Bish" was a bowler and he was very aggressive. Even though you had to bowl underarm it was still delivered at about 100mph if he was involved. When you bat you aren't allowed to move your foot from the peg and, for a ball to be good, it has to be delivered anywhere between the eye and the knee. Bish was baseball's version of a bodyline specialist. Ouch!

On the rugby front, there was a tendency for local players to join the Cardiff club because that seemed to be the best way into the Cardiff and District Youth team, which was a stepping stone to the Welsh Youth team. But several of us broke the mould and we didn't see any reason to leave our clubs. Mike Budd and myself were at St Joseph's, the props Stuart Evans and Dai Joseph were from RTB Ebbw Vale and Phil Davies, from Seven Sisters; most became international teammates.

I went on to play for Cardiff and District in the 1981 Crawshay and DG Griffiths Cup and was then selected for the Welsh Youth trials at South Wales Police ground at Bridgend. Straight after the trial the team was announced for the game against Australian Schools, which was to be held at Neath. As preparation for that game we played against Welsh Students, a game we won comfortably.

So my first taste of the international stage was against the all-conquering Australian Schools side that had given brilliant exhibitions of running rugby and, just before our meeting, had trounced Scottish Schools at Murrayfield. But they almost met their match when they came up against us. Though they eventually won 13-9, it was a game we should have won because we missed seven kicks at goal – including one from yours truly. I had a big boot so tended to be given the long-range shots and, on a filthy night, watched my effort drop just short from halfway. Fly-half Richard Griffiths did manage to put over two penalties and full-back Gordon Thomas, from Haverfordwest, managed to get into position to drop a goal.

Our side was skippered by my St Joseph's teammate Mike Budd. Richard Donovan, who was to become a good mate, was in the centre and Stuart Evans, who also moved to rugby league after playing for Wales in the 1987 World Cup, was at prop. The Wallaby side included several players who were to become all-time greats and was led by back row Steve Tuynman. Michael Lynagh was at fly-half and Matt Burke partnered Brett Papworth in the centre. All four went on to become major cap winners for Australia although I don't recall them making much of an impression on me on that occasion: they failed to shine because the rain was lashing down and the floodlights at the Gnoll were hardly the best in the world in those days. It was a fairly dour game with few opportunities for class players to demonstrate their running skills. The other thing that worked against the Wallabies was the state of the visitors' dressing room. I didn't discover how bad it was until I returned there as a Cardiff player. You couldn't swing a cat around in it.All the family had turned up to support me but I didn't exactly see a lot of ball. The trouble is that everyone wants to impress at that level so its hard shit if you are on the wing because nobody wants to give you the ball. I used to go looking for it and that's one of the reasons why I tried to get myself moved into the centre, something I didn't achieve at senior level until I started playing the other code.

From that day. I started to view my rugby career differently. I

14

found that I enjoyed the atmosphere of the big games and decided I wanted more of that even though I have always been laid back about the whole thing. I certainly never got a taste for the manic build-up to a game that seemed to be a necessary element for a lot of people. Some players go around headbutting the wall and I've known players wanting to fight a teammate in the dressing room just to get themselves wound up. Sometimes coaches would go fucking mad and players would get so keyed up that they would be physically sick. When I played at Sale Sharks, Phil Winstanley, the prop who was known to everyone as "Philly Wink", used to stick his fingers down his throat and throw up into the bin in the dressing room whereas I would sit in a corner and have a laugh with anyone in the mood for joking around. At Sale it was usually Shane Howarth, the star of "Grannygate", who was another laid back character who took everything in his talented stride. The pair of us found Philly Wink's antics quite hilarious.

We may not have beaten the Aussies but, a couple of months later, I did something I never achieved as a senior international: I was on a winning Welsh side in France. We travelled to Libourne, near Bordeaux, beat French Youth 9-7 and discovered that Gallic crowds don't take defeat too well. After the game, which we won 9-7, we were pelted with fruit as we left the pitch and the authorities had to extend the roof of the tunnel to provide protection. Mind you, one or two of the Welsh players were amusing themselves by hurling the stuff back into the crowd, which incensed the French spectators even more.

Mike Budd again led the side and was the outstanding player on the field. Lyn Jones, a flanker from Cwmafan , now coaching Neath, who was upholding a family tradition because his father had also played for Welsh Youth, scored our try and fly-half Richard Griffiths converted and also kicked a crucial penalty.

Schools and youth rugby had been great fun but I was poised to step up onto a stage where top players were in the limelight, where the rugby was harder and faster but also where the opportunities to travel and enjoy yourself were far greater. To say that I was up for it would be an understatement.

CHAPTER TWO

Black and Blue

AS MY SCHOOLDAYS came to a close, decision time had arrived in more ways than one. Playing with my mates at St Joseph's had been great fun but it was pretty obvious that I was too talented to stay at that level and needed to move to one of the senior clubs, of which there were quite a number to choose from in South Wales. The other decision revolved around getting a job. My boyhood ambition had been to join the police force. I passed the necessary exams, went to Bridgend for my interview and then got a letter back saying, "No thanks." That was a huge disappointment but, rugby being the game it is in South Wales, I was offered the chance to join later, once I had made my name playing international rugby. It was my turn to say, "No thanks."

I ended up having an interview with the Inland Revenue in Cardiff and was asked if I had applied for any other jobs. I said I had sent applications to the police and to a company looking to employ a trainee draughtsman, which was something else I fancied. They asked which I would choose if I was offered all three.

"The Police," I said.

"And your second choice?"

"Draughtsman."

"So we would be your third choice?"

"Yes."

You can guess where I ended up. I don't know why but the Inland Revenue still offered me a job and that's where I earned my first wages after leaving school. It was as boring as hell but the job certainly had its compensations. More of that later.

On the rugby front both Mike Budd and myself were looking for a senior club and a guy called Dennis Hughes, who looked after the St Joseph's Youth side, would take us to training with Wales Youth at Porthcawl on a Sunday. Dennis did a lot of work for the club and was a great bloke but he must have been the worst driver in the world because he drove over every cat's eye he could find. Mike and I were usually suffering from a very liquid Saturday night and were invariably ready to throw up by the time we reached Porthcawl.

Club scouts were approaching both Mike and myself and I ended up with an offer from Bridgend and a trial at Pontypridd. A teacher from school, Les Gauntlet, was a local referee who used to train pre-season with Cardiff and he offered to take me to the Arms Park, so I ended up with three options. I quickly ruled out Pontypridd after playing in a trial game at Sardis Road. It was the old, old story of everyone wanting to impress, which meant the ball never reached the wings. The heavens were opening and I was bored, wet and cold. Afterwards the committee said they were keen to sign me and asked me back for another trial but I thought, fuck that for a lark. Nothing against Ponty but it just didn't feel right at the time.

In any event I had a problem because I couldn't drive and Cardiff's was the only ground I could reach relatively easily from home. Having said that, Bridgend did look a good prospect because Mike Budd was definitely going there and the club, that already had Glenn Webbe on its books, thought the three of us could travel from Cardiff in the same car. I came very close to agreeing to go to the Brewery Field because Mike had no interest in going to Cardiff. That had a lot to do with being overlooked at times by Cardiff Schools.

In the meantime, Les took me to a Cardiff training session during that summer of 1982 and it was a bit daunting to be on the same pitch as the likes of Terry Holmes, Gareth Davies and Bob Norster. And it didn't help when I upset the coach, Roger Beard, as soon as I walked out of the changing room. I was wearing an Aston Villa shirt and he just stared at me and said, "What the fuck is that?"

He gave me a bollocking and insisted on calling me "Aston Villa" at the sessions, which weren't always to my liking. If it was sprinting then I was perfectly happy but I hated the long runs. After all, I considered myself to be a greyhound rather than a donkey. Fortunately, I had good hands and ball skills to add to my pace and I clearly did enough to be selected for the second team after impressing in a trial game. The season wasn't very old, however, before I was called upon to make my senior debut. And what an evening that turned out to be.

Nobody at the club had said anything about my being selected and even though I knew the club had injury problems, especially at wing, it was like a bolt out of the blue when the teamsheet arrived in the post at home. I was in for the injured David Thomas. I had already found it difficult walking into a place where I hadn't known anyone apart from Mark Ring and back row Owen Golding, who had done some of his teacher training at Lady Mary School and who suffered the same fate as Neil Back in being unfairly considered too small for the international stage.

Although I didn't find it easy joining such a distinguished group I can't fault the top players at Cardiff in those days. They were very down to earth and had no edge to them whatsoever. Even so I was still shitting myself, an unusual experience considering I was always so laid back, when I walked into the home dressing room at the Arms Park on the evening of my debut game against Penarth. At St Joseph's you had to provide everything yourself but I noticed I was the only Cardiff player walking in carrying a bag. Once inside the massive dressing room I realised why. Literally everything was provided. All the kit was on hangers, towels were on the benches and, when you walked through to the showers, the club had provided soap, shampoo and even talc. That was when I was first introduced to Albert Francis, who was the groundsman at Sophia Gardens and Cardiff Arms Park and, if you wanted anything at all, he was the man to speak to.

I was so overawed that I didn't like to sit down in case I took someone else's place. So I just stood around until the rest had settled down and then slipped into a spot between Terry Holmes and one of the subs. I needn't have concerned myself because the great thing about Cardiff was that you were never ignored if you were involved in the team. It didn't take me long to get close to "Holmesy", who was a great character. People used to stand off him a bit because of who he was, a second Gareth Edwards in the eyes of many, but, despite the aura that surrounded the guy, Terry was very approachable.

Bob Norster was a good guy too and probably the best second row I have ever seen, whilst I always got on with Gareth Davies and number eight John Scott, who has a decent bloke considering that he was an Englishman! I became very close to Mike Rayer and Gerald Cordle. I was Mike's best man when he got married and I later played Rugby League with Gerald. Scotty and hooker Alan "Thumper" Phillips were the two jokers in the pack and used to spend a lot of time taking the piss out of people. Scotty was good at receiving it in turn but Thumper tended to get a bit irate when he was the butt of the humour for a change.

Cardiff had been very keen to do well against Penarth because they hadn't started the season particularly well. In the event we hit them with 14 tries and referee Brian Davies blew up early to prevent further punishment. I celebrated with a debut hat-trick and Gerald Cordle grabbed two on the other wing.

Alun Rees, writing in the local newspaper, said that my "pace, style and awareness" had helped me to three tries and also helped to create others. Describing it as a very promising first outing, he said I had handled well and shown speed and confidence when going outside my marker and had demonstrated an ability to make the inside break too whilst remaining alert on the rare occasions when I had had to do some covering.

Nice sentiments, and I was duly retained in the side to play Coventry at the Arms Park a few days later. Even though it didn't prove to be one of Cardiff's best seasons, I also did enough to attract the attention of the national selectors.

The "Black and Blues", as Cardiff are known, duly saw off Coventry and then brought Aberavon's excellent start to the season to a somewhat abrupt end. Gareth Davies put me over in the corner and I scored two more when we travelled to Franklins Gardens to beat Northampton. Dave Thomas, on the other wing, went one better by scoring a hat-trick but the real stars of the show that day were Terry Holmes and Gareth Davies. Not many players get the opportunity to launch their senior careers in a back division that was able to boast that duo as the playmakers. They were great as individuals and Terry was just outstanding because he could do all the scrum-half bits and also play like a flanker.

I seemed to have become a fixture in the Cardiff side. The first really tough contest was in October when we entertained the New Zealand Maoris and I marked Robert Kurangui, who was a big lump. All I remember is that they were big and very physical and beat us 17-10 in front of a 12,000 crowd at the Arms Park (which, for the uninitiated from outside the Principality, was the Cardiff club ground. What many refer to as the Arms Park, where international games were staged, was actually called the National Stadium. Just thought you would like to know that).

Anyway, I had to put my defensive skills to the test that evening and had limited attacking opportunities. The best one came when I found space on the left flank, but perhaps I was too eager because the final pass went behind me. Dave Barry, later replaced by Chris Webber, had kicked us into a 6-0 lead but the tourists came back strongly and we couldn't complain about the outcome, even though we didn't like it.

Our bogey team at the time was Bridgend but we saw them off at the start of a successful Christmas period. Gareth was in scintillating form but the platform for victory was laid by the Cardiff pack that won the forward battle hands down. Llanelli were going well too but we beat them at the Arms Park, with Gareth putting me away for a 50-metre sprint to the line, and I scored twice when Moseley paid us a visit on New Year's Day.

By that stage people were talking about me possibly making the national squad. The first step on the ladder came in the form of the senior Welsh trial at Neath. Richard Donovan, who had also played with me in the Welsh Youth side, was also in the Possibles side and I had Mark Ring as my centre and Gareth at fly-half. Unfortunately, from our point of view, Terry Holmes was in the Probables team but we did have my Cardiff teammates Bob Norster and Alan Phillips on board. I was up against Clive Rees and although I didn't get called into the senior squad for the up-coming Five Nations games, I had clearly made enough of an impression to be drafted into the Wales A squad that was scheduled to tour Spain.

On a personal note my first season with Cardiff had been both a success and an education. Until that stage rugby had simply been a winter recreation but playing with what was probably the top club in Europe at the time, and alongside top class players, opened my eyes to the game's possibilities. Although the club was to go on to enjoy far more successful seasons it was a good one for me as I achieved my best strike rate in six seasons in the colours of the Black and Blues.

I ran in 24 tries in 32 outings. The last of those tries was against the Barbarians, when we came from way behind to earn a 32-32 draw. Full-back Paul Rees started the fightback with a try and Terry Holmes gave us hope when he forced his way over from a five-metre scrum. Not that it was easy stopping Terry from that range if he had the bit between his teeth. Then it was my turn to get over and we had given the home crowd plenty to shout about as we came back from the dead.

From a scoring point of view the highlight of that first season was snatching a seven-minute hat-trick against London Welsh, one of the fastest on record. It all happened at the end of the first half, Ringo setting things up in midfield and John Scott and Paul Rees taking the ball up before putting me clear for the first. Then "Thumper" Phillips flung out a long pass to unleash me again and the final try was down to centre Alun Donovan, who chipped ahead from deep inside our own half. I managed a bit of fancy footwork to get the ball into my hands on our ten-metre line and then raced 60 metres to the touchdown. Journalist Rob Cole wrote at the time that I had answered critics who claimed I was too lethargic and lacking in pace!

The big disappointment of my first season was that Cardiff failed to reach the Welsh Cup Final – something we achieved in each of the four succeeding seasons. We had enjoyed some big victories over more junior clubs but eventually went out to the old enemy Pontypool. They won 13-9 and my old pal Dave Bishop scored a crucial try for them. I thought he had put his foot into touch but that was in the days when each club provided a touch judge, rather than relying on referees to run the line, and Bish just happened to be on the wing being marshalled by the Pontypool official. I'm not saying the guy deliberately let it go. Just that he and I obviously saw it differently.

The big problem during the season had been inconsistency. We did pull off some good wins, including a 32-0 demolition of Leicester. They were good then but not as good as they have been in recent seasons when they have tended to dominate the English scene.

As the season drew to a close I had two things to look forward to. The Welsh A tour to Spain and a pre-season tour the club was undertaking to Thailand. Neither country was noted for its rugby prowess but at least Thailand, with its famous fleshpots, seemed to have plenty to offer a group of fit young men, even if it wasn't going to be on the rugby field. I'm not sure the Far East was the best possible place to prepare for a new season and it is interesting that these days pre-season is often confined to the strict boundaries of an army camp!

The Spanish venture was really a development tour and was my introduction to John Bevan, who was to be my coach when I graduated to my full cap. I didn't get on with the guy from day one and that situation never changed throughout his time as national coach. When we played the test in Spain I wasn't included because he went with Elgan and Clive Rees on the wings and that got up my nose. I could understand why the selectors didn't pick me for the Five Nations' Championship after the senior trial because I was, after all, a first-year rookie but I felt a development tour should have been treated differently.

John also had his own little clique, which included the more senior players and skipper Eddie Butler. There was one occasion when we had all been told to be on the team coach at a certain time and we were there on the dot, only to be kept waiting for 40 minutes whilst John and his coterie decided to carry on drinking in a bar they had found. That wasn't a good move in terms of building team spirit but, fortunately, there were some good young lads on the tour and we tended to stick together. In the main I hung around with the likes of Gareth Roberts, Richard Donovan and Mark Davies, who ended up as the British Lions' physiotherapist on the most recent tours to South Africa and Australia.

I scored seven tries on the short tour, including a hat-trick against a Valencia Select XV when we romped to an 83-3 victory. Paul Moriarty, destined to become a popular travelling companion and teammate in both rugby codes, gave an inspired performance in a dominant pack and I was surrounded by quality backs. Malcolm Dacey was at fly-half and Mark Ring and Bleddyn Bowen were the centres. They were all good footballers and I always rated Bleddyn very highly.

A disappointing tour it may have been but three weeks in Thailand beckoned and what a great time we had, even though it didn't get off to the most auspicious start. The tour organiser was Fred Rumsey, the former Test cricketer, and, in his wisdom, he decided to fly us via the Indian sub-continent on a "dry" airline. You can imagine the scenes at Heathrow when 30 rugby players discovered that they weren't going to get a drink whilst incarcerated in a metal tube for hours on end. By the time we were all telling poor Fred what a wanker he was, his wife, who was accompanying him on the trip, had decided to make herself scarce. We made ourselves scarce too by legging it to the duty free shop to load up with gin, vodka, brandy and whisky. Well, we knew we would be able to get bottles of tonic on board.

It went from bad to worse. We were all decked out in Cardiff blazers, shirts, ties and flannels. Once on board, the lads started stripping into shorts and tee-shirts but that led to a bollocking from the flight captain. Apparently it wasn't the done thing to undress in front of women. The only thing that stopped us turning around and going home was the sure and certain knowledge that the ladies in Thailand wouldn't mind one little bit if we started taking our clothes off.

We had a five-hour stopover in Pakistan and Fred had arranged for us to spend the time at a hotel to relax in the pool or snatch forty-winks on a sun bed. What I hadn't been prepared for was the poverty and squalor that faced us when we walked out of the airport. There were beggars in rags everywhere and young kids with no legs who scooted along on home-made skateboards. They all pleaded for money but we had been told not to give anything at all and get straight on to the bus that had been provided. We were all tired, very hot and pretty pissed off and this young lad clambered up the side of the bus and poked his head through an open window. The poor mite only had one eye and had his arm held out inside the bus asking for money. One of the lads, who was probably at the end of his tether, turned to him and said, "Sod off or I'll poke the other one out for you."

Not the most Christian thing to say but you don't always think straight when you are shagged out. But the kid had the whole bus load of us forgetting our own trivial discomfort and falling about laughing when he pointed at the player and, in a little voice but in perfect English, said, "Why don't you fuck off!"

I don't sleep well on aircraft so crashed out on a sunbed at the hotel. The only problem is that I fell fast asleep and, by the time we boarded another aircraft for the final leg to Bangkok, I was sunburnt all down one side from head to toe and looked a bit like a vanilla and strawberry ice cream on a stick.

Fortunately, Thailand was well worth the lengthy flight but I was soon wondering about my room mate, full-back Paul Rees, who was known to all and sundry as "Pablo". I went straight into the bathroom and by the time I got back into the bedroom Pablo had emptied the contents of both our bags into a pile in the middle of the floor. I asked what the hell he was doing and he said that as we were both about the same size we didn't need to waste time and effort putting our clothes into drawers. Instead, we would simply grab the first item of clothing we saw from the pile each morning and put it on. Suffice it to say, Pablo was a complete nutcase and he also liked a drink, so I don't know why they put him with me.

He was a great bloke and a highly entertaining room mate. Pablo was also a very talented player who would certainly have played for Wales had he been a goalkicker. He was the safest thing I have seen under a high ball.

Taking a rugby team to somewhere like Bangkok must be a bit of a nightmare and we were all read the riot act before we set off. We were told to stay away from all the knocking shops — a bit like asking a young lad to spend three weeks in a chocolate factory without sampling the produce — to beware of prostitutes and to limit ourselves to watching what goes on. We assumed that meant we could watch the live sex shows in the Patphong district of the city without demonstrating our own prowess in that department. Needless to say, we hadn't been there five minutes when one of the young players was on a diet of penicillin and had to stay teetotal for the remainder of the trip. He'd been walking back to our hotel by himself the first evening, been approached by a young lady and ended up doing what comes naturally to a healthy young man.

Let's not beat about the bush. When boys go away you can't expect them to behave like saints and I am the first to hold my hands up and admit that I didn't have a tendency to look a gift horse in the mouth. Not that top class rugby players need to go abroad to enjoy themselves in that department because most clubs I have been involved with have their had quota of groupies who have more notches on their bedposts than most Wild West heroes had on their guns (stay with the dialogue to find out more).

One of the funniest moments on our Thai tour was going with one of the other players, rather surreptitiously, to one of the many VD clinics in Pattaya Beach to be checked out. The two of us walked past the place a couple of times and had a beer before plucking up the courage to go in. These clinics are all over the place and we thought we would see what it was like inside one of them, as we were fairly confident that we hadn't picked up anything nasty. We needn't have bothered trying to be surreptitious – we discovered that we were on first-name terms with everybody else in the waiting room! A load of our teammates were already in there: I think they had gone in for the same reason as ourselves, curiosity. Mind you it wasn't a bad idea to get checked out, although we weren't so sure when the staff stuck cotton buds up our jacksies. That made the old eyes water but it did prove valuable for one of the lads. He discovered that he didn't have a sexually transmitted disease but did have a waterworks infection.

The craftier members of the party even found a way around the business of paying a fee to the nightclub for the privilege of taking a girl back to the hotel for a little action. They would wait by the lift until a girl was departing after performing her nightly duties, and simply offer her a little overtime on the black economy.

There was also a serious side to the pre-season tour and it is perhaps significant that Cardiff had a good season in 1983/4, culminating in victory over Neath in the Schweppes Cup Final. I'm not sure which physical activities contributed most to that success, however.

The rugby authorities in Thailand had provided us with good training facilities and really looked after us well. We even had an Olympic sized swimming pool to work out in and the heat was so intense that it was a blessed relief to throw yourself into it. We did actually train quite hard and those who had perhaps over indulged the night before on the local brew would be collapsing like ninepins.

We played a couple of games in Bangkok and our coach Roger Beard really lost it with Martin Daly during one game. I was on the touchline with Roger when Martin made a lovely break and then got tackled just inside the Thailand 22. He didn't get up for several minutes and we were getting worried about him until he manage to crawl on to his knees and promptly starting spewing up all over the place. In the heat of the moment Roger declared that Martin would never play for Cardiff again. A threat that wasn't, of course, carried out.

Martin wasn't the only one to be under the weather. My room mate Pablo excelled himself one day. He went down with a dose of the shits and, as we were about to leave for training, asked the club doctor if he could help. The doc lent him his room key and told him he would find a bottle of kaolin and morphine on the dressing table. Pablo, of course, never did things by halves and, instead of using a teaspoon to measure the dose, just took a long swig from the bottle. He then joined in the training but was practically dying afterwards. The doc was a bit puzzled until he realised that Pablo hadn't bothered to read the label on the bottle and had, instead of kaolin and morphine, helped himself to the equivalent of several tablespoons of calamine lotion.

Pablo recovered after two days in bed and was fit and ready for two weeks at Pattaya Beach, where he was able to join us at a Thai boxing evening. We had all had a few beers and hooker Jose Souto, a lad who could look after himself, decided to challenge one of the local boxers. All the Thai money went on their guy and we put ours on Jose, in an act of great faith in our own. Second row Tony McLean and Mark Ring offered to act as his seconds.

The bout seemed to be going well for Jose. He was punching the crap out of the Thai guy who seemed to rely solely on kicking Jose in the thigh. We were sure Jose was winning but, when the fight ended after three rounds, the Thai's arm was raised in triumph. Apparently, he had scored more points with his feet. We, not unnaturally, thought the whole thing an outrage and the place erupted when Tony McLean picked up a huge metal tray, used for putting the stools on in the ring, and clobbered the referee over the head with it. The next thing we knew the police were in there waving their truncheons and we all legged it back to the hotel. Roger Beard was less than amused when Jose was unable to train for the rest of the tour because of the severe bruising to his legs.

We were up for everything but even we decided that discretion would be the better part of valour when the locals told us to stay out of town after we had asked why the prices in the bars had suddenly shot up. The answer, they said, was quite simple. A US aircraft career was in the process of docking at Pattaya Beach and the locals didn't fancy Cardiff's rugby finest trying to take on the might of the US Navy. We could get into enough trouble without tangling with the overpaid, oversexed and over here guys, especially as one of our props was suddenly taken aback when he was chased by a machete wielding Thai. Having been taken short, all he had done was have a piss in a jug he found in the street. How was he to know it was a shrine.

I had my introduction to the traditional court session, a popular feature of rugby tours. Terry Holmes acted as judge and jury with Gareth Davies as the prosecutor. The attorney for the defence was a dull fucker, whose name I can't for the life of me remember. George Carman would not have been worried about the competition, that's for sure.

I was sentenced to drink a bottle of whisky and smoke twenty fags in an hour along with Alan Donovan, who was sentenced to drink a bottle of gin and smoke twenty fags in an hour. I can't recall what my particular crime had been because, by the time I had carried out the sentence, I was sufficiently brain dead for it to have slipped my memory. Dave Barry, like everyone else, lost his case too and was sentenced to wear the complete Cardiff kit, including boots, for the remaining four days of the trip – twenty-four hours a day.

All considered, it was a great tour and Cardiff had others in a similar vein. Unfortunately, that was the last Cardiff tour I would go on because I was poised to start an international career, with Wales having first call upon my time in the summer months. The days of summer evenings spent playing baseball had also ended but there were new things to keep me entertained.

CHAPTER THREE

Day of the Dragon

BY THE TIME the 1983/84 season started, I was well established in the Cardiff side, had already sampled life in the Welsh development squad and was going through the motions in my job as a clerical assistant with the Inland Revenue in Cardiff. I was later promoted to tax officer, don't ask me how because I was never there, and hated every minute of it but there was the considerable compensation of the place being a bit like a holiday camp. I had joined just before Christmas and the first two weeks of my new career were spent attending office parties.

The amount of shagging that went on was incredible. People were at it all over the place and I remember one very pleasant coupling on the fire escape. It got so bad that you had to knock on office doors and wait to be invited in so that you didn't catch one of your colleagues with his trousers down and one of the girls using the hem of her skirt to keep her neck warm. It was probably all down to the fact that the job was so unbelievably boring that we were all looking for any diversion possible. After all, most people only have to plough their way through a tax return form once a year. Try doing that all day, every day.

My officer was a little Scottish guy who took me on one side to say that it wasn't always like that and that I would have to knuckle down once the festive season was over. I never did, and he certainly didn't, and I suppose I really took the piss, especially once I had graduated to full cap status, which affords you certain privileges in Wales even now. You couldn't walk down the street in Cardiff without people coming up to you and, although in a way it's very nice and complimentary that they do, it can become a bit of a bind and you find yourself seeking out places with your mates where you are largely left alone.

My old pal Shane Howarth will have found that when he played for Wales before the so-called Grannygate rumpus revealed his lack of Welsh ancestry and put an end to his career with the national side. He would be immediately recognised in the street but back in Manchester, when he played for Sale Sharks, he was able to walk about without anyone having the faintest idea who he was. When I played rugby league for Salford Reds it was only occasionally that someone would acknowledge me as I walked through the centre of town.

The other downside to being a top class player in such a rugby-daft area as South Wales is that there is always some idiot who fancies taking a pot at a player, usually the biggest for some strange reason, and especially if he plays for a club they don't support, such is the inter-club rivalry in the country. Just to make things more entertaining, they would all forget their own little rivalries to unite in their hatred of the Cardiff club. Later in my career, when I was married to Ann, we had gone out for a meal with Mike Rayer and his wife Debbie. A group of six lads at another table, who were clearly Caerphilly supporters, realised who we were and started having a pop at us and you reach the stage where you wonder if you ought to simply get up and leave.

In the end I went to the toilet and, on my way back to the table, I suddenly grabbed the mouthiest of the bunch and poked him in the eye, telling him that if he had anything to say I would be only too happy to discuss it with him outside. Thankfully they got the message and stopped their barracking. Just as well really because there were six of them and only one of me because Mike had his arm in plaster at the time.

Life at the Inland Revenue was definitely not taxing and I gave flexitime a new meaning, which didn't please some of my colleagues because I managed to spend most of my time in the pub. You see, I was well into the drinking culture, even for a supposedly top athlete. Friday was the best day because I would go with colleagues to the Church Inn in Cardiff at lunchtime and drink there until 3pm, when they had to close under the licensing laws.

As the closing hour approached, we would order another round of drinks and a taxi to take us up the mountain to the Travellers Rest at Caerphilly, where closing time was 4pm. Before being shown the door there, we would order another taxi to take us back into Cardiff in time for the city pubs to open again so that we could carry on drinking until about 8pm. Then I would go home to sleep it off before my game for Cardiff the following afternoon.

Any young player reading this should do it by the textbook rather than by the example given in this book. Rugby employers and coaches wouldn't stand for that sort of match preparation these days and, the way the game is going, you wouldn't last long if you didn't look after yourself. But you have to remember that I started playing top class rugby twenty years ago when we were all amateur players – despite what some people assumed if you played for Cardiff – and rugby was still a recreation. A lot of top players may stick to orange juice and a strict training regime today but then rugby is now a full time job that pays the mortgage.

That's not to say we didn't give of our best on the field. Your attitude in a game doesn't necessarily change just because you have lived like a monk. Ability is largely God-given and, when it comes down to hey lads hey, you can be the finest trained athlete in the world but you will still finish second best if you lack bottle and heart. I knew a lot of world class players who drank like it was going out of fashion but still produced the goods on a Saturday afternoon.

When I wasn't sliding off for a drink, or on to the fire escape for refreshment of another kind, I was getting out of normal duties because I was away on special leave with Wales, receiving treatment for injuries or playing rugby for either the Inland Revenue or the Civil Service. The Revenue's main base was Newcastle and games were played midweek, which meant one day off for the game and two further days off for travel. Then there were sevens tournaments all over the place and that was great fun because Mark Ring played for the Department of Trade and Paul Turner for the Ministry of Defence. A strange choice for Paul as I always thought him more suited to tearing up defences rather than providing one.

Cardiff, fortunately, didn't do a great deal of travelling. All the Welsh opposition was within easy reach and we never got further than places like Leicester, Northampton and Harlequins on our expeditions over the border. Even then we would travel on the day of the game.

The previous season had been a difficult one but we had clocked up a club record 1,198 points and blooded a lot of young players like myself, Mark Ring and Gerald Cordle. We all had a little more experience under our belts as the new campaign got under way. The target for me was a full Welsh cap and I was awarded the next best thing when I was picked for the game against Japan in the October. Unfortunately, the game didn't turn out as hoped and, playing in front of 25,000 people at the National Stadium, we only managed to scramble home 29-24.

For a time it had looked as though we would run the Japanese ragged as we swept into a 29-10 lead, running in five tries in the process, the first of which came from yours truly. We launched an attack down the left and I was tackled but managed to keep the move alive. I then scrambled up and raced to the opposite wing, just in time to provide the extra man outside right wing Mark

Titley and take a scoring pass. My Cardiff teammate Ian Eidman provided the link to send in Pontypool flanker Mark Brown for the second and Bleddyn Bowen and skipper Eddie Butler combined to open up the Japanese defence for Swansea fly-half Malcolm Dacey to get over.

Malcolm and Mark Titley put Bleddyn in for number four and it seemed to be all over when Malcolm demonstrated his ability by engineering an opening for scrum-half Ray Giles. At 29-10 we were cruising but the Japanese came back so strongly that we were almost hanging on at the end. Our coach John Bevan wasn't exactly amused and gave our pack a bit of a roasting but did concede that one of the most pleasing features, from his point of view, had been the way the young three-quarters – Kevin Hopkins was the fourth member of the quartet made up by Bleddyn, Mark Titley and myself – had played.

Eddie Butler said it had been insane to ease off when we thought we had it sewn up and we were all left wondering just how many of that side would survive to face a sterner test against Romania in Bucharest the following month. In the event, five of the backs survived: Mark, Bleddyn, Malcolm, Ray and myself. Gwyn Evans, the Maesteg full-back, was bought in for Mark Wyatt, who hadn't had a great day with the boot, and Rob Ackerman replaced Kevin Hopkins in the centre. My club mate Jeff Whitefoot lost his place at loose-head prop to Pontypool's Staff Jones and Swansea's Mark Davies lost his place in the back row to Llanelli's Dave Pickering.

Caps were being awarded for the game in Bucharest and there were six new boys in the end, which I suppose was a bit of a gamble. The others were Mark Titley, Bleddyn Bowen, Ray Giles, Mark Brown and Terry Shaw, the Newbridge second row. The side hadn't been announced and I was worried if I would be fit enough anyway because I had picked up an injury playing for Cardiff. I knew John Dawes quite well and often had a beer with him in the Old Arcade, a well-known Cardiff hostelry. I told him that I needed to know if I was in because, if I was tested fit and not selected, I would play for Cardiff that week. As it was I took time off from the Revenue to have treatment with Cardiff physio Tudor Jones, who was also the Welsh physio, and then went home to ring John Dawes. He asked me if I was fit to play for the club and I told him that I was.

"Well," he said. "You won't be playing for Cardiff."

He congratulated me on making the Welsh side but told me to keep it quiet because the team hadn't been announced. There was nobody at home at the time and I just sat in a chair not really knowing what to do. I ended up ringing my mother to tell her I was playing for Wales and she just burst into tears. It took a while for the full implications to sink in and, once the team had been announced, I found myself having to get used to all the media attention. Journalists came round to the house to do interviews, often with photographers and television camera crews in tow and it was completely manic for a time. It was almost a relief to get into training camp for the game.

With hindsight I certainly wouldn't choose Bucharest as the ideal place to win a first cap and the whole shambolic episode got off to a bad start. John Bevan had organised a Sunday morning training session on the beach at Aberavon but had forgotten to check the tide tables. The tide was in and we had to wait ages before we could get down to business. That was another black mark for John in my book as he was still not my favourite person. It wasn't his ability that I questioned, just the arrogant way he treated me, and we were to head towards a couple of bust-ups before long.

One was in Ireland, where we were having a team run before an international and I just ambled over the line to touchdown at the end of one practised move. He obviously felt I should have raced over as I would have done in a match situation and he bellowed at me, "You'll never score like that on Saturday. How many tries have you scored for Wales?"

36

People were filming the session so I snapped back, "What's more to the point, how many tries did you ever score for Wales?"

That episode was in front of all the Irish and Welsh camera teams and in full earshot of all the Welsh players and committee. There was deadly silence for a minute and then he just called another move to be taken from the halfway line. As I jogged back, Ringo was chuckling away to himself. It obviously amused him but Bevan never mentioned the incident again.

The side flew to Bucharest on the Thursday morning by charter and we were given some inkling of what conditions might be like in Romania when we were each handed a goody bag containing chocolate, chewing gum, writing paper, pencils and Welsh badges to give to our opposite numbers after the game because they were so poor. The reception was something else.

The moment we entered Romanian airspace we were joined on either side by fighter aircraft that were to escort us to the airport. We were all shitting ourselves wondering just what sort of regime we were getting involved with. And to think that my mum and dad were making their own way to Bucharest to watch their son win his first cap. On arrival at the airport there was nobody about except military personnel, and the road into the city, which was like a four lane motorway in each direction, was completely deserted. No traffic, no cars. Apart from army types, we didn't even see ordinary people until we got close to where we were staying and then they were just waiting in long queues that seemed to stretch for miles. We supposed they were trying to buy food and its amazing how much we take for granted because anything you want is on tap 24 hours a day. We dreaded to think what the hotel would be like but it wasn't too bad except that, for reasons we never really understood, we had to walk to another hotel down the road in order to eat.

As a precaution we had taken our own food but that didn't work out well either because we hadn't taken our own chef. The first morning Tudor Jones took our supply of bacon and eggs into the hotel kitchen but when it came back the bacon wasn't cooked properly and you could see through the white of the eggs. We ended up living on bread and, sorry chaps, we decided that charity began at home and ate all the edible contents of the goody bags we were due to hand to the Romanians.

Any doubt about the genuine poverty of the Romanian people was brought home to us by the hotel chambermaids. They were so poor that they were offering sex for ridiculously small amounts of money and weren't backward in coming forward because they would simply waltz into your room and offer themselves. Hardly the ideal scenario when you are nervously preparing for your international debut. Goodness knows what the girls would have done for a bar of chocolate. It was absolutely unbelievable. One of the boys was taking a shower when a maid walked into the bedroom, realised where the occupant was and, without invitation, stripped off and joined him. For a fee, of course.

The game itself was quite unreal. The stadium was packed but everyone was in uniform. On the way in everyone was being given a flag to wave but they then had to hand them back on their way out after the game. As for the on-field action, to put it simply, we got a good old fashioned battering, going down 24-6. The forwards never really got into it but you had to question why they had picked two front jumpers in John Perkins and Terry Shaw, with the result that we got stuffed in the lineout.

With very little ball to play with, we never really had a chance to use our young, quick backs and Ray Giles was left trying to stem a flood at scrum-half. If ever we needed the Herculian Terry Holmes then that was the day. Unfortunately Terry was still recovering from a serious knee injury that had put an end to his British Lions tour that summer. We backs did our best with what little ball we saw but even our cause was hindered when Malcolm Dacey had to leave the field with an injured jaw. Swansea's David Richards was ushered on to the field with Bleddyn Bowen switching to fly-half to further demonstrate his all-round talents.

Just to rub salt into a very open Welsh wound, the Romanian captain, Mircea Paraschiv, said afterwards that his most dangerous opponent that afternoon had been French referee Jean Claude Yche, who accidentally poked his finger into the scrum-half's eye.

Most of my work was in defence but at least I must have impressed Steve Bale, writing in the *Western Mail*, who said, "An outstanding debut by the 20-year-old who confounded the doubters with his great determination and courage. Like Mark Titley he was underused but managed several fine runs out of defence."

It was almost a relief to get back to the Inland Revenue and club rugby with Cardiff. There was also a reunion of past and present players and officials at St Joseph's to mark the rugby club's 25th anniversary. I was an "honoured" guest, which was quite something, and the club had certainly enjoyed an eventful first quarter century, having reached the final of the Mallett Cup on eight occasions and ending up as winners on four of them. The club had also picked up wins in the Harry Parfitt Cup, Ninian Stuart Cup and also reached the final of the Welsh Brewers Cup one year. A great many players had gone on to play for top clubs like Cardiff, including my brother John, who is now back playing at St Joe's.

Early in 1984 I had my first experience of what was then the Five Nations Championship but it wasn't the most auspicious of starts. We played host to Scotland and were beaten 15-9 at the National Stadium. Just as in Bucharest, I saw very little of the ball and it wasn't an exactly inspiring game. Again, I didn't get too nervous before the start but I always liked to do my own thing. I might go out on to the pitch just to sample the atmosphere before the game but I preferred to quietly warm up by myself rather than indulge in the lengthy sessions involving everyone that seem to be the norm these days.

I loved playing in front of a Welsh crowd at the stadium, however. It really does get to you when they sing and anyone watching on television will have noticed that I was one of the few players who never sang the Welsh anthem. A lot of players cry when the anthem is played and I had to concentrate on not bursting into tears, which I would have done had I joined in the singing. It is a highly emotional experience when there is a full house at Cardiff and I remember taking one of the backroom boys from Sale, Robbie Dixon, to watch a Wales v Ireland game there years later. Although Robbie is a Scot, the tears were also flowing down his cheeks when *Land Of My Fathers* was sung. It is so powerful a moment that it even affects people who aren't from Wales. You also pick up on the singing when there is a lull in the game and it really does inspire you. The support from the Welsh fans, even when things aren't going well, is brilliant. I still have to fight back the tears even now when I hear the anthem.

My second cap passed with little glory and I had still to be on a winning side. In fairness to the Scots they did go on to perform the Grand Slam and their skipper Jim Aitken led a Scottish fight back with a crucial try after we had taken the lead when Mark Titley got over on the opposite wing to myself and Bridgend full-back Howell Davies, who was making his debut along with Llanelli scrum-half Mark Douglas and Newport prop Gareth Morgan, kicked the touchline conversion to add to a penalty.

At least we tried to play some rugby and our fortunes changed when we crossed the Irish Sea to play Ireland in Dublin. For some reason we invariably did well over there and they had a tendency to get their own back in Cardiff. And I loved going to play in Dublin just as much as I hated playing in Paris. I never had much to do with my opposite number after games but one major exception was Ireland's Trevor Ringland. He was a hard, strong player too and neither of us liked to give an inch but we got on really well and after internationals he always took me around the Dublin bars for a few beers. Being in Ireland used to remind me very much of being back home in Wales.

For the Dublin visit the selectors had made changes. They completely changed the front row, bringing in Bridgend's Ian Stephens and my Cardiff club mate Ian Eidman at prop and Newport's Mike Watkins not only came in at hooker but was handed the captaincy on his international debut, with Eddie Butler retained in the back row but reduced to the ranks. Mike, who was a great character and motivator, became only the second player since the Second World War to lead Wales on his debut. On this occasion our pack got the better of the exchanges and we had already opened a 12-6 lead through two Howell Davies penalties and two more by Bleddyn Bowen when centre Rob Ackerman sold a dummy to Irish full-back Hugo McNeill and raced half the length of the field to score. Howell kicked the conversion and I was able to celebrate victory with a generous Trevor Ringland.

Our next outing was against France in Cardiff. Playing at home spared me the dreadful French food. I don't know why people make such a fuss of French cuisine because I have yet to be fed properly on my many excursions over there for a variety of teams. I know I'm a fussy eater but it wouldn't be so bad if they actually cooked the meat. No matter how many times you tell them that you like your beef well done, it still comes back rare. I can't handle all that blood. I don't mind it on the rugby field but I can't stand it on my plate. More often than not I would live on potato crisps and bread and get my hands on as much fruit as possible.

The French are also a pretty anti-social lot. The players never seem to want to mix with you after games and even the English would do that to a certain extent! Once the formal dinner was over the French would shoot off into Paris on their own so we would give them the same treatment in Cardiff. One year Terry Holmes and myself decided to hang on to Serge Blanco and Philippe Sella and follow them wherever they went in Paris. I don't think they particularly wanted us along but we thought, fuck it, you're not shaking us off. Not surprisingly we ended up in some fabulous places and the champagne was flowing the minute we walked through the door and the owners realised who we were with.

More often than not we found the French to be completely obnoxious, so all we could do was go out and get shitfaced. Then it would be a problem because we would jump into a taxi and ask to be taken to the Concorde Hotel, where we usually stayed in Paris. The problem is that there are apparently several Concorde Hotels in the city and we would end up at all manner of strange places before being taken to the correct watering hole. By which time we would have run up an astronomical bill.

In Cardiff in 1984 we should have beaten the French. We outscored them two to one in the tries department but we missed a lot of kicks at goal and, no disrespect to Mark Douglas, we were missing the very special qualities of Terry Holmes at scrum-half that season. Howell Davies and Eddie Butler scored our tries but Howell could only convert one and land two penalties whilst Jean-Patrick Lescarboura, the tall French fly-half from Dax, was kicking everything in sight, including the conversion of a try by Sella.

That meant we had lost both our home championship games for the first time in 21 years and that put pressure on us to redeem ourselves by beating the old enemy, England, at Twickenham a month later. I had played there for Cardiff against Harlequins and loved the playing surface so, apart from the fact it was the English HQ, I always looked forward to appearing there. Fortunately, I was only once in a Welsh starting line-up that lost to the one side we loved to beat. In some ways, perhaps, the Welsh always set too much store by beating England. If we lost our other games it never seemed to matter quite so much, just so long as we triumphed against the English.

The selectors kept faith with the side that had lost to France but for one major change. Terry Holmes was considered fit for duty and that was a tremendous boost to our morale because he was destined to have a mercurial battle with our club skipper, John Scott, all through the game.

Playing at Twickenham was an odd experience because it was totally different to playing anywhere else. In the early days we used to stay at the Angel Hotel across the road from the ground for home internationals and it was a case of walking straight into the stadium. When we played at Twickenham the team coach would pull into the West Car Park and we would have to walk past all the English fans, in their Barbour jackets, tucking into their picnic lunches at the back of all the Range Rovers, Bentleys and Jaguars, all in a line. So far as I was concerned we were the working class valley boys and they were the toffs. I never thought they were as knowledgeable as Welsh crowds either and remember walking towards the dressing rooms some years later when an impeccably accented woman implored her husband to point out Terry Holmes. By that stage Terry was long gone to rugby league and I just looked at her pityingly and shook my head.

England were first to latch on to the hospitality and corporate thing and it's ironic that life would one day go full circle for me and, in my role as director of rugby at Sale Sharks, I would be back in the West Car Park entertaining the club's corporate clients out of the back of a Land Rover – as close to the Guinness tent as possible. I refused to wear the Barbour jacket though!

Back in 1984 we came away with the spoils again and I celebrated with the only try of the game as we won 24-15. Dusty Hare kicked five penalties for England but Howell Davies matched him with four penalties and the conversion of my try, which came with the sides level at 9-9 and the game delicately poised. The move came from a lineout when Terry Holmes fed Malcolm Dacey and Bleddyn Bowen took it on. The English defence drifted out and Bleddyn sold a lovely dummy to step back inside to make some space. I came off my wing, took Bleddyn's pass and then drew Dusty before doing a one-two with Eddie Butler and crossing under the sticks. I didn't do too badly considering that my shorts had ripped and Tudor Jones had had to run on with a spare pair. Unfortunately, they were for a 40-inch waist and I was still only a 34 in those days. We had to tape them down to stop them flapping around my legs like sails in a Force Nine.

Just to stop England getting any ideas of a comeback after pulling back to just a three point deficit, Malcolm Dacey dropped two goals. Meanwhile, Howell's kicking feat that afternoon gave him a Welsh record of 39 championship points in a season.

The real feature of the game was the running battle between Holmesy and Scotty. Their respective positions on the field meant that they were often in opposition and it was no place for the faint hearted. Afterwards I was walking out of the dressing room when I felt this smack at the back of my head. When I looked around ready to smack somebody I saw that it was Scotty who said, "Don't ever do that again you Welsh bastard!"

Cardiff had a lot of great players and characters in those days and Scotty really was a top man. When I arrived at the Arms Park he had taken me under his wing and I have nothing but respect for the guy. He may have been English but the players and fans really took him to their hearts in Cardiff.

The season, of course, was far from over after the Twickenham visit. Wales had the little matter of playing a WRU President's World XV to dispense with and a suitably subdued Scotty was soon back in Cardiff colours and leading the club towards what was to be the first of four successive appearances in the Schweppes Cup Final.

The World game had been organised to celebrate the completion of a £9 million development programme at the National Stadium and was the first fixture in which I had been involved where politics came into play. The Welsh RFU had invited three Springboks to play but news that South Africans had been included in the side caused something of a stir because this was long before Nelson Mandela had been released from prison and elected to steer the Rainbow Nation to a new beginning. As a result, anti-apartheid demonstrators made their presence felt in the city before the kick off.

I found myself facing Peter Grigg, the Aussie wing I was destined to tangle with on more than one occasion, including a World Cup third-place play-off. He had more opportunities to run than I did and they outscored us by three tries to two. The crowd didn't like it when we went for goal rather than run our penalties but coach John Bevan was interested in victory above everything else and Howell Davies and Belddyn Bowen obliged with a succession of kicks. By half-time we had been trailing 13-6 but bounced back to take the game 27-17 with tries coming from Terry Holmes, who finished off a powerful drive at a five-metre scrum, and Rob Ackerman, who benefited from some clever work by Bleddyn.

On the domestic front Cardiff had a better season despite losing away to several of the top Welsh sides. But it wasn't a league in those days and we had good results against English sides and struck form in the Schweppes Cup.

The early stages of the competition were certainly interesting, especially when we clashed with Treorchy at The Oval in the second round. We won 31-4 but referee Clive Norling, never one to stand for any nonsense, sent off four players as things got out of hand. Three were from the host club and we lost Jeff Whitefoot. I kept out of it and scored a try instead.

We beat Newbridge 12-7 in the quarter finals on a very wet day and won through to the final by beating Llanelli 26-9 at Swansea in the semi-final. It was fantastic playing at the National Stadium and I must say my first national final was a very enjoyable experience. Mind you, it did help that we beat Neath 24-19. So the season ended well for me, having started with me being voted the best newcomer in Wales with the top award for Player of the Year deservedly going to Terry Holmes.

CHAPTER FOUR

Blown Out by Bevan

CLUB RUGBY WITH Cardiff continued to be a great experience in the 1984/85 season. We had developed into a very good side and were the team to beat in Wales even though a glance at the merit tables that were popular in those days didn't exactly demonstrate our dominance. Instead of points, your place in the table was worked out on a percentage basis, which enabled clubs like Pontypool to take top billing because their fixture list was nowhere near as strong as ours.

Any doubts concerning Cardiff's standing were swept away when we did what Wales couldn't manage – beat the touring Australians in October of 1984. Not that beating the Wallabies ever seemed to present a problem to Cardiff: our 16-12 success was the sixth on the trot. In meetings between the sides since 1908, the Wallabies had yet to successfully put the city club to the sword.

Beating Australia that year was some achievement because they had a number of world class players in the line-up such as hooker Tommy Lawton, second row Steve Cutler and a back row of Bill Calcraft, Steve Tuynman and Steve Poidevin. Mark Ella was at fly-half and the team was led by skipper Andy Slack. They held Michael Lynagh and David Campese in reserve for the

47

international but it was still a very strong Aussie team. Just how strong was proven by the fact that they went on to achieve a coveted Grand Slam, beating England, Scotland, Ireland and Wales. The 28-9 win over Wales was fairly comprehensive but was memorable for my pal David Bishop. He won his only full cap in that game and scored the only Welsh try.

Gareth Davies was the man of the match despite playing with a heavily strapped ankle after injuring it playing against Pontypool a week earlier. He controlled everything behind a solid pack that was superbly led by hooker Alan Phillips, who had also taken over the captaincy for the afternoon because Terry Holmes had ruled himself out by dislocating his shoulder in the Pontypool clash. Steve Cannon stood in for Terry at scrum-half and did a great job in a high pressure situation.

I got on to the scoresheet when I turned inside the cover to dive over and a second score came from a penalty try after Aussie flanker Bill Calcraft had been caught diving into our side of a scrum that was easing its way to the line. Gareth got the rest of the points with his boot and we managed to hang on when the tourists started clawing back our 16 points lead.

It was a different story when Wales played the Aussies. They were well beaten, 28-9, and I wasn't involved because I had been having treatment on a hamstring injury. I still believe I could have played because the problem had been around for a while and it hadn't stopped me playing and scoring against the Australians for Cardiff. I took the call from John Bevan at the Inland Revenue. It didn't come in on my usual line but on a desk at the far end of the office. Once they knew who it was, everyone clustered around to try to hear what was said, knowing full well what it would be about.

"You have this hamstring problem, you haven't played the games we wanted you to this season and we are leaving you out," said John.

I asked who was playing in my place and he said, "Phil Lewis."

My response to news that the Llanelli wing was to take my place was, "But he's a right wing."

"Yes, we know, but we are playing him on the left wing instead."

"Well, it's your decision," I said.

"Look, we are not writing you off but this is a big international match."

I was bitterly disappointed because my condition was no different from when I had played against Australia for Cardiff and I wondered if they wanted Phil in and me out and were using the hamstring injury as an excuse. Fortunately, Cardiff were going well, so I concentrated on my club rugby and, by the time the Five Nations' came around the weather had intervened. It is rare these days for international matches to be postponed due to the weather but the games against France and England had to be put back and that may have played a part in my regaining pole position on the left wing.

With the postponements, the first game for Wales wasn't until early March 1985, when they travelled to Edinburgh to face Scotland and came away with a 25-21 victory. Terry Holmes captained the side and Phil Lewis was on the left wing. You always want your team to do well, even when you aren't playing, but I have to be honest and say that I always secretly hope that whoever is in my position doesn't exactly cover himself in glory. So I wasn't unduly unhappy when the ball was kicked over the Welsh line and Phil was beaten to it by Scottish number eight Iain Paxton, for one of his two tries.

Phil did score a try of his own two weeks later in Cardiff but my old adversary Trevor Ringland pulled one back for Ireland, who went on to win 21-9 as Mark Wyatt had an off day with the boot for Wales. As a result the selectors made three changes, one of them positional. Paul Thorburn was brought in for his debut at full-back in place of Mark, and Stuart Evans earned his first cap at prop at the expense of my Cardiff club-mate Ian Eidman. I was recalled on the left wing with Phil Lewis moving over to the right in place of Mark Titley. So, there I was, delighted to be back but thinking there could be better places for a comeback than Paris.

As I said earlier, I hated the place. I didn't like the food and didn't much care for the people, although I always enjoyed the coach ride to the Parc des Princes. This was my first experience of an international in the French capital and old heads suggested I should sit at the front of the coach to watch the antics of the police motorcycle outriders. It was incredible. Everybody has to get out of the way and, if they don't, they get battered over the head. Even the cars come in for some stick as the riders lay into them with their truncheons or simply aim kicks at the vehicles.

Serge Blanco was largely instrumental in guiding France to a 14-3 win by setting up tries for left wing Patrick Esteve and scrum-half Jerome Gallion. All we had to show for our afternoon labours was a penalty by new boy Thorburn. There was a bright side for me when my Cardiff buddy Gareth Roberts got on to win his first cap as a replacement in the back row for Richard Moriarty. Gareth is an absolutely brilliant bloke but must have been the tightest player in Welsh rugby because he never had any money on him. There was even a rumour that he once left a party early because he realised the newly installed central heating at his own home would have come on . . . and he didn't want to waste any of the heat. He also bought his wife a parcel shelf for her Ford Fiesta as a Christmas present! When on tour we used to get an allowance and Gareth and Bob Norster were the only players who managed to come home with more than they had left with.

One thing I do remember from that game is that drug testing had been introduced and the authorities decided to pick out Stuart Evans. We had to wait on the coach for the best part of an hour whilst Stuart, who hadn't had a chance to take a drink after the game, desperately tried to have a pee. Drug testing is important but I have to say that there are players who are prepared to take a chance with performance enhancing drugs and others who owed their sudden bulk to the use of steroids (let me quickly add that Stuart was not one of them).

Here I have a confession to make. When Wales played Scotland in Cardiff in the 1986 Five Nations, I had been feeling a bit rough and I wasn't the only one. That was not surprising because we used to go in the team coach to training and return, often wet through, to have a shower back at the hotel. That's hardly an ideal scenario and I was sniffing and feeling pretty miserable at the hotel when one of my teammates said he could give me something that would help. He told me to see him about an hour before kick-off.

Once we were at the ground, he was as good as his word. An hour before the match was due to start, we got together in a corner of the dressing room – it was all rather clandestine – and he produced a little white tablet and told me to take half. I can't remember which of us broke the tablet but I went off and swallowed it down with a drink of water. A couple of the other boys had the tablets, one helping himself to more than the recommended dose. I can't remember whether he took a whole tablet or even one-and-a-half but it seemed to affect him later.

Unbeknown to all three of us we had taken a tablet called Dexedrine. I hadn't a clue what it was for but I made enquiries recently and discovered that it was an amphetamine. It seems I had been introduced to what is commonly known as "speed" and was apparently used by youngsters keen to rave the night away. I was to discover just how effectively it worked too.

As I say, I was feeling pretty shitty as I sat in the dressing room before the game and I can't claim that I noticed any very sudden change in my condition. But, gradually, I started to feel better and better and during the game I felt that I could just run and run. I had so much energy, scored a try and was still flying at the end of the game – which we won 22-15. Normally, after an international match, you are physically tired, compounded by the stress and emotion of the occasion. But on that afternoon I felt as though I could have gone out and played another full-blown international.

I felt like the Million Dollar Man and it was some time before I was really back on terra firma. After a game I normally slump on to a bench in the dressing room and am never one of the first into a shower. Being laid back, I tend to take my time but I was bursting with energy so rushed into the shower, got dressed and raced across to the Angel Hotel. I was in the bar on the balcony, where we all liked to meet before heading for the formal part of the evening, as fast as you could say Billy Whizz. The fellow who had taken more than he should was so out of it that we had to put him to bed. Yet I continued to feel great and had no adverse reaction. I suppose that by the time the drug started to wear off the alcohol had kicked in.

The person who had given me the tablet said that he used them regularly but, although I was offered them again, I declined. It was obvious to me that there were others in the international squad who were prepared to use a little help but I suspect that practice died out as drug testing became a regular feature of the game at top level.

One of my Cardiff colleagues claimed that he took the same drug before a Schweppes Cup Final against Swansea and was crapping himself when he heard that there were to be random drug tests after the game. Fortunately for him, his number wasn't selected and he got away with it but that might have frightened him off for the future.

I hold my hands up and admit taking the tablet before one international but I hadn't a clue what it was. I suppose I thought it was some sort of vitamin but, in reality, I'm told it helps you to take on board more oxygen. It is obvious that players are not going to admit using performance enhancing drugs but I said at the start of this book that I would tell it warts and all and I can guarantee that I wasn't alone. I am not, however, prepared to name the players that I know used the tablets.

Recreational drugs also feature in both rugby codes – as they do in all walks of life and all sports. I've known loads of professional rugby players who smoke dope socially: I've even known one who sold it in the changing room. I smoked it once myself when I was at Salford and got a stinking headache: it never interested me again after that. However, when I was at Sale Sharks in the mid-Nineties, one of my teammates, back row Dylan O'Grady, was caught in a police operation into a drugs ring and went to jail. He was an Irish international at the time and it effectively ended his international career. He was a mate and it really hits home when one of your friends loses his liberty over something like cannabis. Dylan was a good lad and when he came out of prison I even invited him back to train with us when I was Director of Rugby. I figured everyone is entitled to make one mistake and anyway, who was I to judge him?

For a wing I grew quite big naturally, perhaps it was the lager, but I never felt any need to use steroids and, quite frankly, they scared the shit out of me. They could bring about a sudden change in a player's physique and I prefer tits on my women, not on myself. I didn't know much about steroids until I switched to rugby league where they would be offered to us occasionally when we went to the gym. They were mainly body builders who knew we played rugby professionally. Big hits are a part of every day life in rugby league and some players used to take steroids to bulk up although most were clever enough to do it in the summer when there was less chance of detection.

I know of one top RL team that was well known in our circles for using steroids although they would never admit it. Even some rugby union players resorted to them and you would get raised eyebrows at the way some of them suddenly bulked up. You need to shift very heavy weights to do it naturally and that takes a long time, not just a couple of months, because you have to build up gradually. Two players, who figured at Sale at different times, took steroids to my knowledge and I am sure you would hear similar stories from other top union clubs.

The big thing these days is Creatine which, although banned in France, is considered safe here, if used properly, and is not a banned substance. As I understand it, the idea of the supplement is to enable you to train more often. That was hardly something I would have wanted to do anyway, training never having been one of my "just can't wait to do" activities. John Mitchell was a great advocate of Creatine when he was in charge at Sale Sharks but he would sometimes just take a spoonful of the stuff and wash it down with a drink rather than mix it first. He went a bit funny on a couple of occasions and once, as we were warming down at the end of a training session, he collapsed and looked so rough that we sent one player to ring for an ambulance. Fortunately he came round and was all right and although one can't say that Creatine was a factor, one couldn't rule it out either, especially as you should clearly use these things as recommended by the manufacturers. That's if you should use these things at all. I think any athlete has to have all the facts available to him before he takes anything.

The other thing there is debate about is the use of painkilling injections. God knows what damage cortizones do and, when I was director of rugby at Sale, I would never tell a player that he had to have one to help him play a game. That would have to be his decision. But I used to have injections at Salford in order to play in a game. When you are a professional sportsman, it's a little more difficult. If you don't play then you could not only lose your appearance money but your place in the side too. And being out of the team for a lengthy spell because someone else has had his chance and taken it can cost you a lot of money.

It was towards the end of April before we finally got to grips with England in Cardiff. I stayed in the side but three more players were called up to make their debuts. Swansea centre Kevin Hopkins took over from Mark Ring and soon-to-be relatives Jonathan Davies and Phil Davies were brought in. Jonathan was to launch his glittering career at fly-half and Phil, later to marry his sister, was drafted in at number eight.

Beating England is always high on the list of priorities for a Welsh lad and we didn't disappoint our faithful fans, winning 24-15. England had been working on plans to halt the mercurial Terry Holmes but they hadn't bargained for yet another masterful fly-half straight off the country's conveyor belt. Jonathan dropped a goal to ease himself in and, when England full-back Chris Martin dropped the ball over his own line, Jonathan was on to it in a flash. England had been leading by a point at that stage but our tails were up and, with Paul Thorburn kicking well, good old Gareth Roberts finished off the English with a try engineered by David Pickering.

It was tradition in the Welsh camp for the left wing to room with the fly-half so Jonathan and I were together in the build-up to the game and I decided to look after him in the post -match celebrations as well. After international games in Cardiff we would go across to the Angel to meet up on the balcony for a few beers before the formal dinner and, after that, we would all meet up with wives and girlfriends. I used to get bored with dinners and never stayed for the speeches if I could help it, so Jonathan and I sneaked out as soon as we were able. I've always been a big lad who could handle his drink but, for a relatively little guy, Jonathan was fairly handy too and the pair of us had a rare old time at a couple of Cardiff nightspots called Jacksons and The Bank. It was very late when we finally rejoined the rest of the party and received a very frosty reception from the ladies, who had been wondering where we had been and what we had been up to. And who with!

Wives and girlfriends had good cause to wonder about their rugby playing partners because the path of a top class player is literally strewn with temptation of the female variety. Cardiff had its share of groupies too and a particular pair of sisters attained a certain notoriety for their love and passion for the game and its exponents. They travelled the world in pursuit of rugby pleasures and were featured in one tabloid newspaper when photographs of themselves with various top class players didn't exactly go down well with the loved ones at home. At one time there was a rumour that they were planning to write a book giving players a score out of ten for performance between the sheets.

They were, for all the rumours about them, great fun to be with and I remember, when I played back in Swansea with the Wales RL side, a reception was held at the hotel after an international game for the players and their wives. Nearly all the players, naturally, were former Welsh rugby union internationals so had been around the club scene in the past. And most of their wives had heard all about the fun loving pair – although probably not from their partners. As it happened, my wife Ann wasn't going to be there because she was expecting our youngest, Craig, and myself and one of the other players found ourselves with a spare ticket each and no partners. We needn't have worried because, when there were international rugby players around, you could almost guarantee that the sisters would be around too. So it was with tongue in cheek that we waltzed into the reception with them in tow. If looks could kill, from both genders, the four of us would be dead now.

The 1984/85 season ended a little brighter on the international front but we didn't finish as we would have wished as a club. Cardiff reached the final of the Schweppes Cup for the second successive year and the game against our old rivals Llanelli attracted a record crowd of nearly 45,000 at the National Stadium. Further proof, if any was needed, that the cup was the biggest prize on the club calendar in those days. It was a close contest throughout and I thought we had safely arranged for the trophy's return to the silverware cupboard at the Arms Park for another season as the game moved into injury time.

We were holding on to a 14-12 lead and the game was in the

fourth minute of injury time when Llanelli won a scrum in a position that was well within the range of their fly-half Gary Pearce. Jonathan Griffiths fed him from the scrum and Gary popped over a drop goal to take the match. We threw everything into what we knew would definitely be the last play of the afternoon but Gareth Davies watched his own desperate drop goal attempt at the other end veer wide of the target. I still have a loser's tankard with a big dent in it — the result of me hurling it against the wall of the dressing room. I hate losing and that was a horrible way to lose. Fortunately, we made up for that failure over the next two seasons.

CHAPTER FIVE

South Seas Adventure

MY FORM KEPT me in the national side throughout the following season and I warmed up for the Five Nations by running in a brace of tries for Cardiff against the touring Fijians at the National Stadium in the October. It was tough on the tourists because we had lost our unbeaten home record to Bridgend a week earlier so were in the mood to take it out on somebody. In typical Fijian style the tourists threw the ball around at every opportunity but our pack was so dominant that day that they had fairly limited opportunities. In any event, we weren't exactly deficient in the "throwing it around" department either.

Not for the first time, Gareth Davies ran the show superbly from midfield and opted to release the backs rather than relying on kicking for field positions, as he had done when we tamed the Aussies a year earlier. Terry Holmes did his best to batter his way over the Fijian line all afternoon and, eventually, John Scott was able to set him up for one of his familiar charges. Gareth Roberts got our other try to make up for letting the lively Fijian scrum-half Paulo Nawalu escape his grasp and wriggle over our line.

I was back in action against Fiji for Wales a month later and we romped to a very comfortable 40-3 victory, running in seven tries in the process. It was raining cats and dogs in Cardiff that afternoon so the conditions were hardly conducive to the Fijians' favoured style of rugby and our pack destroyed them. Number eight Phil Davies led the charge with a brace of tries and the others came from myself, Dave Pickering, Mark Titley, hooker Billy James from Aberavon, and Terry Holmes, who had to leave the field with a knee injury. The hard man really did suffer more than his share of injuries and they were to plague him after he had made the switch to the other code with Bradford Bulls, or Bradford Northern as they were in those days.

We opened our Five Nations challenge against England at Twickenham and that's the only time I ended up on the losing side against them. Even then we only went down 21-18 and still managed to score the only try of the match when Jonathan Davies sent Bleddyn Bowen racing over. That had given us the lead at 18-15, after Paul Thorburn had kicked the conversion, but Rob Andrew had arrived on the international scene and kicked the last of his six penalties before dropping a goal in injury time to win the match

Maurice Colclough, the big second row we knew only too well from Swansea, was another influential figure in the English second row that day but I felt we had done enough to win. We were the much better footballing side and threw the ball around well but "Squeaky's" boot kept the English in the game. I was never a great Rob fan and we had occasion to differ when he was director of rugby at Newcastle Falcons, but I have to admit that he was a decent player who served England very well over the years.

Wales had blooded three new caps that afternoon. It was the start of what was to become a very illustrious career for scrum-half Robert Jones but appearing on a losing side against England had hardly been the start his father-in-law, Clive Rowlands, had been hoping for. Clive had been the last Welsh captain to lose to England in Cardiff in 1963 and had been desperate not to have his record taken from him. I know this game was at Twickenham but Clive won't have enjoyed the setback one little bit. John

Devereux was brought in for his debut in the centre, having played his way in by getting the better of Rob Ackerman in the Schweppes Cup game between South Glamorgan Institute and Cardiff, and Dave "Muddy" Waters finally got his chance in the second row alongside John Perkins. He should have played against France the previous season but missed out when the game was postponed because of the weather.

We got ourselves back on track by beating Scotland 22-15 in Cardiff, even though they outscored us three to one in the tries department. I got over for the Welsh try and, apart from a typical Jonathan Davies drop goal, all our other points came from the boot of Paul Thorburn. Paul made sure of victory with one of the most amazing penalty kicks every recorded. We were holding on to a one-point lead when he opted to have a go from a spot that was later measured as 70 yards and eight inches from the posts. He had a chat with our skipper Dave Pickering and told him he thought it was worth having a blast at it because, if nothing else, it would take play out of our half and deep into Scottish territory. It was a good day for Paul because he also became the fastest Welsh international to reach 50 points – his 54 were achieved in just five games for the Dragons.

Next stop was Dublin and another battle with Trevor Ringland, contests we both enjoyed to the full. Games in Ireland were never easy but we came away with a 19-12 win although Trevor had the satisfaction of scoring a try – and letting me know about it. I'm claiming that it wasn't my fault because the match video showed that Jonathan Davies had gone for an interception, and missed, leaving me with a two-on-one situation. I took the ball carrier and Trevor was given a free run in, so that night he kept reminding me that the score had been one-nil. Phil Lewis and Phil Davies scored our tries, the latter courtesy of his brother-in-law, and Paul Thorburn was on song again with the boot.

Paul Moriarty, the Swansea flanker, made his debut in that game and he became a good friend to me as our careers followed similar paths. We both went to the World Cup before switching codes and ended up playing for Widnes together. He was a good man to have around because he was a hard lad who didn't take shit from anybody.

We couldn't win the Triple Crown, having lost to England, but felt we could still have a share of the championship if we could beat France in Cardiff. Tony Gray had taken over as coach and there was a good spirit in the camp. Tony was a very different character to John Bevan and, although both were good coaches, I felt that Tony forged a better relationship with his players.

The omens should have been good for the French game because it was staged on St David's Day, which also happened to be my birthday. But my experiences with the French were never particularly happy ones and we let them in for four tries, being outplayed in all departments. Without Paul Thorburn we wouldn't have got on to the scoreboard to lose 23-15 — a more respectable scoreline than we deserved.

The disappointment was so great that it was a relief to get back to domestic rugby and we were soon back at the National Stadium to face Newport in the final of the Schweppes Cup, determined to wipe out the memory of the previous season's final when we had been literally pipped at the post by Llanelli. This time things couldn't have gone better and the 28-21 winning margin hardly demonstrated the way we had dominated the game.

It was something of a red letter day for me because I became the first player to score a hat-trick in a cup final and the Welsh Rugby Writers' Association voted me as man of the match, something Paul Turner used to rib me about because he felt he should have had it. In fairness to Paul, he was almost a one-man show for Newport because our pack ensured that they had few opportunities to mount attacks. Afterwards our skipper, Alan Phillips, said he thought we had played badly all season, by our own high standards, but that we had proved in the final that we could still play great rugby in the Cardiff style.

We soon had the chance to demonstrate that when we played Pontypool at the Arms Park. They had won the merit table again and we had won the cup so the game was billed as a battle of the giants of Welsh rugby. I have never seen a bigger crowd. The stadium was so tightly packed with rival fans that the police shut the gates and I can remember looking up and seeing fans hanging from the balconies of the flats that overlook the ground. There must have been more than 16,000 people in the ground and the atmosphere simply crackled. We both wanted to win in order to establish ourselves as the best side in Wales but we were the ones celebrating the night away after winning 27-19.

The dust had hardly settled on the season before the Welsh squad was heading for the South Seas for games against Fiji, Tonga and Western Samoa. I had played against the Fijians for both Cardiff and Wales but somehow suspected that they might prove a very different kettle of fish in their own backyard. And backyard was the operative word for the island of Tonga. I've seen better backyards in downtown Cardiff (but more of that later).

First port of call was Fiji and I felt it was important to have a good tour because the following summer Wales would be competing in the first ever World Cup. You didn't have to be an Einstein to realise that form during the 12 months prior to the competition was going to be crucial. Not that I was too concerned because I always had confidence in my own ability. The other wings on tour were Glenn Webbe, Mark Titley and his Swansea teammate Alan Emyr. Tony Gray and Derek Quinnell, guys I liked and respected, were the coaches.

I quite liked Fiji. The hotel was nice and had enough attractions to keep even Paul Moriarty occupied for a time. I've never known anyone like Paul for racing around hotels trying to find things to do. Mind you, by the end of the first morning he had done everything possible and was starting to get bored.

The opening game was against a Western Fiji Select side at

Lautoka and we only managed to win 19-14. All our points came from Bleddyn Bowen except for a very painful try that I managed to score. I slid in at the corner and ended up with a massive grass burn that took a long time to heal. When we went to the reception that evening I was the odd one out in shirt, tie and a pair of shorts instead of flannels. My thigh was such a mess it was impossible to get my trousers on and, even now, when I get sun tanned, you can see that the skin is a slightly lighter colour where the burn had been.

I wasn't able to play in the next game against an Eastern Fiji Select, but it was perhaps just as well because we were beaten 29-13, which made us realise that the Test match, despite how easy it had been in Cardiff, was going to be no picnic amongst the swaying palm trees. My leg was still a problem but they wanted me to play in the Test even though I purposely didn't go to ground in training. In the end I turned out with my leg smothered in petroleum jelly and our physio, Tudor Jones, did his best to put some strapping around it. Trouble was that it was so hot that any strapping quickly came off because we were all sweating so much.

Although normally a fly-half, Malcolm Dacey was picked at full-back and John Devereux partnered Bleddyn Bowen in the centre with Mark Titley on the opposite wing to myself. The main interest up front was the fact that the Moriarty brothers, Richard and Paul, were picked to play in a Test together.

The match was played in the National Stadium at Suva and will always be remembered by me as the game that almost ended skipper Dave Pickering's career. It was a fairly physical game and Dave had his head well and truly kicked by one of the Fijian players. The incident wasn't picked up by either the referee or the touch judge so the culprit went unpunished and Dave was, sadly, out of the tour. He was completely out of it in every other respect too and was very lucky not to have suffered permanent damage. As it was he was flown back to Wales as soon as he felt well enough and the captaincy was handed to Richard Moriarty.

It was a hard game but we managed to win 22-15. We started well to open a 13-point lead but Fiji, roared on by their fans, pegged us back to a single point before we managed to pull away again. I had to grit my teeth and go down on my sore leg for a try, all in the cause of my country. Jonathan Davies scored our other try and dropped a goal, Bleddyn converted one of the tries and Malcolm Dacey kicked three penalties.

I enjoyed Fiji and we certainly had some good times there, although I'm not too sure Tudor Jones would agree. We chartered a boat to a deserted island for a bit of fishing and a barbecue and the boys pinched Tudor's false teeth and didn't give them back to him until two days later. He was even less amused when myself and another squad member entertained a young lady in the bedroom set aside as his physio room – well, it did have a rubbing down table. The Fijians were a very friendly race and some of the young beauties were happy to prove it. We spent a very pleasant hour and put his ultrasound device to a use that we are sure was never intended by the manufacturers: the young lady thought it was the strangest vibrator she had ever encountered. Poor old Tudor was picking pubic hairs out of it for days!

A bunch of touring rugby players can usually find a few girls to spend time with but Tonga was a bit confusing, quite apart from being the biggest shithole I have ever been in anyway. We were told that some boys are raised as girls so there were transvestites everywhere. I ended up hitting one in the hotel bar. Phil Pugh, the Neath flanker, had been kidding one of them – this thing was clad in a blue sequined dress – that I fancied him, or it, whatever the correct terminology is, and the next thing his hand was on my arm. I just lost it and the lads had to stop me from killing him; at least, those lads who weren't rolling around having hysterics at my expense.

After Fiji, which was a nice place, arriving in Tonga was like landing on another planet. We were staying at what I think was the only hotel on the island – I wouldn't like to think there were any more of the same category anyway – and I was sharing a room with John Devereux. The first day we were sitting in the bar after training and watched a huge rat wander across the room. The staff never batted an eyelid and we used to sit in our room armed with a spray for killing all the cockroaches.

One day we were taken to meet the King of Tonga and were confronted by this big fat guy wearing cycling goggles and a hat that made him look like Toad of Toad Hall. Some days we trained in the palace grounds; it was more like the Waltons' house than a palace. We visited the "playing arena" three days before the Test and there was just an open field with some rugby posts. When we went back for the game they had erected a stand made from breezeblocks and wood, with a seat about 40 feet up on the halfway line for the King. We had to use showers back at the hotel but they had erected ramshackle dressing rooms, although a broken window caused us a little aggravation.

Paul Moriarty was working himself up for the Test match – we had earlier beaten a Tonga President's side 13-9 – and punched the window, which smashed to smithereens. The police took exception to that and it was some time before the management could cool things down. Poor old Paul had already been in trouble with the local constabulary for walking back to the hotel minus his shirt after a training session, which is illegal in Tonga for some reason.

The Test was a bloody nightmare. It was the dirtiest game I have ever played in and it's a wonder we got out of there alive. It was a bit like Roark's Drift. I was carried off unconscious after a massive fight behind the posts involving everyone except Malcolm Dacey and Mark Titley who, wisely, stayed on the halfway line. I grabbed hold of somebody who was punching Stuart Evans from behind and got hit from behind myself. The next thing I remember was waking up in hospital and the first face I saw was that of Kevin Hopkins, who'd been sent in the ambulance with me. I had a king-sized headache and don't know if I had a brain scan or whatever. They kept me lying there for about 15 minutes after I had come round and then told me I could go.

We asked for an ambulance to take us back to the ground but hospital staff said there was only one ambulance on the island and that had had to return to the ground to deal with any other casualties. We then asked if they could call a cab but it materialized that all the taxi drivers were at the game so Kevin and I had to walk back. Needless to say, I was still in full kit and rugby boots and nursing a very sore head. In my absence I missed one of the more entertaining moments in the game. Bleddyn Bowen was chased by a big Tongan player and, in the end, jumped into the crowd in a desperate attempt to get away, only to be followed by his assailant. It's a good job Bleddyn had a good sidestep because he had to use it as he dodged between fans before finally vaulting back on to the field of play and the safety of his teammates.

The post match reception was interesting, if you understood Welsh. Richard Moriarty gave his captain's speech in English and then Jonathan Davies asked if he could say a few words, which he did ... in Welsh. Luckily, our hosts didn't understand Welsh and I'm not too sure that our manager George Morgan did either, which may be just as well. I'm not a Welsh speaker but teammates were translating quietly for me. It seems the sum total of what Jonathan had to say, in his lovely lilting accent that was very warmly received by the uninitiated, was: "This is the worst fucking island we have ever been on, the game was shit, the food is shit and we can't wait to get the hell out of here."

Incidentally, I am at last completing my education in that I am learning Welsh. After Ann and I split up during my time in Manchester, she returned to live in Wales with our two boys, Matthew and Craig. They are both doing Welsh at school and I feel that I want to be able to converse with them in what is, after all, our native language.

Oh, and by the way, Wales won the Test match 15-7. Smashing

windows is obviously good pre-match therapy because Paul Moriarty scored our only try and Bleddyn Bowen and Malcolm Dacey kicked the necessary goals. Tonga scored a try but proved less adept at kicking goals than people. My departure during the game did serve one useful purpose: it gave Glenn Webbe the chance to make his international debut. Interestingly, Tonga toured England in 1998 and played an evening fixture against Sale Sharks. Talk about *déjà vu*, it was hardly a vicarage tea party.

Our party then moved on to Western Samoa which, like Fiji, was a nice place although very Americanized. We only had the one game there and I was definitely ruled out, having been to space and back. The boys played quite well to win 32-14, despite the presence in the home team of Michael Jones. The great All Black flew in on the same aircraft as ourselves.

We had a good party that night because it was the end of the tour and a crowd of us went skinny dipping when we got back to the hotel in the early hours of the morning, only to be relieved of all our gear – clothes, shoes, wallets, watches. So half of Western Samoa must have been walking around in Welsh number ones after we had returned home.

CHAPTER SIX

Wales Take on the World

THE WORLD CUP has become the ultimate rugby competition and it is very satisfying now to look back at where it all started in 1987 and be able to say, Max Boyce fashion, "And I was there."

So long as we didn't cock things up in the Five Nations, the players knew they were going to be in with a shout of a history making trip Down Under. It is ironic then that we nearly ended up with a whitewash, which would hardly have endeared us to the selectors, and the only success was against England in what will be remembered as the battle of Cardiff. Without the fighting, and I was on the bench so couldn't legitimately join in, I have a funny feeling we might have lost that one too.

It wasn't that we had a poor side that season and, as most of the boys went to the World Cup, the fact that we finished third in that competition supports that view. When we lost we didn't lose by much and in international rugby, when games are tight, it can often be a case of not getting the rub of the green. I don't think we got the breaks that season.

Perhaps we all felt that so much was at stake in terms of our individual ambitions that we failed to gel as a team in the Five Nations that season. In any event, I ceased to be first choice in that championship campaign after believing I had made the left wing berth my own. When Wales travelled to Paris to face France the selectors had decided to give Ieuan Evans his debut on the left with Glenn Webbe switched to the right wing. Kevin Phillips made his debut at hooker and Dave Pickering had recovered sufficiently from the shoeing in Fiji to lead the side again. Wales lost 16-9 and then squared up to England down in Cardiff.

I was on the bench and could only watch as the game deteriorated into little better than a brawl. The nonsense started as early as the sixth minute when Wade Dooley, the giant England lock, flattened Phil Davies. Had he walked, as he deserved to, the game may have followed a different pattern but, instead, it went from bad to worse and England did drop several of their players for disciplinary reasons afterwards, including Dooley and skipper Richard Hill. Wales didn't take any such action but then we hadn't started it.

Wales won 19-12 but the quality of our performance had done nothing to suggest we would be challenging for honours at the World Cup just weeks later, especially when we then went down 21-15 to Scotland at Murrayfield. I was on the bench again and got on when Ieuan was injured but we were being so comprehensively beaten up front that most of my work had to be in defence. Unfortunately, Stuart Evans had broken a bone in his foot and Peter Francis, the Maesteg prop, had been drafted in for his one and only cap. He won his wings that day but that's only because he spent most of the afternoon up in the air. It was a step too far for poor Pete and we struggled in the scrums all afternoon.

At one stage New Zealand referee Keith Lawrence said, "I'm having a problem with your prop."

At which one wag in our pack quipped, "We've got a fucking problem with him as well."

With Ireland due to visit Cardiff we at least could aim to end up with a 50-50 record in the championship but instead went down 15-11 to finish at the foot of the championship table. Hardly an auspicious start to our World Cup challenge. At least I was retained in the side and Ieuan moved to the right wing whilst my Cardiff clubmate, Steve Blackmore, took over at tighthead prop from Peter Francis. Ieuan and Rob Norster scored tries but Mark Wyatt had an off day with the boot so we were all left with an anxious wait to see if we had made the World Cup squad.

In the meantime we had the little matter of the Welsh Cup to deal with, having beaten Newport and Neath on the way to a final meeting with Swansea. It was a close run thing that went into extra time but we sneaked home 16-15 to make it three wins in four years. To the Cardiff boys it was the highlight of the season and I just loved the atmosphere. Leagues, of course, have changed things a bit because winning the title has assumed greater importance, as it means being measured over a whole season.

We had another head-to-head with Pontypool in front of another full house and were losing until I came off Mark Ring, went straight through a gap and rounded the full-back under the sticks to win the game. As I walked back John Perkins looked at me and said, "You complete wanker. That's the only time you've touched the ball." Well, it's not about how many times you get your hands on the ball, it's about what you do with it when you get hold of it. As a wing you get used to perhaps being offered just one opportunity to strut your stuff in a game.

With the final out of the way, our thoughts turned to the World Cup and, once the squad was announced, and despite a very indifferent Five Nations, we were all confident of at least reaching the quarter finals. We didn't expect too much trouble from Tonga and Canada in our pool games. The fourth side in the group was Ireland and, even though they had just beaten us in our own backyard, the sides had rather developed a habit of disregarding home advantage. We certainly seemed to find it easier to beat them in Dublin than Cardiff and hoped Wellington would prove a lucky venue for us too.

We were capable of playing some good rugby, especially when we had the ball in the backs. We loved to throw the ball around and, with Jonathan Davies at fly-half, we did just that as often as possible because he ran things in midfield and liked nothing better than demonstrating his ability with ball in hand. He also had confidence in those outside because, in the centre, we could pick from Bleddyn Bowen, Mark Ring, John Devereux and Kevin Hopkins, with myself, Ieuan Evans and Glen Webbe on the wings. Paul Thorburn was first choice full-back and Tony Clement was in reserve.

Wales being Wales, there was massive press interest in the event but, despite the expectations of our fans in South Wales, we did little in the way of extra preparation because the squad had been working hard for the Five Nations. We were also at the end of a long season, so it would have been senseless to have gone in for the headbanging variety of training and our South Seas tour the previous simmer had helped to lay the foundations for the challenge. All we needed was some fine tuning. We did, however, go away for a few days to Saundersfoot with our coach Tony Gray, who was being helped by Derek Quinnell. They were very meticulous about what they wanted us to do but were both good blokes off the park too and would enjoy a beer with us.

Tony was pretty laid back and nothing like his predecessor, John Bevan. I recall him taking one session at the Arms Park when we were working with the backs at one end of the field and Derek was organising the forwards at the other end. Tony stood in the middle of the pitch with a fag in his hand just watching what was going on. When I ended up as director of rugby at Sale Sharks I found that to be a good technique, minus the cigarette. At the time Jim Mallinder and Steve Diamond were the coaches but I involved myself in every training session. I would stand apart to watch the patterns of play and there were always things you picked up by watching from a distance or elevated in the stand. There was no blame on Jim and Steve for not spotting certain things because they were too close to the action and didn't have the overall view that I enjoyed. Towards the end of my time

71

at Sale I used to occupy a seat at the end of the press box and send messages to pitch side by walkie-talkie. The only problem with that is that the media boys sitting close by easily picked up on just what I thought of the game, or certain players!

The spell at Saundersfoot ended with all the wives and girlfriends being invited up for a farewell dinner on the Saturday night. Naturally, we had quite a few beers but there was a charity fun run for locals on the beach the following morning and Tony thought it would be a good idea if we all joined in to show a little solidarity and to sweat out all the beer we had drunk. It was good fun but a bit embarrassing to get beaten by some of those taking part.

I'm told international squads fly either first or business class these days but we flew all the way to New Zealand in the cattle section. I was tall for a wing and found it pretty tight but the poor old second rows sat with their knees under their chins all the way. It was a busy flight so there wasn't much chance to stretch out on empty seats. We flew from Heathrow with stops in Los Angeles and Hawaii and there's not much you can do except watch the films, play cards and sleep. At least on the return leg we did have a distraction in the shape of a group of New Zealand girls who were travelling to Los Angeles. A little game of cards, complete with forfeits!

The trip was purgatory for Paul Thorburn, who is about as happy in the air as I am on the ocean waves. I can get seasick while the boat is still tied to the dock and I must be the only guy on earth who has ever had to bale out of a pedalo. I turned so green when I went out on one off Crete that I had to jump into the water and swim to shore, leaving my wife Ann to pedal it back to the beach by herself. This problem of mine stems from the days when I played for youth rugby teams on tours to Ireland. We were once stuck for hours in a force nine gale in the middle of the Irish Sea. The engines were going full belt but the boat wasn't going anywhere. And I was as green as the ocean.

72

We landed in Wellington, which is noted as a windy city. Their Super 12s team is called The Hurricanes and it felt like one was blowing as we started on our final approach. The aircraft was being blown all over the place. Mr Thorburn, who would prefer never to leave terra firma, was all over the place too.

Wellington was similar to Wales. In addition to being very windy, it was also very green and very wet. The hotel wasn't the best in the world and the laundry service wasn't very good either. Which was a problem, as our training kit was getting wet through all the time because it never stopped pissing down. You can't train all the time so it's a case of trying to fend off the boredom and drinking isn't the solution during a World Cup although Tony and Derek were very good by not laying down any hard and fast rules in that department. They knew that we wanted to do well and wouldn't abuse their trust. Even though I was one of the biggest drinkers in the squad I gave it a miss because the coaches were guaranteed to pick up on it at training the following morning.

It was different when we all went out as a group or on special occasions. Prop Steve Blackmore was a pal of mine and he was in a bit of a state when his wife gave birth later in the competition when we were in Brisbane. He obviously wished he was back in Cardiff to be with his wife and new baby and was feeling a bit down so the pair of us decided to go out and get hammered. We got sympathy the following morning on the basis that it's not every day you become a father. Steve had to have somebody to drink with and I needed no excuse.

Our opening group game was against Ireland, which was hardly the ideal start and the Irish probably thought the same. There hadn't been any warm-up games so it would have been nice to have eased our way in against either Tonga or Canada. Instead we took ourselves off to Athletic Park to renew hostilities with our old friends from across the Irish Sea.

A very strong wind was blowing, which we thought might give

the Irish an advantage, but they never looked like repeating their Cardiff victory. Jonathan Davies controlled things from midfield and also dropped a couple of goals as we won 13-6. Paul Thorburn kicked a penalty and helped to send in Mark Ring for the only try of the game. We were able to relax after that and start to think about the quarter-finals.

Perhaps we shouldn't have presumed too much because Tonga were next up and they had kicked the shit out of us the previous year. It also meant moving on again to Palmerston North but at least the Showgrounds Oval provided a great playing surface and we won 29-16, wearing green shirts for the first time instead of our traditional red. I got over for a try but Glenn Webbe went two better by running in a hat-trick, even if he didn't know too much about the last one.

He took one hell of a hit in the form of a high tackle, a Tongan speciality, and the poor sod was concussed. Although he still managed to get over for his third try he hadn't a clue where he was and the upshot of it was that his World Cup was over. It was ironic that he had made his international debut against Tonga some twelve months earlier after I had been knocked out. We were all disappointed for him and missed his company because Glenn was a real character, the joker in the pack. He once had John Jeffrey, the Scottish flanker, gunning for him after one of our international meetings. Glenn had given him the old fag ash treatment, rubbing it into his face when he was past the stage of noticing. Poor old John, he unwittingly walked around all night with it all over his fair features and he was fuming when he found out. Stuart Evans also got injured in that game and was also out of the tour so at least they were company for one another on the long, lonely trek back to Wales.

The final group game was against Canada at Invercargill and, if you fancy visiting the arsehole of the world, that is it (sorry, I've forgotten about Tonga). It's at the end of the earth and if you head south from there the first living thing you'll see will be a penguin at the South Pole. Even when the sun shone it was bloody cold but we didn't see too much of that commodity and I remember sitting in the hotel with the rest of the boys, all feeling down in the dumps. It was pissing down outside, there was nothing to do and we sat watching England, who hadn't been dragged from pillar to post for their pool games, playing in Australia. The sun was shining and they were all in short sleeved shirts. Made us feel great, I can tell you, although it probably helped motivate us for our meeting in the quarter finals. Not that we ever needed much motivation to play England.

The hotel had, apparently, been built for a visit by the Queen some years previously but it was antiquated and had massive old radiators in the rooms. Staving off boredom was again a problem and even Paul Moriarty couldn't find anything to do. Paul was always a nightmare on tour because he couldn't simply do nothing. Even in Fiji the previous summer, when the hotel had a golf range, snooker table, table tennis table, gaming machines and a swimming pool, he was complaining by noon on the first day that there was nothing else to do. He had already done the lot. Paul wasn't one for pacing himself.

Invercargill is such a riveting place that one of the trips the locals organised for us was to an abattoir. No wonder the Kiwis are so keen on their rugby if a visit to a hypermarket version of a butcher's shop is considered as entertainment. Most of the time it was a case of train in the rain, back to the hotel for a shower, eat lunch, sit around watching television or videos, have dinner and then play cards and go to bed. One night we went to a bar in town and asked if there was a nightclub. We were directed to a place down the road but when we got in there it was completely dead. Just a bunch of rugby players and a barman but at least he was on the ball when we asked where everyone was. He sorted out the drinks and then asked to be excused. Before long the place started to fill up. He'd been busy ringing local people telling them to get down to the club.

We were back in our green strip for the game against Canada at Rugby Park and the Canadians proved stern opponents for a time. They actually led 9-6 at half time but we weren't worried and romped to a 40-9 victory in the end. Jonathan, who was acting captain for Richard Moriarty, again masterminded the show as we ran riot in the second half. I got over for one of our tries and there were others for Alan Phillips, John Devereux and Bleddyn Bowen whilst Ieuan Evans, on the opposite wing to me, in place of the luckless Glenn Webbe, equalled the Welsh record with four.

A few beers were consumed that night as we had topped the group to earn a quarter-final tilt at England and it was great to fly into Brisbane and feel the warm sun on our backs for a change. Aussie hotels were better too and ours was slap bang in the middle of the city. It had two swimming pools and it was good to be able to just wander around outside, especially as the pedestrianised zone was right in front of the hotel.

That did have its drawbacks, however, because I unwittingly ended up as a bit of a sideshow. I woke up scratching my nether region one morning and took myself off to the team doctor's room to find out what was wrong. He told me to walk over to the window, open the curtains to let some light in and drop my pants. So there I was, standing stark bollock naked in front of the window while the doc got down on his hands and knees to examine me. God only knows what passers by thought he was up to!

The upshot of the examination was that I had picked up a dose of crabs and he told me he wanted me to keep it quiet. He needn't have worried because I wasn't planning to call a press conference and make an announcement. I was too busy being concerned about the implications to my physical well being.

"Don't tell the other boys," he said. "It's not a good thing to have and rumours will start spreading and everyone will get upset."

It seemed to me that someone had already been doing a little spreading and I was left with an itchy crotch. The doc told me to shave myself, which I did ... very, very carefully. I needn't have bothered. I discovered later that instead of shaving the complete area, all I had to do was use a certain type of shampoo and cream, so I toddled off to the nearest pharmacy to buy some. The only problem was trying to explain being shaved in the nether regions when I hadn't needed to shave my pubes off in the first place. I told the doctor that he was a prick for not telling me about the alternative treatment and he told me I was a prick for catching crabs in the first place!

I must confess that I panicked at first when I realised what it was but there was no question of me not playing and, just like Paul Thorburn and Paul Moriarty, I ended up playing in every World Cup game.

The next task was England and the media boys, not surprisingly, latched on to the events of our last meeting in Cardiff and were busy speculating about whether or not hostilities would kick off again. Most picked England to win, especially as we had had our share of injuries and were drafting in nineteen-year-old Dai Young for his first cap at prop. He arrived as the babe (some babe!) in the squad after Stu Evans had been sent home injured. Dai just happened to be playing in Australia at the time with another Swansea youngster, Richard Webster. I don't know whether or not Swansea, or maybe just the players, had been cute enough to foresee what might happen during the World Cup. It was easier to draft them into the squad rather than have someone sent out from Wales and both covered themselves in glory before the competition was over.

The sun deserted us on the day of the game at Ballymore and it rained. It was hardly the weather we wanted but I don't suppose it suited England either because they must have been confident of taking us. Not that we even gave an England victory a thought. We were fired up and full of self belief so weren't as surprised as our old enemy when we ran out 16-3 victors.

In the conditions it was hardly a classic, especially as there was a lot of tension in the air, but there is no doubt about the better side winning that day. I think our forward effort surprised them because I am sure they thought they could put pressure on Dai Young but they lost his opposite number Paul Rendall, to be replaced by Gareth Chilcott. That was a defining moment because England had to defend a scrum with seven forwards before Chilcott got on and, when the ball popped out, our blindside flanker Gareth Roberts picked up and drove over the line.

A kick and chase brought the second try. It was a race between the rival scrum-halves, Robert Jones and Richard Harding from Bristol. The Jones boy did us proud and we were out of sight when John Devereux gratefully grabbed number three. England were chasing the game when their fly-half, Pete "Gobbler" Williams, who was to become a teammate at Salford, passed the ball into the arms of Devs by mistake and the big Bridgend centre strolled over the line with a huge grin on his face and a fist raised in salute. Paul Thorburn converted two of the tries and all England could muster was a penalty by full-back Jon Webb.

It was a satisfying moment and ended England's involvement in the tournament. They had played reasonably well when losing to Australia in their pool game and I thought we had been lucky to beat them in Cardiff. The knowledge that a teenage prop had replaced our rock, Stu Evans, must have had them dreaming of a semi-final spot but we simply played as we always did against them in my day – in their faces. I hold my hands up and admit that, if it was England, I didn't mind smacking somebody off the ball.

That was a night to remember or, in my case, not to remember. In his autobiography, *Flying Wing*, Rory Underwood wrote about how a bad day turned into a bad night when he and the rest of the England side arrived at a disco to find the Welsh team there. I can't remember sharing a disco with the England players so I must have been really enjoying myself!

What I do remember was a session back at the hotel. Bryan Robson, who was playing for Manchester United at the time but was on a visit to Australia, introduced himself to us and paid for bottles of champagne to be brought over. A nice gesture considering he's an Englishman. In return we invited him up to our team room, where we had beer laid on, and he spent the night with us, joining in all the drinking games. Mind you, Bryan could certainly put it away.

Back home I'm sure everyone thought that reaching the semi-finals was a tremendous achievement and, although you never go into a game expecting to lose, even we knew that New Zealand was likely to be a bridge too far. They were hot favourites to win the competition and were undoubtedly the best side in the world at the time, as events proved a few days after our meeting. We were massive underdogs. But it was great to get the opportunity to play in the semis and it felt like a reward when we were taken away to Surfers' Paradise to relax, especially when Tony Gray said he wanted to see us all on the beach.

We expected being allowed to mess about but he ordered us to run up and down the beach instead – it was a long one – to get rid of the all the booze we had consumed celebrating our victory over the English.

Perhaps we should have stayed on the beach because I'm afraid Ballymore wasn't such a happy place for us on our return. We were hammered 49-6 by the All Blacks. At that time it was the heaviest defeat Wales had ever suffered and the fact that Devs scored the try of the game was little consolation considering that the Blacks ran in eight, two of those coming from my opposite number, John Kirwan. One wasn't down to me but I must confess he skinned me for the other when I showed him the outside. The only other player who has ever done that to me is Martin Offiah in rugby league. I was always confident of my pace and angles when I showed an opponent the outside track but John got over in the corner.

Kirwan is the best wing I have played against. I couldn't get over just how big he was. Mark Ring got hold of his shorts after the game but disappeared when he put them on. Then he spotted a thoroughly pissed off Huw Richards slumped in a corner — he'd been sent off —and thought it would be a nice gesture to pass them on to the Neath second row. They didn't fit Huw either. When I got home I presented Kirwan's shirt to St Joseph's rugby club and the chairman, thanking me, told the audience that the closest I had got to Kirwan's shirt was when we exchanged them after the final whistle.

Huw had been sent off during the game and its hard enough playing New Zealand with 15 men. Playing them with 14 proved impossible but, if he deserved his punishment, Wayne Shelford, the New Zealand number eight, should have gone with him. Admittedly, Huw smacked Shelford at a lineout but the All Black hammered him back and should have gone off for retaliation.

There's not much else to say about that game. There was no magical turnaround like the one the French produced at the same stage in the 1999 World Cup but we felt we had gone as far as we could have done and had exceeded all expectations of us. At least we had a chance to clinch third place in the play-off against Australia, even though it meant moving home yet again to set up camp at Rotorua. And, oh boy, if we thought Invercargill was the pits, this place was something else.

Rotorua is famous for its hot springs that send jets of water and vapour shooting out of the ground. The only problem is that the whole place reeks of bad eggs because of the sulphur. And guess where the geysers were – right behind our hotel, if that's what you could call the barracks we were housed in. I can understand now why so many New Zealanders seem keen to come over here. If they're from Rotorua it will be to get away from the pong.

The schedule meant that we had hardly any time to prepare for the Aussie game. The squad had also been badly hit by injuries. Second rows Rob Norster (injury) and Huw Richards (banned) were out of it and skipper Richard Moriarty had to move up into the second row, where he was joined by policeman Steve Sutton. That left a gap that resulted in young Richard Webster winning his first cap because Richie Collins was also injured; not bad, considering Webby had only gone to Australia for a playing holiday. My pal Steve Blackmore took over from Dai Young at prop.

Mark Ring teamed up with John Devereux in the centre, Robert Jones and Jonathan Davies were at half-back, Paul Thorburn was at full-back and Ieuan Evans and myself were the wings. Australia put out a strong side that included talented players such as Matt Burke, Michael Lynagh, Andrew Slack, David Campese, Steve Cutler, Steve Tuynman and Steve Poidevin.

The best thing about the day was that International Park in Rotorua was impressive and we had the full support of the local crowd because New Zealanders can't stand Australians. We didn't get on too well in the opening exchanges either because it was very, very physical. I was marking Peter Grigg and the pair of us were warned in just the third minute for fighting. A minute later Aussie flanker David Codey was sent off for stamping all over Gareth Roberts. The referee was "Fearless" Fred Howard so there was no way he was going to let Codey stay on the field after that.

Fred was a good referee and I always got on well with him, although I came close to walking when he warned me for a high tackle on Campese in the second half. I enjoyed that tackle because I can't say I got on with the guy. I found the Aussies pretty arrogant and Campo was gobbier than most.

Australia scored tries through Burke and Grigg, who later went off injured and was replaced on the wing by scrum-half Nick Farr Jones. Both were converted by Lynagh, who then drilled over two penalties and dropped a goal. We replied with tries by

Paul Thorburn and Gareth Roberts with Paul converting one and adding two penalties. That still left us 21-16 adrift until the final minute when the boys managed to work me over in the corner to cut the deficit to a point. Paul banged over a pressure conversion from the touchline to give us a third place spot that exceeded our wildest dreams.

Our opponents were their usual graceless selves at the reception after the game, with their coach Alan Jones saying the Aussies hadn't been interested in third place, their tournament having ended when beaten by the French in the semi-final. Just a load of sour grapes really. Truth is they "don't like it up 'em" and, despite what they say about the whingeing Poms, they can whinge with the best of them when things don't go their way.

We were driven to the post match reception by Steve Blackmore, who worked as an electrician for a bus company back in Cardiff. I don't think the driver was very happy about it but he didn't really have a lot of choice in the matter as the rest of us were egging Steve on. Afterwards, the inevitable happened. We ended up in the same nightclub as the Aussies and the whole thing nearly kicked off again. One thing that has struck me is that this business of making friends for life with opponents simply doesn't happen any more. It may have done in the old amateur days but, as professionals, I don't see how you can get too close. You make acquaintances, nothing more. The real friendships are forged with teammates if you stay with a club for a long time but, these days, professional players tend to move club far more frequently than the amateurs did.

The squad was flown to Christchurch to watch the World Cup Final, when New Zealand beat France. I always had a problem with official dinners so it wasn't long before a group of us sneaked off for a few beers to fortify ourselves for the long haul back home. At least we took the return trip in gentler stages. We stayed in Hawaii long enough to stroll along Waikiki Beach and in Los Angeles long enough for me to crash out by the hotel pool while some of the lads went off to Disneyland. I was happy to lie around in the sun with a few beers by my side so that I could get shitfaced. I can't say I like America much anyway. The place is too busy for me and, even though I hail from Cardiff, I think of myself as a country boy who doesn't like a lot of hustle and bustle. The other thing I can't stand is the accent, which tends to grate on my nerves.

We did have an interesting session at Los Angeles airport when we arrived from Hawaii. The duty boys were looking after all the kit so Mark Ring and myself disembarked pretty smartish and, as the bus hadn't arrived to take us to the hotel, we made a beeline for the bar. We had just ordered a drink when we heard someone with a Welsh accent asking, "And where are you boys from then?"

Ringo and I turned around and found ourselves face to face with Tom Jones. Mind you, Ringo said, "I know you from somewhere," and I had to jog his memory. The next thing the rest of the boys were in the bar too and it wasn't long before we were all reminiscing with the singer about Wales and the World Cup. As soon as word got around that Tom Jones was drinking with us, "Thumper" Phillips came charging into the bar and greeted Tom as though he had known him all his life. He even invited Tom to our hotel for a few beers but he was noncommittal because his wife was sitting by herself in a corner of the bar. They had been back to Wales for a family funeral.

When we got outside, Tom's limousine was as big as our bus. That evening I was having a beer with Steve Blackmore and Gareth Roberts and we positioned ourselves opposite the hotel lifts. We then rang reception and got them to ring Thumper to say that Tom Jones' chauffeur was waiting in reception for him. A couple of minutes later he came bouncing out through the lift doors, took one look at our grinning faces and said, "You bastards."

We flew back to Heathrow and then took the coach back to

Cardiff for a fantastic reception in the city centre. Wives and girlfriends and kids were there to meet us and the place was a madhouse for a time with newspapers, radio and television lining up to do interviews. It was something we were all able to look back on with pride. We had surprised the pundits by taking third place in the inaugural World Cup and had only been beaten by one side ... the best in the world.

CHAPTER SEVEN

Hello Corrie Street

LITTLE DID I know that the autumn of 1987 would herald the start of my last season with Cardiff and Wales. At least I went out on something of a high on the international stage as we got within a whisker of a Grand Slam. Clearly, finishing third in the World Cup had done wonders for our confidence and, whilst we wouldn't claim to have been a match for the dominant Welsh side of a decade or two earlier, we did have some decent players. Had a few of the more notable ones not switched codes, it is possible that Wales would have enjoyed a dominant period again in the northern hemisphere.

We warmed up with a game against the USA in Cardiff in November and ran in eight tries in beating our cousins from across the water 46-0. Bleddyn Bowen was switched to fly-half and made skipper in the absence of Jonathan Davies and there were new caps for Neath prop John Pugh, back row Rowland Phillips, who ended up playing rugby league for Warrington, and a second row who was completely unknown to us, Stuart Russell. He had been born in Kenya but had a Welsh qualification and was playing at London Welsh.

Bleddyn revelled in his new role and celebrated with two tries, as did Tony Clement, who came on as a replacement in the centre for Kevin Hopkins. Dai Young, later to become a Salford teammate, also scored along with Glen Webbe, Rob Norster and Paul Moriarty, who was destined to become yet another of the World Cup side that switched codes. At the time I'm sure a move wasn't in our thoughts as we prepared to start our Five Nations campaign against England at Twickenham. We had got the better of them in the World Cup and saw no reason why we couldn't do so again. Anyway, there was no Rob Andrew, who had done all the damage on our last visit to Twickenham. Rob's place at fly-half was filled by Les Cusworth from Leicester and his lack of hair caused me some embarrassment before the day was out.

We went into the game without a recognised goal kicker because Paul Thorburn was injured, whereas England had Jon Webb, the doctor from Bristol, kicking for them. Tony Clement started at full-back, Bleddyn retained the captaincy but led the side from centre because Jonathan was back in the fold and Phil May made his debut in the second row. Much has been made of the ability of Welsh fly-halves over the years and this game was remarkable for the fact that we had four top class number tens in the side: Jonathan, Bleddyn, Mark Ring and Tony Clement. Ieuan Evans and myself were on the wings and, although not big hitters in the centre, there was nothing wrong with the defence of Bleddyn and Mark.

Not surprisingly, with so many visionaries and ball players in the side but without a kicker, there was only one way we were going to play against England and that was to throw the ball around at every opportunity. For all our endeavours to do just that the scoreboard was still blank at the interval, which is unusual in a rugby match at any level, but our intent to run the ball paid off and I scored twice to help Wales to an 11-3 victory. Ringo and I had been playing for and against each other since our primary school days and we combined in an inter-passing move that ended with me getting over in the corner. Ringo was involved in my second try too although on that occasion he opened up the English defence with some neat inter-passing between himself and Jonathan and I took a pass from Bleddyn to go through Les Cusworth on the way to the line.

Immediately after the game I was interviewed for *Grandstand* and they asked me to talk them through the try as they put it up on screen. I told how I had taken the pass and gone through Dusty Hare's tackle to get over in the corner but Bob Norster, who was standing alongside me, was creasing himself laughing. The interviewer realised my mistake and Bob took great delight in telling me that Dusty hadn't been playing. Well, I knew it was a little guy who didn't have much hair.

The scoring that afternoon was completed by Jonathan, who had made a bet before the game that he would drop a goal in all four matches in the championship. True to his word, he popped one over.

That was one of our best victories, and scoring twice in a Welsh victory at Twickenham remains one of my greatest rugby memories. The evening was good fun too, especially when myself and Bob Norster, along with our wives, walked into the celebrations at the hotel and helped ourselves to a few glasses of champagne before we realised that we had gate-crashed a wedding reception by mistake. My second *faux pas* of the day.

As I have said earlier, I hated the formal dinners after games and physio Tudor Jones and myself found ourselves on a table with a few suits and Rory Underwood. Everyone was being very respectable, and Rory doesn't drink and was due to fly the following day anyway, whereas Tudor and myself were just intent on drinking ourselves shitfaced. I don't think that went down too well and we made our excuses and left as soon as we reasonably could. Later, in the bar, Staff Jones, the Pontypool prop, ended up getting a serious ticking off. A very old guy was walking through carrying a ball he had clearly had signed by the players so Staff, who was full of pop, decided it would be a good idea to go thundering across the room and tackle him. The poor chap was so badly winded that they had to call a doctor.

I had all the headlines in the Welsh press on the Monday and rather spiked my boss's guns in the process. By that time I was working for Clive Thomas, the former soccer referee, who was managing director of the Welsh operation of OCS, a large industrial cleaning group. Fellow international Malcolm Dacey also worked there and scrum-half Robert Jones also had a spell with the company. Two days after my Twickenham success, we had to go to a reception in the line of duty. Clive was used to being the centre of attention at these things but he had to take a back seat that day because I was the one everybody wanted to talk to, that being the way of things in rugby-daft Cardiff. I don't think Clive was impressed. I remember going into his office once and opening a cupboard door. I was immediately buried under a mountain of copies of his autobiography. I don't know whether or not Clive had bought all the books himself – so don't lend this book to anybody or I'll end up in the same boat!

After that we entertained Scotland in Cardiff, winning 25-20. It was a really close contest with Jonathan winning the day for us as we came from behind to take the points. We deserved to win if for no other reason than we scored three tries to their two and the first came about when Jonathan indulged in a kick and chase and beat Scottish number eight Derek White to the touchdown. The second was an absolute cracker from Ieuan Evans. Paul Thorburn started what was a planned move and I took it on. I then threw out a poor pass to Mark Ring but he recovered the situation well to feed Ieuan, who came off his wing to wrong-foot a string of defenders before scoring at the posts. As a wing myself I could really appreciate that one.

Hooker Ian Watkins grabbed the third try but we still trailed by a point as time started to run out. Then Jonathan, who had promised to drop a goal in every game, went one better than that, he dropped two!

Suddenly, a Triple Crown and Grand Slam was starting to look like a distinct possibility and we travelled to Dublin with our tails up. Once again I was up against my old adversary Trevor Ringland but it was honours even as neither of us managed to score and the hero for Wales was Paul Thorburn. Having said that, Jonathan started the ball rolling by dropping yet another goal and his boast that he would drop a goal in each of the four games was starting to look a distinct possibility. But Ireland came back at us strongly. We conceded a try to their prop Terry Kingston and a conversion and penalty from Michael Kiernan left us trailing 9-3.

Fortunately Paul Moriarty got over from the base of a scrum close to the Irish line and Thorburn's conversion levelled the scores. A draw looked the likely outcome as the game moved into injury time but the Irish killed the ball at a ruck and Paul kicked a real pressure goal to give us the Triple Crown. There really was a good party that night and we returned home on Sunday without Rowland Phillips. He must have been having a wonderful time because he missed the flight.

Sunday was usually a day of relaxation and drinking for me. If I was in Cardiff I would go to the City Social Club for a lunchtime drinking session with my mates and then go home for dinner and to watch *Rugby Special*. Then I would meet up with my mates again and we would go to 6.30pm Mass at St Peter's before going to the club for a few frames of snooker and a bag of chips and back home for a good sleep in readiness for work on Monday morning.

With a Grand Slam at stake the hype was tremendous for the visit of France to the National Stadium. By that stage I had already had talks with Salford and knew there was a possibility it could be my last game for Wales. It would have been wonderful to have gone out with a bang, or Slam preferably, but, in the end, the game was a damp squib. The weather was dreadful too and it's a myth that you pray for rain when you play the French. We might have done better on a dry track whereas the French adjusted better to the conditions and, despite the fact that they only beat us by a point, 10-9, we made too many mistakes and they had the better of things overall.

France led throughout and a kick and chase try by Ieuan Evans, converted by Paul Thorburn, came perhaps too late. We weren't really able to put pressure on their line again. Needless to say, Jonathan did his level best to drop a goal in the closing stages but, on this occasion, his amazing powers left him. He failed in his personal quest to drop a goal in every game but at least he averaged out at one per match, which was quite an achievement.

My move to *Coronation Street* country came about after I had received a telephone call from a *Western Mail* reporter asking if I had ever fancied a switch to the other code. He had been called by a fellow scribe from "up north" who said that a couple of clubs were looking to recruit centres and wings. Playing rugby league was an option I had considered, although maybe not too seriously, but once the bones of the idea had been given meat by the knowledge that a club could be interested in me, I thought it was something I should have a crack at.

Although Cardiff looked after their players and I had a decent job, I had achieved everything in rugby union except playing for the British Lions. The next Lions tour was some time in the future and I felt that if I didn't switch codes, then I never would. It was a case of grabbing the nettle then or not at all and I told the reporter that I might be interested if someone wanted to give me a call.

The call that came soon afterwards was quite bizarre. At the time there were two Hadleys playing for Cardiff, myself and back row Matthew Hadley, who is unrelated and worked as a painter and decorator. The guy who called was Salford's chief scout, Albert White, who was a brewery rep, and I was left wondering if he had been in the sampling room because he asked if I was Matthew when I answered the telephone.

I told him no, it was Adrian and he said, "Yes, but it is Hadley isn't it?"

I said that that was my name and he said that Salford wanted me to sign professional forms with them. "You're not married are you?" he asked.

When I told him that I was, he said, "Well, you're a painter and decorator so we can get you a job doing that during the day."

I told him that I was a rep for a car leasing company, was married with a baby on the way and that he had clearly got the wrong guy. Although Salford wanted a wing, Albert had got all the background on Matthew so I suspected he had never seen me play.

Soon after that I had a call from the Salford chairman, John Wilkinson, who is a really nice guy. Once he had ascertained that I was interested in following a well-worn path from the valleys of South Wales to the industrial North, we arranged to meet at a hotel in Ross-on-Wye

I asked Mike O'Brien, an accountant pal of mine, to go with me to deal with the financial stuff. I had played rugby at St Joseph's with his brother Martin, who was known to everyone at the club as Sloppy because his shoulders were forever popping out. His other brother, Laurence, was a hooker at Cardiff and had a couple of seasons there playing mainly second and third team rugby.

Once I had talked in general terms to John, I left Mike to agree terms with the club and I went to wait in the bar. The deal, barring my signature, was done and dusted and I then had to concentrate on playing the final international of the campaign against France.

With the tour to New Zealand looming I had also had to make a decision. I hadn't thought it right to go on tour if I was likely to switch codes but wanted to keep my options open and didn't actually sign for Salford until a week before their season started. After the French game, I gave a letter to Rod Morgan saying that

I wasn't available to tour and gave as my excuse the fact that Ann was pregnant with Matthew. Paul Thorburn gave him a letter saying he wasn't available either and I don't think the authorities were too pleased about losing two key players for what was going to be a tough tour and one that turned out, in the end, to be a complete disaster.

Interestingly, Warrington had also come in for me and I went through a period of indecision. One option was to stay where I was in Cardiff. I was playing with a great club side, was enjoying international rugby as a bonus and was doing well in the car leasing operation. Another option was to see what sort of deal I could cut with Warrington. Or I could stick with my original idea of moving to Salford. In the end it was a case of going with my first instinct and I went up to sign on a Friday afternoon, two days before Salford were due to play their first game at home to Hull KR.

At the time I had never even been to Manchester, let alone Salford, so it was quite a big step. As I was being provided with a club car I was accompanied by my pal Mike, who was going to drive my car back to Cardiff and make sure the signing went ahead without a hitch. After booking into a hotel in Manchester we drove to The Willows, Salford's ground, for the press conference.

Before that I had a medical that turned out to be a bit of a joke. I expected a lengthy and intensive examination – after all I was an expensive £100,000 signing, which was a record at the time – but after having my blood pressure taken and a thermometer stuck in my mouth, it was all over. Oh, I was asked if I had broken any bones or had any illness during the last 18 months but I could have told them anything because nobody asked to see my medical records.

When I had gone to meet John Wilkinson initially I had had no preconceived idea of the size of fee that might be involved. I felt I was getting stale, having done everything anyway in rugby union in Wales, and would probably have signed regardless of the figure. If John had known that, he could have saved himself a lot of money. I had left the financial side of the deal entirely to Mike and it didn't really register with me that it was a record sum. It was a lot of money in those days but my only concern was how it was going to be paid to me.

After the press conference I was taken to Heald Green, a Manchester suburb on the more affluent south side of the city and not far from the airport. Just how close, I was to discover. A club house was part of the deal for six months and then I was expected to buy one of my own, which was fair enough considering the deal I had just signed. I liked the area so eventually bought a house just around the corner but we were right on the flight path and aircraft used to almost skim the roof. You do get used to the noise after a time and when the boys were growing up they were so used to it that they wouldn't even look up when one went over, although visitors would be craning their necks or diving for cover.

I was dropped back at the hotel and found Mike in the bar, where he was looking worried and said he needed to talk to me. When I asked how serious it was, he told me I would need a drink. My first thought was that something had somehow gone wrong with the deal or that the cheque I had been given was of the bouncy variety but, fortunately, Mike had only smashed up my car as he tried to find his way from the ground to the hotel. He didn't know the streets and had gone flying around a corner and hit something. I assured him that so long as there wasn't a problem with the cheque it was all right and he eventually started to relax.

Finding my way in and out of Salford became a nightmare for me. I was continually getting myself lost but that may have had something to do with the drinking culture I got into. I know, you shouldn't drink and drive, but it's what we did in those days and I paid the price during my time at Salford when I found myself off the road. More of that later.

The pair of us went back to Cardiff and I went to watch the boys play at the Arms Park. I can't remember who they were playing but I remember being turned away when I tried to walk into the downstairs bar afterwards. Officials had known for a while that I was leaving to turn professional and most were fine about it and I continued to have a good relationship with both officials and fans. But I had run up against a jobsworth who was a stickler for protocol and he reminded me that as I wasn't a Cardiff player any more and wasn't a member of the club, I wouldn't be admitted. Fortunately Terry Holmes realised what was going on and came over to sign me in.

I had sold my soul as far as the doorman was concerned but, fortunately, most people had a grown up attitude to my departure, despite the way in which rugby league had raped Welsh rugby for years. My switch seemed to spark something of an exodus. David Bishop had already gone north and it wasn't long before I was followed by Jonathan Davies, John Devereux, Paul Moriarty, Dai Young, Rowland Phillips and Allan Bateman.

Rob Ackerman returned after he had taken the coin and I remember a bit of a spat with some of the committee but I don't think Rob had got on that well with them anyway, whereas I had had a good relationship with them and that continued even after my switch.

The following day I was back in Salford and I was back and forth so often in the early days that it's a wonder I didn't wear out the road. Although I wasn't ready to make my debut, Salford wanted me so that they could introduce me to the fans. There was a big enough media presence too, especially from Wales, because in addition to mine being a world record signing at the time, it was also my old pal Dave Bishop's debut for Hull KR.

Sadly, Dave only lasted about 45 minutes before getting injured so doesn't have happy memories of his first visit to The Willows. Nor does my old Wales teammate and now famous ghostwriter for gobby England tourists, Eddie Butler, who was working for

BBC Wales. It was a very angry Eddie who stormed back into the clubhouse a few minutes after having left it. The ground is in what some would consider a rough area and Eddie's car had been well and truly trashed by the local worthies.

I never found the area a problem. Cardiff has its rough parts too but I find that people who live there do look after each other to perhaps a greater extent than they do in some of the more affluent areas. What I did find a problem was being there rather than back in Cardiff. Truth is that I missed my mates and it didn't help that I was living on the south side of Manchester and well away from most of the Salford players, who lived mainly in Salford, Swinton or Wigan. The result was that I used to dash back to Cardiff between training sessions – we trained Tuesday and Thursday evenings and Saturday mornings – to go drinking with my old mates simply because I missed the "craic".

The other problem was that it took a while to establish myself with my new teammates. Not surprisingly there was some resentment over the money I was receiving, although I wasn't the first to experience that. It was a bit the same for Peter Williams, even though he came from a rugby league town like Wigan and his father Roy, a Welshman who had played for Llanelli, had moved north to play the 13-a-side code. But then Peter had played rugby union for England so he was "one of them" to the bread-and-butter boys in the Salford camp.

It didn't help that I was also well out of condition at the time. I hadn't trained since the Spring when Cardiff's season finished. That was partly because my wife Ann was pregnant and we were awaiting the arrival of Matthew and partly because I had been undecided for much of that summer about where I was going to play in the new season.

Keith Bentley was very good and helped me a lot in the early days when the rest of the squad were probably wondering why their employers had paid out what was then a very large sum of money for an out-of-condition Welshman from the other code.

Unfit or not, I still classed myself as a good footballer and I think that, at least, came out in my first training sessions. Not that I had many before I was pitched in for my debut, a week after my arrival. There was no gentle introduction in the Academy side but then I suppose John Wilkinson was keen to get an early return on his investment.

So that left me making my debut, at home, against Warrington, the other club that had tried to secure my services. That brought me up against Des Drummond, a big name in rugby league and a player I later considered one of the best wings I played against. It was rather a baptism of fire but I came through all right even though I didn't exactly set the world alight. Having said that, I didn't exactly receive much ball and was involved more in a defensive capacity. That wasn't a problem because I prided myself on the quality of my defence in either code.

We did win the game but it all passed in a bit of a haze and I can't remember much about the detail. What I did find was that the game was much quicker at that time. Rugby union has moved on since going professional but, back in the Eighties, it was a yard or two slower than the 13-a-side version. The game was also harder physically and one thing I had to get used to was the fact that you tended to get man-on-man all the time. It was perfectly normal to be twatted by two opponents at the same time, especially when you played on the wing. Unlike in union, there was rarely the opportunity to take your opposite number on the outside.

I was never that quick off the mark anyway, unlike Des Drummond, John Bentley, Jason Robinson and Martin Offiah. But I was a handful when I got up a head of steam because I was a big lad and pretty physical. From the first training session Keith Bentley said he could tell that I was a good footballer, so that was some consolation.

After the Warrington win we won 36-8 at Wakefield, beat Oldham away 18-2 in the Lancashire Cup and I scored twice, my first tries for the club, when we beat Widnes 15-12. When we beat Warrington again in the semi-final of the Lancashire Cup I started to think the world was wonderful. Six games and six victories. I even did the goalkicking in that game and popped over three as we won 15-2. But it was all going to change. We didn't have a big squad and that had a major effect on progress once we started to pick up a few injuries to key players.

Along with the injuries came the defeats and we lost to Wigan in the final at Knowsley Road even though we later beat them 24-16 in the league at The Willows.

After a couple of months I started to settle in and it helped when I cut out the mad dashes back to Cardiff just to go drinking with my mates. You might find that rather strange behaviour in a semi-professional sport but drinking was very much part of the culture and some of the sessions the day before a game were among the more memorable. One reason why drinking was part of the culture was the lack of something to do. Some of the players had jobs during the day but people like myself and the overseas players tended to just hang around and it got very boring. I see the same situation now in rugby union although professionalism has grown to the extent that the majority sit watching television rather than prop up bars.

It was heading towards my first Christmas at Salford that I decided the trips back home – which had meant Ann being stuck at home in a strange town with Matthew – had to stop. My money was guaranteed and we were comfortable but I just needed something to get me out of the house, and the pub, and spoke to John Wilkinson about it. He fixed me up with a car leasing company that he had dealings with so I started working during the day almost in the shadow of Strangeways Prison. I wasn't new to the job because I had been involved in a similar position in Wales, where I ran the Cardiff end of the operation and Ieuan Evans ran the Swansea office. The company logo was "Winging our way to success." I got on well with the other lads at the

Salford operation and it wasn't exactly a stressful occupation. I was on a basic salary, plus commission, but I was happy with the former and didn't exactly bust a gut to boost my wages.

It was three months before I felt I was playing well and really getting into the game. I was also getting on terms with a sport I had expected to be more professional. Training sessions were hard, with the emphasis on defence and a good deal of time was devoted to holding and hitting tackle bags, but we trained no more than they had at Cardiff and the facilities were far worse. There was no training ground so we always trained on the first team pitch and the only facility was a multi-gym stuck between the dressing room and the showers. There was no planned programme for using it and, although they were supposedly part-timers too, we knew the Wigan boys had weights sessions every morning. Salford were always behind teams like that in terms of preparation and conditioning.

By comparison, Cardiff trained at the National Sports Centre across the road from the Arms Park and that came complete with pitches, astro-turf and all the training aids you can imagine. Afterwards there would be a hot meal in the clubhouse rather than the sandwiches and cup of tea provided by a couple of charming old dears at The Willows. The other big difference between the two set-ups was in medical back-up. The only way you could get physiotherapy treatment at Salford during the day was to go to the local university where the physio was a lecturer. Later, a girl called Linda from Wigan took over so it meant a drive out there to receive treatment, which was the last thing you wanted if you were suffering with an ankle or knee injury. In Cardiff that sort of treatment was always on hand at the club.

The back-up wasn't there if you needed speedy treatment after an injury in a game either. I remember Dai Young having to sit for hours in the accident and emergency department of Hope Hospital, Salford, before a medic had a look at him, after his back had gone when he bent down to play the ball at a training session in Buile Hill Park and couldn't get up. If you got injured playing for Cardiff you would be in hospital that night and the club would arrange for a specialist to see you straight away.

Having said all that, I enjoyed my time at Salford. It was a great club and the people there were fantastic from chairman John Wilkinson down. Graham McCarty was the secretary and money man and he was a good bloke. He would hand out the wages on a Thursday and even though my signing money, which came in stages, was invariably late, you knew the cheque would arrive. Which was rather different from my experience at Widnes a few years later. The thing is that John Wilkinson was a man of his word. If he said he would do something for you then it would be done.

When I arrived, the team was being coached by Kevin Ashcroft and Tommy Grainey. I wouldn't say that Kev was the best coach in the world but he was a brilliant guy to work with even though he used to go crackers with us on Tuesday evenings if we hadn't used the drills he had drummed into us before the game. He was a typical mouthy hooker. We used to crease ourselves sometimes when the chairman would come into the dressing room when we had lost a game and Kev would hold up his hands and say, "Can't blame me for that chairman. We were prepared and had the tactics but it was all down to those fuckers," waving his arms in our direction.

Kev was a typical Lancashire lad who had done the round of clubs as a player, including Doncaster, Rochdale Hornets, Salford and his home town club, Leigh. He had played for Great Britain and had two spells as a coach at The Willows but clearly found it hard going and had handed over to Kevin Tamati by the start of my second season there.

Tommy was a likeable character too. He was a total fitness fanatic although his sense of direction wasn't too good. When the pitch was too frozen to train on he would take us all for a run around the Salford streets so it was a bit like training on the set of

Coronation Street. At every street corner he would have us doing press ups and sit ups, much to the amusement of passers by.

One evening he set off with Ian Blease at the front but Tommy didn't know Salford too well and turned left at a roundabout instead of going straight on. A few minutes later 30 rugby players were running along the hard shoulder of the M602 motorway and it wasn't long before the boys in blue turned up and gave us an escort to the next exit with their blue lights flashing. That was fine but then most of us didn't know where we were and had to find our way back to The Willows. Tommy and Bleasy knew where they were going, eventually, but the stragglers hadn't got a bloody clue and we were left jogging between high rise flats in one of Salford's toughest areas, where even the Rottweilers are said to patrol in pairs. It was an absolute shambles.

If I thought the drinking culture I had enjoyed in Cardiff would end in my new professional environment, I was very wrong. A few of us, Antipodeans Shane Hansen and Steve Gibson, Martin Birkett and Ian Blease, with occasional appearances by Ian Sherratt and Francis Leota, formed ourselves into a little group that took advantage of the many opportunities to get wrecked and to keep tabs on the local talent. I was married at the time, with a young family, but I happily fell into the honeytrap that is the sportsman's lot. There were simply too many temptations around, whether in bottles or tight skirts and, needless to say, some of our marriages paid the price. I'm not proud of that fact, as I'm sure they aren't, but being married to a fit rugby player with time on his hands can't be the ideal scenario for any woman.

One of our favourite haunts was a pub called the Inn of Good Hope, close to Hope Hospital, and it was our habit to go there straight from training. It was very much a young persons' pub and that included the usual percentage of attractive young ladies. I discovered that rugby league clubs had their groupies just as Cardiff had. Martin had a house close to the Salford ground and I used to take one particular young lady there for a little horizontal training. Trouble was that her husband found out, assumed it was Martin doing the dirty work, and slashed his car tyres. A let down for him and a let off for me!

One night the normal crew were in there after training having a "quiet drink". The pub was up a flight of stairs, with burly doormen at the bottom to keep out troublemakers. We were just chatting among ourselves and eyeing up one or two of the local beauties when we heard a succession of sharp bangs coming from the car park outside, like a Chinese firecracker going off. Most people didn't seem to notice but one or two of us were a bit concerned.

Suddenly one of the doormen came charging up the stairs, his face white and his whole body shaking. 'Get an ambulance, get a fucking ambulance,' he screamed. 'Someone's been shot.'

Two of the doormen had been gunned down in the doorway in a drive-by shooting. We heard the getaway car wheel-spinning away. Someone immediately dialled 999 but there wasn't much the rest of us could do – so we carried on drinking.

Within minutes the bar was swarming with police. They wouldn't let anyone leave at first and went through the bar asking everyone what they had seen. I discovered that there was a "door war" going on in Manchester and Salford at the time for control of the doors on various licensed premises and the two bouncers had been victims of that. They were both taken to hospital but their injuries weren't life-threatening and they both recovered.

The only inconvenience for us was that the scenes of crime officers forced us all to leave our vehicles in the car park overnight while they checked for forensic evidence, so there was no chance of drink-driving that night!

Normal practice was for the side to train at the ground on a Saturday morning to prepare for the following day's game. We would then all repair to the Inn of Good Hope after training for a drinking session. We would stay there until five or six in the evening and then go home to sleep it off. Now that might not seem the perfect preparation for a hard game of professional rugby league but our recovery rate was good because you would never have known the following day, even if the club didn't have a great season. The problem is that Salford were never really strong enough to beat the biggest clubs except on a strictly one-off basis.

Having been a prolific try-scorer for Cardiff, I wasn't able to match that when I switched to league and only managed nine tries from 23 appearances in my first season, when we just managed to stave off relegation. In my second season I fared even worse, with seven from 20 appearances, even though I felt I was playing well. That was the season when we were relegated after finishing in 13th spot in the Stones Bitter Championship. If you are a wing in either code, you largely rely for your scoring opportunities on those around you.

The campaign started with a 46-18 hammering at Widnes that turned out to be just the warm up for a 56-12 battering at Wigan. Leeds at Headingley and Bradford at The Willows followed and you could see the writing on the wall. We went out of the Lancashire Cup on the wrong end of a 27-4 scoreline at Warring-ton and our only success from the opening six games was a cup win over second division Rochdale Hornets. In many ways it was a continuation of how we had played in the second half of the previous season.

I also missed a slice of the action in mid-season. I had been troubled with hamstring injuries and was finally sent to the National Rehabilitation Centre at Lilleshall to see if they could sort me out. And what an interesting interlude that turned out to be because that's where I met Alan Hansen, John Barnes and Ian Rush, who had all become my heroes by then, as I had turned into an avid Liverpool fan. Having been involved in rugby I hadn't realised just how much top soccer players enjoyed letting their hair down. I thought they would behave a bit like monks but I was in for a surprise and we had a good laugh. Barry Venison and Michael Thomas were also there at the same time and it was good to see that they were all human.

We used to finish training at 5pm and by 6.30 John Barnes and Michael Thomas would be in the bar and into Jack Daniels and Coke. After a little "warm-up" we would take ourselves off to the local pub to get blitzed. One evening Alan Hansen came up with the idea for a pool tournament at the pub and we all stuck money into a pot for the winner. When we got there Alan went to the boot of his car and produced his own pool cue. No need to ask who cleaned up!

New Zealander Kevin Tamati took over from Kevin Ashcroft before the end of the season and, as you would expect with a Kiwi, there was a change of emphasis, as Kevin Moran discovered. He had to travel from Widnes and was invariably late for training, so Tamati warned that if he was late for the Thursday session he would be out of the side come the weekend. When he eventually walked in, late, Tamati asked, "And where the fuck have you been?"

Moran's response broke us all up. "Sorry boss but a plane landed on the motorway," he replied in his Scouse accent.

He was out of the team but he had been telling the absolute truth: a light aircraft had been forced to make an emergency landing on the motorway in Lancashire, causing a serious hold-up.

There wasn't a great deal Tamati could do to stave off the inevitable. Barrow were in bottom spot in the table and we were next with an unbridgeable gap between ourselves and the other strugglers, Leigh and Sheffield Eagles. Getting relegated was a real blow for the club and I started getting itchy feet in the sense that I fancied a move to a more successful outfit. But I had signed a four-year contract, I was being well paid and decided that I simply had to get my head down, do the hard work and do all I could to get the Reds back into the top flight at the first attempt.

We still had some good players in the squad and that was demonstrated by the fact that we lost just one league game in the 1990/91 season, going down 7-0 at Workington. The successful run – we also did well in the cup competitions – gave us confidence as a side and, from my own point of view, things couldn't have gone better because I played in 38 of the games and picked up the top try-scorer trophy with 31 to my credit, more than I had ever achieved in any of my six years at Cardiff.

Our first target was the Lancashire Cup – after the Challenge Cup and the Regal Trophy the Lancashire and Yorkshire Cups were much sought after by the clubs – and we excelled ourselves to reach the final. Rochdale had taken our place in the top division and we saw them off in the first round before beating Oldham 27-25 at home. Oldham had also just been promoted but our young loose forward Andy Burgess grabbed a brace of tries and the old drinking firm of Steve Gibson, Martin Birkett and myself contributed the others.

Our cup was overflowing when we turned over St Helens 21-7, again at The Willows, a week later with the Birkett, Gibson, and Hadley trio being joined on the try-scoring list by Tex Evans, playing on the opposite wing to myself. Steve Kerry kicked a couple of goals and hooker Mark Lee, who was quite handy with the boot – in a legal sense – dropped a goal. That win did confound the pundits and I was pleased with my try when I chipped over the head of Gary Connolly, who had just gone on as replacement full back, and then beat him for pace in the chase to the line. Gary was only a youngster then and he has developed into a brilliant player, especially defensively. Like Jason Robinson, he would make the switch to rugby union without any difficulty and probably wasn't used to best advantage when he did have a short spell at Harlequins. Still, it was good to pip him for a try when I had the opportunity and, with the season only a few weeks old, I had already seen more of the ball than I had in my previous seasons put together.

Ten days later we came up against Leigh in the semi-finals at The Willows and triumphed again. We won 16-7 courtesy of a brace of tries from Dave Fell, one of several former Orrell players who ended up at Salford. Centre John Gilfillan was another and both later reverted to rugby union with Sedgley Park. The third ex-Orrell player was Peter Williams, who had gifted John Devereux a try when playing for England against Wales in the quarter-finals of the 1987 RU World Cup. He was my centre for quite a time at Salford and I feel we worked very well together. Peter was a great lad and he would occasionally join our drinking group.

We met Widnes in the final at Central Park, Wigan, on September 29 and, for a time, it looked as though we might capture another notable scalp and take the trophy back to The Willows for the first time in 18 years. Peter Williams, Dave Fell and Ian Blease scored tries and it took a late effort from the Widnes flyer Martin Offiah to deny us at the death. That was a real sickener but we had proved to ourselves that we were capable of mixing it with the top sides.

Oldham gained their revenge for the Lancashire Cup defeat when they knocked us out of the Regal Trophy 26-6 at Water-sheddings and we came unstuck again at the same venue when they beat us 40-3 in the quarter finals of the Challenge Cup. That was a tremendous blow after earlier victories over three Yorkshire sides. Amateurs Cutsyke were first up and my mate Martin Birkett ran in a hat-trick of tries. We then dispatched Batley and Sheffield Eagles, but the really important business of that season was securing promotion at the first attempt. By the end of October we had opened a lead at the top of the table with Halifax and near neighbours Swinton as our closest challengers.

Our biggest win was at home to Barrow, when we won 76-10, and we chalked up 50 more at Chorley. It wasn't all plain sailing, of course. We had a narrow escape when we just pipped Doncaster 14-12 and I had to save the day at Keighley, despite a hangover after we had celebrated my birthday the night before. Kevin Tamati wouldn't have been too chuffed if we had gone down and that looked eminently possible until Keighley dropped the ball in a tackle when they tried to spin it following a scrum in our 22 and I picked up the ball, did a little one-two with Tony Howard, and raced the length of the field to go under the sticks. Steve Kerry, who topped more than 400 points that season, kicked the conversion, the hooter went as the ball cleared the crossbar and we had sneaked home 22-21. Steve's wife got so excited that she wet herself!

Despite our stumble against Workington Town in March, we made sure of our place as Second Division champions when we drew 10-10 with Swinton, who finished third. We managed that draw with just 12 men on the field after one of our props had been sent off early in the game. That saw us heading for Old Trafford, Manchester United's ground, for the Second Division Premiership Final clash with Halifax.

Because there were so many sides in the division, you didn't play everybody, and we hadn't come up against Halifax, who had finished as runners up. We still had the play-offs to negotiate and, despite our successful league campaign, that proved harder than it looked. Carlisle didn't pose too many problems at home and we won 26-12 but the semi-final saw us drawn against Working-ton, the only side to beat us in league action during the season. They travelled with massive support and, even though I scored from a Pete Williams-inspired chip and chase, we could only draw 9-9. The Cumbrians were cock-a-hoop.

I can't say we looked forward to returning to the one ground where we had come unstuck and a replay just before the final was far from ideal. We shouldn't have worried because we won fairly comfortably 26-6 when it really mattered. So we booked our trip to Old Trafford although, favouring the other Reds, I would have preferred a trip to Anfield. I did get that honour some years later when I managed a Premiership All Stars team there that had been hastily and chaotically assembled to provide cannon fodder for England as they prepared for the 1999 World Cup.

The Stones Bitter Second Division Premier Final was played on May 12 and our game kicked off early, with the main event being between Widnes and Hull. Because they needed the dressing rooms we had to change at Lancashire County Cricket ground and then get bussed across to the home of Manchester United. I must admit it was a great experience playing there, although I didn't finish the game because of injury. The important thing is that we won 27-20 despite a massive brawl at the end, the hooter coming at just the right time. There had been a bit of niggle in the game and Peter Brown, the Halifax forward, took a bit of a battering. He had played for Salford but missed kicks in a Lancashire Cup Final and I think the boys were out for retribution for doing them out of a bonus!

After that it was party time again and we collected our wages in cash before flying out to Magaluf where we got shitfaced for a week. Tex Evans drank for four days and then slept the remaining three but the rest of us managed to keep the tempo all week. We had a kitty made up of fines collected during the season for a variety of internal misdemeanours and Tamati was determined to get his share. One night we were on Tequila Slammers and I remember him collapsing at one stage. I think that was the occasion when Steve Kerry made a complete mess of himself and had to be carried back to the hotel. It was a big week but we had to enjoy ourselves because we knew that the following season would be no picnic back in with the big boys – and so it turned out.

Kevin Tamati was flavour of the month for taking us back into the Premiership and I always got on all right with him. I wouldn't call him a brilliant coach technically but he was okay. I remember his arrival at The Willows. We were in a huddle on the pitch and John Wilkinson brought him over to meet us. Kevin told us he wouldn't hold any grudges and then his eyes lit on Mick Worrall, who had broken his jaw a few years earlier. They didn't get off to the best start.

It was shortly afterwards that he asked us what our pre-match routine was. Nobody said anything so, after a lengthy period of silence, Steve Gibson's Aussie twang was heard to say, "Well, to be honest Kevin. I usually have a couple of wanks."

Needless to say it was some time before order was restored. Kevin must have wondered what he was dealing with when there was a bit of a rebellion during a pre-season training camp at Lancaster, of all places. They wouldn't allow us a drink of water during the training session and there was no food, so one of the directors, John Oakes, went out and bought sandwiches. Then they were wondering why we were cramping up by tea-time. The boys weren't happy with things and made their own arrangements. I'm not sure what Kevin thought when a fleet of taxis arrived that evening to take us all into Morecambe, where we got nicely shitfaced. The next day, perhaps as punishment, we were sent out on a long run. Mick Worrall, the former Oldham and Lions forward, had better ideas and slipped into the bushes at the side of the road, planning to wait there until we had gone and then rejoin us as we made our way back. Unfortunately for him, Terry Cassidy was following on five minutes behind the rest of us and caught Mick redhanded.

Our success the previous season resulted in our being invited to a function at Buile Hall thrown by Salford Council. That's when I had a run in with Salford's new Aussie scrum-half, Dave Cruickshank, who had just got off the plane. I can honestly say that in my entire career there are only two players I have disliked. One was Crookie and the other was Sale Sharks second row Dave Baldwin. At the reception Crookie was staggering up to the bar whilst the Lord Mayor was speaking and he was drinking pints of wine whilst the rest of us were on pints of beer. He was a complete pain and at one stage tried to pull the chain from around the Mayor's neck.

He was a very good rugby player but a complete dickhead as a bloke and he managed to spill beer all over me. That was the final straw. I smacked him and he fell across a table sending booze and broken glasses everywhere. I got the feeling that our chairman, John Wilkinson, was not amused. I had more reason to dislike the guy after we had all gone to a bar in Eccles, a Salford suburb. My leg was in plaster at the time because I had an ankle injury. Crookie was doing his best to touch up the barmaid but the guy standing next to him just happened to be her boyfriend. He took a swing at Crookie with his pint pot, Crookie ducked and it smashed me in the face instead. A large brawl ensued with me sitting on the bar bashing people, using my crutches instead of fists.

As expected, life was harder once we were back playing with the big boys and, in any case, Salford was a yo-yo team that never really set the world alight. The season started on the wrong note when we lost by a solitary point to Warrington; it was a very dubious pass from Mike Gregory to Kevin Ellis, that we were convinced was forward, that cost us. I missed that game because I had been recovering from a hernia operation but returned to score a try against Castleford in our next game. Unfortunately, that one went down the pan too and, although we turned the tables on Warrington in the Lancashire Cup, we were tonked by 40-odd points by Bradford. The writing was already on the wall.

Rochdale Hornets were back in the second division but they still managed to knock us out of the Lancashire Cup. I remember just lashing out at someone, I haven't a clue who, in sheer frustration. We saved our best for the Sky TV game at Hull where we won 24-12. I scored the final try and Martin Birkett sold an outrageous dummy with two men outside him to cross under the posts.

I hoped that might spark a revival and, for a time, it did. We beat Halifax at home and Featherstone away before toppling Wigan at The Willows. After beating Trafford Borough in the

Regal Trophy and winning at Wakefield, we found ourselves facing Wigan again in the Regal Trophy quarter-finals. The game was on BBC *Grandstand*, I scored a try and we beat them 24-14. Beating Wigan twice in 17 days was no mean feat but it all started to go downhill from that point, especially for me.

We travelled to Bradford to play Leeds in the Regal Trophy semi-finals where I found myself marking my good friend from Cardiff, Phil Ford. In the first half I went into a tackle on a pitch that alternated between soft and very hard. It felt as though someone had stabbed me in the ankle. I was stretchered off and we lost 22-15. We had chances to win but little kicks through bounced unkindly for us. I should have been taken straight to hospital to have the ankle attended to but they just strapped it up and gave me a pair of crutches. When I eventually started trying to run on it you could hear it clicking; the sound used to reverberate around The Willows. All the boys knew when I was around, as I trained by myself. It was three weeks later that I saw a specialist at a hospital in Bolton and he said I needed an operation.

Losing the cup tie was disappointing but it was even harder for me because it was one of the worst days of my life. I ended up losing my licence. I had a couple of beers in Bradford and a couple more back at The Willows before driving home. Luckily it was an automatic car although, when I think about it, it was my right ankle that was strapped up. After running the babysitter home I had a can of beer and then, because I felt peckish, I drove to a nearby village to get a Chinese takeaway.

I wasn't pissed by any means but I made the mistake of pulling away from the kerb outside the takeaway without having switched my lights on, something I corrected almost immediately. It was only a short drive home and as I headed in the direction of Manchester Airport I noticed a Peugeot car behind flashing his lights at me. I assumed he was some sort of idiot and accelerated away from him only to be stopped a short while later by four

My debut for Wales, against Japan in October 1983. Though I scored a try, we only just scraped a win. I had some great times with the Welsh side but we did generally under-achieve throughout the decade, despite having some brilliant individuals.

A proud day for my parents, Ernest and Margaret, as mum graduates from South Glamorgan Institute as a mature student.

A gathering of the gang: On the back row is my brother Anthony (left) and cousin Paul and in front are me (left), cousin Robert and my younger brother John.

Me (left) with brother John. We shared a bedroom and used to fight like mad. I don't know why Anthony isn't on the photo but it's such a nice picture I had to use it. Sorry Anthony!

Above: The line-up for East Wales Schools under-12 XV at Cardiff Arms Park in 1974. I'm the fourth boy from the right in the back row. Mark Ring is grinning third from left at the front.

Left: Holding the Brennan Shield, in 1973 (when I was 10). My primary school, St Joseph's, won it jointly with another team and their captain and I broke the trophy when we had a tug-of-war over it after this photo session

My pal and Cardiff teammate Terry Holmes (left) brandishing his Welsh Player of the Year Award for 1983 while I picked up the Most Promising Player Award.

Finding the corner for Cardiff against London Welsh in December 1983. Power, pace and a decent body-swerve were my main qualities as an attacking player.

I join the Welsh squad. **Back Row:** K.Townley, I.Eidman, J.Whitefoot, R.Donovan, M.Davies, H.Davies, M.Ring, M.Dacey, B.Bowen, P.Hopkins. **Second Row:** A.Hadley, M.Douglas, J.Perkins, R.Moriarty, T.Shaw, C.Dennehy, J.Thomas, G.Roberts, G.John. **Front Row:** G.Lewis (Physio), C.Williams, H.E.Rees, Hermas Evans (President WRU), E.T.Butler, R.H.Williams (Honourary Manager), J.Bevan (Hon Asst Mgr), C.F.W.Rees, R.Giles, W.James.

One of my favourite action shots as I burn away from the hands of a flying tackler while playing for Cardiff against Fiji in 1985. I scored two tries in the game.

Signing for Salford with chairman John Wilkinson. The fee was £100,000, a rugby league record at the time. It was a smashing club and John was a man of his word.

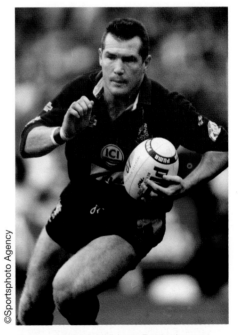

Having a laugh for Salford against my future teammates Widnes in 1988. I enjoyed the camaraderie at Salford – though not the bullets flying outside the pubs!

On the charge for Widnes. Rugby league was a different culture than union but the drinking sessions could be just as lively.

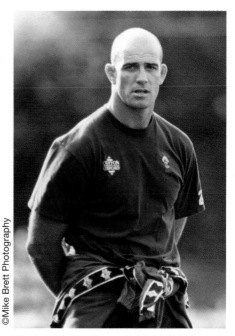

Maestro Paul Turner in full flight. A genius with the ball in his hands, he was instrumental in my move to Sale Sharks. He also spoke his mind, a trait we shared.

The intimidating figure of John Mitchell, the tough Kiwi who bossed Sale and became England's forwards coach. His team-building techniques could be a little eccentric.

Sale's millionaire owner, Brian Kennedy, unveils a new signing from rugby league, Jason Robinson. Jason is a one-off, a performer I admire greatly. Brian I'm not quite so keen on!

With my boys, Craig (left), the youngest, and Matthew. They both like their sport. They are also learning the Welsh language now at school, so I'm having to as well.

Looking at life: With my playing days over, I still want to be involved in rugby in some capacity. The game has been good to me and has given me the chance to visit places, meet people and experience things I otherwise wouldn't have. It beats a career in the Inland Revenue anyway!

policemen in two vans. Within seconds, Mr Peugeot raced up and two police officers jumped out of what I had, by that stage, realised was an unmarked police vehicle.

The Peugeot driver marched over and demanded to know if I realised what speed I had been doing. I asked what he expected me to do when an unmarked car started flashing me from behind. The next question, inevitably, concerned whether or not I had been drinking. I admitted to having had a couple. I was invited to step out of the car. He opened the driver's door and I literally fell out on to the road, because I could only use one leg. Having got me upright, he asked me to walk over to his vehicle. I said I would be happy to oblige if he could rescue my crutches from the car.

As I was still wearing my Salford club gear, the other officers realised who I was and started chatting about the game and how they thought we had been unlucky and could have won. It was nice to have them on my side but I knew it wouldn't stop them asking me to blow into the bag. That was the next thing on the agenda. Can't say I was unduly surprised when it turned red and one of the officers drove my car whilst I travelled to the local nick in the back of one of the vans. Once inside they put me in a cell and removed my tie, I suppose in case I tried to hang myself, although I wasn't sure whether they thought I might commit hara-kiri because I had been caught for drink-driving or because Salford had just missed out on a Regal Trophy final.

I thought my luck had changed when they sent a policewoman into my cell but it was only to ask if I wanted to make a telephone call and I contacted Ann to tell her what had happened. The policewoman then said I didn't seem to be that drunk, which didn't surprise me because I could certainly take my drink. She said she would breathalyse me again and thought I might just get away with it. I blew into the machine and she told me my reading was 74.

"Have I got away with it then?" I asked, somewhat optimistically.

She shook her head and told me that I hadn't because the limit was 35 and I was more than double that. They charged me and said my car would have to go into the police compound and I would have to get a taxi home because they couldn't spare a patrol car to take me. The miserable bugger in the Peugeot asked if there was anything I needed from my car.

"Yes," I said, "my bloody supper."

"You can't want that now, it will be stone cold," he said.

"I don't care. I'll warm it up because I'm starving, I haven't had anything to eat since this morning."

I wasn't proud to lose my licence and it was certainly bloody inconvenient. But I suppose I had been heading for a fall because I took a lot of chances driving home from some of our sessions. I frequently got lost and once even lost the car after I crashed out at a mate's house. I ended up wandering the streets the next morning trying to remember where I had been and it was some time before I found it.

The next thing was the court appearance at Stockport and a newspaper reporter approached my solicitor and asked him to confirm that I was Adrian Hadley the rugby player. My brief, who fortunately wasn't on oath, told him the name was merely a coincidence and that I was, in fact a company rep. In the sense that I was working part time for the car leasing company, he was telling the truth. Although I was never identified as rugby player, my name still appeared in the *Manchester Evening News* Hall of Shame, a regular pre-Christmas feature in which they name and shame those done for drink driving.

I thought I might get the book thrown at me but got away with a 12 months ban and a £350 fine. I felt more sorry for the guy up before me in court. He had just got his first job as a driver after being out of work for four years. He had a couple of drinks to celebrate and was marginally over the limit. He copped a ban and lost the job he had waited four years for. And all because he was waiting at traffic lights that were on red and someone ploughed straight into the back of him.

I injured my ankle on December 7 and didn't play again until March 29 because the injury simply hadn't been sorted out as it should have been. By that stage Salford were deep in relegation trouble and my first game back was another defeat at the hands of Warrington. There were three games left – Widnes away, Hull at home, and Swinton, who were going to get relegated anyway – and we really needed to win all three. Five sides were in danger of joining Swinton: Featherstone, Hull, Bradford, Hull KR and ourselves. Nobody thought we could beat Widnes away but we did, by 24-20, and I scored from our own 22 when I followed up one of our forwards, took the pass and then went the length of the field to score under the posts. We then beat Hull KR but it all depended on the last game of the season and Swinton was always going to be a tricky one. It was a local derby, they were already going down and didn't really want to leave us in the first division.

It was a massive game because it was all going to go down to points difference. It set the old nerves on edge when the public address system announced that we would stay up if we won. We did, 26-18, and I scored a hat-trick. An impressive way to end my Salford career, although I wasn't aware at that stage that the Swinton finale had been my swansong.

CHAPTER EIGHT

Widnes Woes

MY CONTRACT WITH Salford was up at the end of the 1991-92 season and, although I had thoroughly enjoyed my time at The Willows because the atmosphere and the people were great, and had an option to stay, I wanted the chance to taste some real success and knew that wasn't going to come my way with Salford. The call from Widnes came from Jonathan Davies, who was playing for "The Chemics" – now the Vikings – along with two more of the old Welsh national side, John Devereux and Paul Moriarty. He said that Martin Offiah had just left to join Wigan Warriors and they were looking for someone to fill his shoes.

They could forget that idea because I was never going to fill Martin's shoes. He was a legend at Widnes. Anyway, as players, we had totally different styles and strengths. But the idea did appeal to me because Widnes had some good players at the time, even though the ground was a bit dilapidated. The place was falling apart structurally but they were nice people and the team was well supported when it was winning. They also had a fellow Welshman as chairman in big Jim Mills, who was one of the game's great characters.

The next step was a call from the club's manager, Frank Myler, suggesting we meet up at Birchwood service station on the M62.

As the motorway runs from Liverpool to Hull and links the two strongholds of rugby league in the north, I suspect a great many deals have been done in the various service areas.

I went to the meeting and that's where I first came into contact with Phil Larder, who was the Widnes coach. First impressions always stick in your mind and I'm afraid I was never a fan of Mr Larder. There was nothing wrong with him as a coach but the man was so far up himself it was incredible. He acted as though he was the best coach in the world but his man-management was shit. Wherever he went he used to strut around as though he wanted everyone to be aware of just who he was. Yet he hardly had a record that justified placing himself on a pedestal.

He had played for various rugby union clubs, including Sale, before switching to rugby league, where he played in the centre or wing for Oldham before finishing his playing career at White-haven. His first senior coaching appointment in rugby league was at Widnes, so I caught him early in his coaching career. To his credit the side reached the Silk Cut Challenge Cup Final in my first season but he then left to coach Keighley Cougars, taking them to the Division Two Championship and Premiership in the 1994-95 season before being sacked by the Yorkshire club.

The next port of call was Sheffield Eagles, where he was sacked after just 12 matches. He had obviously impressed somebody because he was put in charge of the Great Britain squad that toured Down Under in 1996; they chalked up the worst ever record by not even managing to win one of their six matches in New Zealand. In fairness to the guy, he had worked under the experienced Malcolm Reilly for a few years and had been expected to coach Great Britain in 1994 against Australia but declined because he didn't want an overseas coach, New Zealander Graham Lowe, as part of the set up.

So you will get the impression that Phil and I didn't exactly get along, although I was fine with Frank Myler, who was a down-to-earth character and a good laugh. When you are involved with people you either click with them or you don't and I certainly didn't click with Phil. Not that it made a lot of difference because I was at Widnes to play rugby, not necessarily get along with the coach. I had never seen eye to eye with John Bevan back in Wales so I was accustomed to ignoring the personalities and just getting on with my job.

Mind you, my job was made difficult in my first season because I was still banned from driving, so just getting to training sessions, never mind games, turned into a major logistical exercise. I had to walk from my home to Heald Green station to catch the local train into Manchester. Then I caught a train to Warrington, where I changed again for Widnes. Paul Moriarty used to pick me up from the station and we would go back to his house for a coffee before heading for the club. After the session Ann invariably got a babysitter in and drove out to Widnes to pick me up, which was quite a round trip. We had to put up with that scenario for five months until I had my licence restored to me.

From a purely rugby point of view, things started well. I made my Division One debut in August, 1992, against Castleford and played really well in the 16-6 win at home. I didn't score but did manage to lay on a try for Richie Eyres and brought off two try-saving tackles. The next game was at Hull KR, where we won 16-2 and I got another good report that said I was the difference in the team. At about that time I bumped into Kevin Tamati and he said, "That's typical of you, you Welsh twat. As soon as I get rid of you, you start playing well." Actually, I thought I had played well towards the end of my time at Salford and was even drafted into the provisional Great Britain squad at one stage.

Despite those two early successes it was a difficult September. We had a tough game against Bradford Bulls (or Northern as they were then) and trips to Wigan and St Helens. We lost them all but bounced back by beating Hull KR for a second time and I got among the scorers as we rattled up 52 points. It was a painful experience because I was tackled late in the game and a Hull player came over the top and smashed me in the face with his elbow. I can't say it was deliberate but it probably was. My nose was all over the place and I got quite a shock when I had been led off the field and saw it in the mirror. Blood was everywhere and there was a big dip in my nose where the cartilage had dislocated. The doctor told me not to worry as it would simply click back into place. I couldn't believe that was right and finally solved the problem with the help of my old buddy from Wales, Rowland Phillips who was playing for Warrington at the time.

He called round to my house and I said I would have a go at straightening the old Roman myself. So we both got tanked up first then I stuck my fingers up my nose and Rowland yanked my head back. The cartilage just popped back into place but rough treatment over the years has resulted in my nose being devoid of a cartilage now. Which means I can play party tricks like shoving a piece of cotton wool up one nostril and bringing it down the other.

The Welsh lads tended to stick together a bit because the culture at Widnes was very different from what it had been at Salford and we were often joined by lads like Andy Currier, Darren Wright and Bobby Goulding, who was always game for a couple of beers. At Salford we were always out on the piss after training but I suppose Widnes were a little more professional and that culture simply didn't exist. Quite a few of the boys were internationals so tended to take it easy socially, although a few of us would gravitate occasionally to Steve O'Neill's pub in the town.

In some respects the driving ban and the much-reduced alcohol intake probably did me a favour because I found myself playing well. I was certainly enjoying my rugby. My first bust-up with Phil Larder was not far away, however, and arrived shortly before Christmas. I had scored a try at Headingley when Leeds beat us 48-16 but was dropped to the bench for the Regal Trophy game against Rochdale, which we duly won 30-2. I stayed on the bench for the 21-10 defeat by Bradford at Valley Parade, the Bradford City soccer ground, and was less than happy at finding myself on the bench again for the visit to Salford.

I did, however, come off the bench to a rapturous welcome from the local fans – I don't think – and rewarded them by scoring a try within two minutes of arriving on the field. Faimalo, who we called "Flymo", made a break up the middle with me in support and, when the pass came, I ran clear to score under the sticks. The crowd had given me the bird when I warmed up before the game but, in fairness, a lot of them came up to me after the game to ask how I was.

Larder kept me in the side for the visit to Hull four days later but, in spite of playing well, he dropped me back to the bench for the home game with Swinton in the Challenge Cup. Jonathan Davies had been injured and was fit again and I lost my place in the re-shuffle. We used to be given regular reports on our progress so I went to Larder armed with my stats, which said I had been playing reasonably well, and asked him why I was back on the bench.

He said, "We can't go into a Challenge Cup game without a recognised goalkicker so we have to have Jonathan in the side."

"We are only playing Swinton, for fuck's sake, so why do we need a kicker against a Second Division side?"

"We do if it's a cup game."

"You are so full of shit."

Obviously, I didn't expect to be picked ahead of Jonathan but I had played well at Hull and just wanted some justification as to why I had been dropped rather than be given a limp excuse about goal-kicking.

Widnes thrashed Swinton 62-14 just to prove my point. I did get on but the game turned out to be my last for some time. I went to a training session soon after our little debate and I just felt absolutely knackered. I was never the first in training but I was never the last either, but I really struggled that day. The boys were all having a good laugh as Larder had a right go at me and called me a lazy twat. Afterwards he gave me a lecture about knowing that I wasn't happy about being dropped for the Swinton game but saying that I needed to pull my socks up and show some professionalism. I hadn't the strength to argue with him and woke up that night soaked to the skin, shivering and with a king-sized headache. I was perspiring so badly that the bedding had to be changed three times during the night. The doctor sent me straight to hospital where they diagnosed pneumonia.

That kept me out for several weeks and, as a result, I missed the rest of the Challenge Cup ties. Even though I played in all the other games after my return against Bradford Northern at the end of March, and played against Leeds in the semi-final of the Premiership, I knew the way Phil Larder worked and was sure I wouldn't be included in the side to play Wigan at Wembley in the final. I was not only right but was joined on the not-needed list by Paul Moriarty, who broke his hand in the game against Leeds just a week before the final. He was the one I felt really sorry for because he had played all the way through. There were tears in his eyes as we drove up to Wembley for the game.

Of course, the trip wasn't without a little knuckle-rapping from Mr Larder and I must admit to being involved in that little upset. We had been to look at the ground the day before the game and then it was a case of hanging around the hotel. That's bad enough if you are playing but it's far worse if you're not, so I suggested to Paul Moriarty that we should go for a beer in London. As Craig Makin and Les Holliday weren't in the squad either they decided to come with us. The rest were just sitting down to dinner as we staggered back into the hotel. Poor Les, who had been left out because Julian O'Neill had been flown in from Australia just for the final, was dragged to one side and given a dressing down because he had been on stand-by in case any of the chosen went down with sickness overnight.

The final really was the one that got away. Widnes lost 22-18 and John Devereux had a bit of a shocker. Wigan kicked long, Devs picked up but was then tackled and dropped the ball. Wigan picked up and Martin Offiah rubbed salt in the Widnes wound by scoring a vital try against his former club. There was an upside even in defeat. By getting to the final I am sure Widnes staved off a serious financial crisis because they desperately needed the money the cup run gave them. The only problem was that it simply delayed the inevitable and the side started to fall apart the following season.

We won more games than we lost over the season as a whole but still finished tenth in the table despite hard earned victories over Leeds and St Helens. And the side that had reached Wembley was starting to break up. It was also obvious that cash was becoming a problem because contract money could be three or four months late.

Before our Challenge Cup tie with Castleford, we were taken to Blackpool for a training weekend and ended up being asked to leave the hotel after an old lady had been knocked over in the bar by a golf buggy the boys had "borrowed" from a local golf course and carried up the stairs into the hotel reception. It also didn't help that Rodney Howe, who later went on to play for Australia, started to run a bath at 3am. The trouble was that he was pissed and fell asleep only to be awakened by screams from the room below: the ceiling had collapsed on to the occupants when the bath had overflowed. That made all the newspapers and led to a massive bollocking from Mr Larder.

We lost the game at Castleford, so there was to be no Wembley Way that year, and our Regal Trophy ambitions came to a frozen end at Hull when Larder took a gamble that didn't come off. The game was played on a Wednesday evening and when we left the hotel, where we had stopped off for a bite to eat, a blizzard was blowing. Amazingly they decided the game should go ahead but it was a nightmare out there and, when the sides were level at half time, the referee came to our dressing room to say that the Hull players were in danger of getting frostbite and suggesting that the game should be called off. Phil decided that because the blizzard would be at our backs we should carry on, which we did. It backfired on us because we lost 10-6.

My report afterwards said that I had been badly affected by the weather. It was bloody freezing, for Christ's sake. We later got stuck on the motorway: we managed to get to the Hartshead Moor service area near Bradford, on the M62, but no further because of the depth of the snow on the road and it was 6am the following morning when we arrived back in Widnes. You can imagine the telephone calls home – "I'm stuck on the motorway, love." They had heard it all before only this time it was genuine.

At the end of the season there was an exodus of players and Phil Larder took himself off to Keighley. Tony and John Myler took over in his place but only for a season whilst our fortunes tumbled even further, finishing in 14th spot. On a personal note it wasn't a bad season because I still managed to score eleven tries from 28 appearances and also kicked 68 goals. It's a little-known fact that I can kick goals but didn't do it at Cardiff because we had Gareth Davies. I kicked at school along with Mark Ring. Of course, I was left with the touchline jobs just so that Ringo could keep up his average by taking the easy ones!

The pressure of kicking never got to me but, in a professional game, it was easy to see why it might. We drew 12-12 with Doncaster one day and I missed a last-minute penalty. In the clubhouse afterwards one of the players was a bit off and I asked him what his problem was. He said that if I'd kicked the penalty we would have been on a win bonus. I won't tell you what I called him.

I was probably one of the most experienced players left in the Widnes squad and the knowledge that we weren't going to make it into the new Super League wouldn't have helped much in terms of encouraging new faces. Not that there would have been the money to attract them, I suspect. Even so I signed a new two year contract and had been around the game long enough to know that we weren't equipped to survive in the Super League anyway.

So Widnes found themselves in the Northern Ford Premiership at the start of the 1995/96 season and we had another new coach in Doug Laughton, who was a bit of a nightmare. Not that I had too many dealings with him because I knew I would be joining the Welsh squad for the RL World Cup at the end of September.

We did well in the run up to the World Cup, winning all but one of our opening seven games. The one defeat, ironically, was at Salford, which rather destroyed the pattern that appeared to have been set. When I was at Salford I always scored tries against Widnes but when I switched clubs I invariably got on to the scoreboard against my old club. On this occasion we went down 45-4 and I didn't score, even though I was doing the goal kicking. In the other games I managed three tries and 33 goals and when I left to join the Welsh squad I didn't realise that the 34-29 victory over Huddersfield on September 30 would turn out to be my last for the club.

With the Welsh RL side I found myself on the periphery more often than I was comfortable with. But it was nice to be with a bunch of lads I had played international rugby union with and one year we even won rugby league's version of the Five Nations Championship, except that this one only included England, France and ourselves. But it was quite an achievement beating England because the majority of lads playing for the top clubs were English and we were so few in number that we were happy to find any players with a Welsh connection – such as having visited Wales (now, where have I heard that before).

The first game I played for Wales at rugby league was against Papua New Guinea at Swansea on October 27, 1991. I hadn't played international rugby for three years and had missed both the build-up and the craic with the boys that playing on that circuit involves. It was a big thing for Wales to have a national rugby league side and the players knew each other well. After all we had played with and against each other in Wales before switching codes. The initial squad included people like Alan Bateman, John Devereux, Jonathan Davies, Jonathan Griffiths, Kevin Ellis, Mark Jones, Paul Moriarty, David Bishop, David Young, Rob Ackerman, Rowland Phillips and Gary Pearce. The only three who hadn't played together in rugby union were Phil Ford, who had been at Cardiff, Anthony Sullivan and a guy called Barry Williams. Jonathan Davies, as one would expect, was one of the stars of that Welsh side but Phil Ford was also impressive at full-back, where he played until Iestyn Harris arrived on the scene. Paul Moriarty was a major influence up front and another who did well at front row was Rob Ackerman, who had played in the centre for Wales in his rugby union days. It just goes to show how different the two games are.

I was involved in all the international games from the moment the team was established to the time when I made the move back to rugby union. Unfortunately, I only got on in nine of them but I wanted to be involved, quite regardless of anything else, and if I ended up on the bench then so be it.

We made a good start against Papua New Guinea, winning 68-0, and a lot of people turned out to support us. Clive Griffiths was our coach and the following year we played France, again at Swansea, and I got on as a substitute as we won 35-6. At that time England, apart from Australia, was the strongest international side around because England, or at least the northern part of the country, was where the game had its base. We were just getting started as a national side whereas they had been up and running for years and beat us 36-11 when we clashed at, you guessed it, Swansea, in the European Championship. The abiding memory of that game was Gerald Cordle breaking his jaw.

It was at the championships that we realised what a bunch of cheapskates the organisers were. We were provided with red and black tracksuits bearing the three feathers badge of Wales. England had blue tracksuits bearing the rose on a square background.

One of the lads undid the stitching on the badge and, underneath, was the Nottingham Forest football club badge. The England lads undid theirs and, lo and behold, the badge of Chelsea FC was revealed. They clearly couldn't be arsed with forking out to provide us with new kit but we all had a good laugh about it.

We then travelled to Perpignan to play France for the second time that year and I started in that game, which we won 19-18. New Zealand were next up at Swansea and we lost 24-19. I went on to play in the second row and probably cost us the game. Late in the match Jonathan Davies delivered an up and under, the Kiwi full-back spilled the ball under the posts and John Devereux fell on it. Unfortunately, the referee disallowed the try because I had been offside at the play-the-ball. The ref got it right but it was a tough call because I hadn't been interfering with play. So, we could have won the game and I don't think the coaching staff were too pleased.

In October 1994 we played Australia who were, not surprisingly, the World Champions. By that stage the boys were getting together as a team and we had, after all, mostly played together for Wales in the other code. The game was played at Ninian Park and, despite being a lifelong supporter of Cardiff City, it was the first time I had been on the pitch. Despite the fact that the Welsh side had played together at rugby union, and had a few games under our belt in rugby league, we were no match for a superb Aussie side that included the likes of Mal Meninga, Alan Langer and the great Wendell Sailor, who has now made the switch to rugby union in Australia (it will be interesting to see what impact he has). They hammered us 46-4.

There were a lot of injuries in the game and the player who came off worst was John Devereux. I was on the wing and Devs was playing as my centre. He was up against Mal Meninga and I told him that Mal was so strong that the only way to stop him was to go low to make sure he was brought to ground. But Devs went in a bit high early in the game and he was caught in the face, accidentally, by Mal's elbow. It was one of the worst injuries I have ever seen on a rugby field. His jaw was at 90 degrees and blood was pumping from it. In a long career Devs certainly seemed to have more than his share of injuries.

The following year we made our mark in the European Championships. We took on England at Cardiff and won 18-16. Iestyn Harris had been drafted into the side and it will be good seeing him playing in Wales as a rugby union player after switching codes. Kelvin Skerritt and Wigan's Neil Cowie were also in: the fact that we were up and running as a national side had started to attract players with a Welsh qualification.

France were next up and the game was played at Carcassone. I got off the bench to play and we won that game 22-10 to take the championship for the first time.

As a reward for beating England and France, we were taken on tour to the USA. It was a complete shambles. We played two games in Philadelphia, both against the American Patriots, but it was no contest, even though I didn't know some of the players Wales drafted in through other players pulling out. I can't remember their names, which is hardly surprising because I didn't know who they were even then.

Among the youngsters drafted in was Kieran Cunningham, a lad from St Helens who ultimately turned down the chance to switch to a Welsh side with an almost guaranteed place in the international squad despite his total lack of experience in the old amateur code. Another player drafted in was an Aussie called Gavin Price Jones; I suppose the authorities decided that with a name like that he had to have a Welsh qualification.

We won the first game 66-10. It was played on a college pitch normally used for American Football so the pitch ended before the posts that, in any case, were completely different from rugby union posts. The opposition wanted to fight a fair bit but we coped with that and our second game resulted in a 92-4 scoreline in our favour.

From a rugby point of view the trip was a complete waste of time but at least we had a bloody good time. Mike Nicholas was the manager and he was on a very tight budget. He took us to pubs where we were provided with typical bar food and it wasn't until later that we realised it wasn't costing him anything because the food was free as part of Happy Hour.

As a tour it wasn't much use as a build-up to the RL World Cup, which was next on the international agenda. Most of the lads on that tour were never going to be involved in the tournament anyway and training in the US was a bit hit-and-miss. I remember one session when the heavens opened and we all raced into the stands to shelter, leaving our coach Clive Griffiths doing his nut in the middle of the pitch and trying desperately to get us back out there. Sorry Clive, it was a case of, 'No way, José.'

Wales still relied heavily on the old rugby union brigade for the world event and we were all delighted to be based in Cardiff. The opening game in the World Cup was against France at Ninian Park. We won 28-6 and I got on as a replacement. Next up were Western Samoa and I started that game, at Swansea.

It turned out to be a real bloodbath, the hardest game I have ever played in. Among the Samoans was Apollo Perelini, who I was later to sign to play for Sale Sharks when he decided to return to his first love, rugby union. There was a lot at stake in the outcome because whoever went through would play England in the semi-final. The Samoans, who also had the likes of "Inga" Tuigamala and John Schuster in their line-up, are always very physical by nature anyway. It was blood and guts from start to finish. The hits were massive and cheap shots were going in all over the place. There were fights going on off the ball and you knew you might get more than a tackle whenever you had the thing in your hands. The problem was that both sides were really fired up for it because of what was at stake. That was tribal warfare at its fiercest.

Widnes Woes

After the Samoan game we were all given the day off and went on the lash. Being Cardiff boys, Phil Ford and myself knew all the best places to go and we ended up in Stamps, a club owned by a good friend of the Cardiff rugby fraternity, Bob Phillips, and run by the lovely Ceris. They looked after us very well but, after that, it was down to the serious business of preparing to meet England at Old Trafford.

I was well pissed off when they decided to start with Devs and Anthony Sullivan on the wings. They certainly needed Anthony to play against Martin Offiah. He wasn't as quick as Martin but he was the nearest thing Wales had to the Wigan flyer. But I believe I should have taken the other wing spot ahead of Devs. Surprisingly, they played Devs against Offiah. I ended up on the bench with my mate Rowland Phillips, Kieran Cunningham and Mark Jones. England won 25-10 and I was very disappointed that I didn't get on. I thought I had played very well against Western Samoa, when all hell broke out, and even Mike Nicholas came up to tell me so

So Devs played on the wing and didn't have the best of games. Martin Offiah scored twice down his flank although I'm not suggesting that was Devs's fault.

In spite of my disappointment at starting so few games for Wales, I enjoyed being involved and liked the people in the camp. Mike Nicholas was a good laugh, if a little airy-fairy at times. Things didn't always go as he wanted but it was a very difficult job and the authorities didn't look after us moneywise. Clive Griffiths was very intense as a coach but knew what he wanted. I thought he was a good coach who knew his stuff technically and could produce a game plan to win certain matches. He had his favourites, of course, but that could be said of all coaches, whatever the sport. I suppose that is human nature.

It was during the World Cup that I came to realise just how serious the financial situation had become at Widnes. I popped into my bank in Cardiff to draw some money out and it was a case of, "What money?" The club hadn't paid my contract money and, being in the middle of a World Cup in Wales, I was hardly in a position to march into Naughton Park and demand it. But that's just what I did when the tournament was over. I told them I wanted what they owed me and added that I had played my last game for them. The club said I would be in breach of contract if I refused to play but, in reality, the boot was on the other foot.

The next stage was to take the case to the Rugby League Board but I was told that they could put whoever they wanted on the tribunal panel, which could have included Widnes directors. A date was set for the tribunal but I didn't attend, on the advice of my solicitor, and the Board said my case had been thrown out following my non-attendance. My solicitor told them that the tribunal didn't matter because I was suing them. Widnes clearly didn't want to get dragged through the courts without a leg to stand on and telephoned a few days later to make an offer to settle; an offer I took, as I looked back over the great divide and wondered if, perhaps, my future lay back in rugby union now that that game was set to go professional.

CHAPTER NINE

Back in the Union

ONCE I HAD decided to leave rugby league, my first thought was to return to Cardiff and that very nearly came about. I talked to Gareth Davies about it and was actually picked to play for Cardiff in a game but, at the last minute, I was unable to because of a problem over insurance. At around that time, I bumped into Paul Turner at an airport where we were both returning from holiday. He raised the possibility of me joining him at Sale.

At that time Sale were surprising a few people with top four finishes in what is now the Zurich Premiership, having been steered to promotion by Paul a couple of years earlier. It was a small club compared to outfits like Leicester but they had some decent players and were playing an attractive, open style of rugby that I felt would suit me. The club had no great track record of winning things but, in the good old amateur days, had attracted a fairly strong fixture list, including several Welsh clubs. It was also even closer to my home than either Salford or Widnes had been. My sons were in school in the area and there was a certain logic in staying put if possible.

I had known Paul since the days when we played together for the Civil Service back in Wales and against each other when he was with Newbridge and Newport. He had always had a friendly go at me for getting the man of the match award when I became the first player to score a hat-trick in a Welsh Cup Final. He had been the only Newport player to perform that afternoon and thought he should have got the award!

He was a great performer who would have won more Welsh caps had he not been around at the same time as Jonathan Davies. Right up until he was 40, he was able to bamboozle defences with his sleight of hand and the local press in Manchester dubbed him the Welsh Wizard, which wasn't far off the mark. There was an offhand arrogance about the way he played but that's because he had supreme confidence in his own ability. I liked him because he spoke his mind, even if it did go against the grain with authority at times, and I felt that I could work with him.

I was pissed off with Widnes, was taking them to court and was available. He was aware that a couple of Welsh clubs, including Cardiff, were interested in signing me and I had already put my house on the market. It was my respect for Paul, as much as for anything else, that persuaded me to link up with Sale.

Paul wasted no time in putting me in touch with Brian Wilkinson, who was the club's chief executive, and the deal was done – even if I did end up with three separate contracts. Fine detail wasn't Brian's strength.

Brian was the first of four chief executives I would work for during my five years at Heywood Road and little did I know then that, for all his faults, he would turn out to be the pick of the bunch by some distance. At least he understood the game and could relate to the players because he genuinely cared about them as human beings rather than merely treating them as commodities. No matter what anyone else might say, it was the team that he and Paul built that reached the Pilkington Cup Final the following season. Despite the arrival of high profile players, coaches, administrators and owners, it has been downhill ever since.

Although the game had gone open the previous year, the English RFU had decided to stay amateur for 12 months to allow a smoother transition from amateur to professional; not that that stopped Sir John Hall from buying an international-packed Newcastle team to guarantee promotion to what is now the Premiership. That prompted top clubs to follow suit, but paying players was still illegal. I actually went to Sale to work in the commercial department because I arrived a few months before the date of the official switch to professionalism. Which is one reason why I ended up with so many contracts as they tried to find one that would satisfy my former colleagues at the Inland Revenue. A case of gamekeeper turned poacher!

It was still a very small operation when I arrived at Heywood Road. Paul was the full-time player-coach, Wilkie was running the show, a guy called Roy Maddick was in charge of commercial activity and two women, Jean Swales and Yvonne Kenrick, whose son Mike is a former Sale and Lancashire captain, looked after everything else from the confines of a match box of an office that is now a mere annex to the physiotherapy room, which I shared with Roy. Brian had nowhere to sit when I arrived so he moved himself into one of the hospitality boxes in the clubhouse.

I started training with the club and made my debut at Twickenham in the Middlesex Sevens. It was a bit of a makeshift side and a nightmare for me because I was still getting used to the rule changes, so it was something of a shock when we beat highly fancied Saracens in the first round. That success didn't last long. We made a sharp exit against Leicester but the tournament was dominated anyway by Wigan Warriors, who had been invited to take part as the barriers continued to come down between the two codes.

By that time, John Mitchell had arrived from New Zealand. He was a very fit bloke who worked fanatically hard at training and, as a consequence, had a body that looked as though it had been chiselled out of granite. With his shaven head, he looked a formidable character. Mitch had been appointed as Paul's assistant for the following season and was having a look at how things operated. Apparently he and Paul had met at an international tournament in the West Indies and Paul had sold the club the idea of bringing him in to look after the forwards. The backs, of course, were in very safe hands with Paul. That could have been the dream partnership but, unknown to me, the seeds were already being sown to get rid of Paul, despite the fact that he had taken the club back into the Premiership and led them to fourth place in the table at the first attempt, when most people had predicted an early return to Division Two.

Sale had three or four games left so Mitch and I were invited to travel with the first team. The first game was against Wasps at their old Sudbury ground. Even though I had been into a drinking culture in rugby league, it was done out of sight of club officials; once the squad assembled for a game, it was a very serious business. Mitch, who had come from an environment where rugby is almost more important than life itself, couldn't believe what he was seeing.

In those days, when staying away overnight before a game, the team would have something to eat at Heywood Road in the early evening. They then boarded the team coach and, by the time we had got to the M6, just a few minutes drive away, the beer cans were out and porn films were on the video. We wondered what we had got ourselves into and that feeling increased when we arrived at the hotel. As Mitch and I weren't playing, we had a couple of beers in the hotel bar along with the backroom boys Alan Blease and Robbie Dixon. Mitch and I found it absolutely incredible that half the team were still drinking in the bar at one o'clock the next morning.

Sale lost the game and later got a good hiding at Harlequins. After that game we went straight to the Orange Tree in Richmond before going on into London and arriving back in Sale just in time for breakfast. Mitch and I decided things would have to change if we were going to achieve anything at all the following season but the boys did redeem themselves at Bath in the final away game. That's when Paul demonstrated just how influential he could be as a player.

As he was planning to step down as a first-up player and concentrate more on coaching, he was on the bench at The Rec and Bath were all set to win the English title. At half time, when they led 32-12, Bath couldn't have realised how close they were to come to losing out. Paul was fizzing about Sale's performance and, in desperation, pulled off full-back Jim Mallinder just before half time and went on himself. His half-time team talk would have blistered paint and one or two players threw their water bottles away in temper.

But Paul proved himself to be a maestro as he orchestrated a remarkable fight-back against a very talented side that had seemed untouchable in the opening 40 minutes. The game ended in a 38-38 draw and Bath only took the title because John Liley missed a last ditch penalty for close challengers Leicester. Clearly, the wrong Liley was at Welford Road because his younger brother Rob's accurate kicking at The Rec was one of the reasons for Sale's tremendous result.

On that occasion Sale had decided to travel on the day of the game, despite the distance. We had only gone a few miles when the team coach broke down so we had to flag down the spectators' coach, that was following some time later, and take that over. Oddly, considering that without the Sale team there wouldn't have been a game, some of the spectators refused to get off, so we ended up travelling to Bath in a rickety bus half full of spectators.

At the end of that season I went away on holiday but it wasn't long after my return that things started to happen off the field. I had had no inkling that the knives were out for Paul but relations between himself and Brian Wilkinson had broken down and I suppose people didn't tell me much because I was perceived to be one of Paul's pals. The next thing I knew Paul had been shown the door. The club was run by the members in those days and, being an amateur club historically, it was effectively run by the executive committee, which had decided to dispense with his services.

Along with the other players, I was asked to go to the club's annual meeting. Word was that if certain people got elected to the executive then Paul's job would be safe. He had a strong following amongst the fans, who had been meeting in a local pub to mount a campaign to keep him, and there was a feeling that they might win the day. If they didn't then there would be no way back for Paul although, at the time, I knew virtually nothing of what was going on and even now am not totally clear what the issues were, although one heard talk of personality clashes and his financial demands.

We weren't allowed into the meeting but word was relayed to us that things were going Paul's way. One of his chief backers, Nick Lunt, had been appointed as chairman ahead of the executive's nominee, Dave Levings. The euphoria in Paul's camp was short-lived, however, because other appointments ensured that the executive still finished up with an anti-Turner balance.

Paul was very bitter about the whole thing because of what he felt he had achieved for the club. It wasn't long before he was steering Bedford into the Premiership, just to demonstrate his ability to develop and motivate sides. I attended rugby meetings with him in the years after that and he wouldn't even look at Jim Mallinder, who had been Sale's skipper at the time. I always got on well with Jim but Paul clearly felt that he hadn't been in his camp. Paul wasn't over enamoured with Steve Smith either. He felt the former England captain had a far greater influence at Heywood Road than many people realised.

I never trusted Smithy either and I was to discover later, to my cost, that he appears to be the man pulling the strings at Sale. I got the impression, as time went on, that he wanted to run things from arms length, even after Brian Kennedy had bought the club. It is interesting that every time there was an issue, meetings would be held at the headquarters of Cotton Traders, the company run by Steve and Fran Cotton, his former England colleague. I have no respect for Steve and believe he likes to influence what goes on at Heywood Road without having the responsibility if anything goes wrong. He had his little coterie of followers who would wander around after him on match days but he and I had very little to do with one another. I didn't like him and I'm sure the feeling was mutual.

When the game first went professional he was on the board, giving his twopennyworth at meetings and saying who we should be signing, along with giving his dated opinions about the game. He later resigned as a director but at the start of the 2001/2 season he was back on the board as large as life as the representative of the Sale Members' Club.

Paul's departure put John Mitchell in a difficult position. He had agreed to join Sale as a player who would also help Paul by coaching the forwards. By that stage he was back in New Zealand and nobody was really sure if he would come back because taking over total responsibility for the side was a very different scenario to the one he had envisaged. He did return and enjoyed something of a honeymoon period, culminating in a first ever cup final appearance for the Cheshire club. But it wasn't to last.

Not long after that meeting when Paul's comeback bid foundered, Wilkie was hauled before the guillotine and similarly dispatched. I felt sorry for him because I thought he was a nice bloke who really did have the club at heart and the respect of the players. He liked a drink and that didn't go down well with everyone but at least he knew something about rugby, which is more than can be said about those who followed him. He may not have been the sharpest businessman in the world but he worked hard for Sale and assembled a very good squad of players in readiness for the 1996/97 season. Again, I didn't know what was going on except that Wilkie went absolutely ballistic when he was fired by the executive and the dust took a while to settle from the fallout. I gathered later that he had been given a budget by the committee, which was trying to make a go of running a professional rather than amateur operation, and he had been signing players without getting the salary cleared. As a result the salary bill was considerably higher than they had allowed for in their playing budget.

I don't know how they were managing to run the club and rumour has it that they had to borrow heavily from the bank in order to keep going, using land that they owned as collateral. The only executive member I had known was Wilkie and once he went I was concerned for my own position. I could see a Widnes situation arising again and when you have a mortgage and a young family it's very worrying.

With Brian gone the door opened for a new chief executive, Howard Thomas. Although a nice bloke who I got on with very well off the pitch, he hadn't a clue what rugby was all about. I have always been of the opinion that professional sport is very different from any other type of business; having run a company shouldn't qualify someone for running a professional sporting team. With tongue in cheek, however, I suppose Howard did have the best possible qualification to run Sale rugby club – he was about to become Steve Smith's brother-in-law.

He had previously worked in the hospitality business. One of his tasks had been to look after the touring South African cricket team and he had played that game to a reasonably high standard. There were cricketing pictures on the wall of his office and, when you had meetings with him, he would sometimes pick up his bat and play a few practice shots whilst he talked. On other occasions he would lean back in his chair tossing a miniature rugby ball into the air. Then he would drop it and the meeting would have to stop whilst he scrambled around on his hands and knees looking for it.

In the build-up to that 1996/97 season I broke a finger in three places during contact training. I had to have the finger pinned and that condemned me to miss most of the pre-season and the early games. During the summer the club had signed a young wing from Gloucester, Tom Beim, and my old Wales and Widnes sparring partner John Devereux. I could play either wing or centre but ended up in neither position when Sale played a warm-up game at Stirling County in Scotland. As a result I found myself playing for the second team and that was a complete shambles. It involved six or seven players who, like myself, were professionals; the rest were amateurs who simply weren't up to playing at the level at which they were being asked to perform.

I soon realised that it was hardly a viable vehicle in which to vie for a first team place. I hadn't switched back to rugby union to play with the dirt-trackers, especially as Sale had recruited some good players to ensure there would be competition for places. Former England scrum-half Dewi Morris had been enticed out of retirement and teamed up with New Zealander Simon Mannix. Mitch was also on board but his appearances initially were restricted due to a problem with his work permit. After a lot of wrangling he was allowed to play and coach but the following season he was only permitted to coach the side.

He certainly made a difference when he was on the field: he had bags of experience, the sort of commitment you expect from an All Black and was as tough as teak. He was able to lead the pack by example and had some very able lieutenants behind.

The first team made a reasonable start to the season despite losing narrowly at home to Wasps, and there is little doubt that Sale would have picked up the points on that occasion if Mitchell had played. They made amends by beating Gloucester at Kingsholm but, once I was fit to play again, I found myself languishing in the second team.

In fact I missed out on Howard's great *faux pas* on the day that Sale played Bristol in the league at Heywood Road. The executive was so worried about the club's financial position – many other clubs had secured backers by that time – that they had ordered cutbacks on the playing contracts. With a marvellous sense of timing, Howard sent out a letter to all the professional players telling them that their contracts would have to be renegotiated. Those letters arrived on the mat on the morning of the game against Bristol.

The reaction was what you might expect. The players talked about nothing else in the dressing room and one of them, second row John Fowler, refused to go out on to the field until he was paid what he was due. All this was going on in the dressing room and, after much debate, John was actually given his money before the game. John was a really good guy off the pitch. He was bright and an accountant, so was right on the ball when it came down to money. Some would call him mercenary but he was in the game for the money and he knew that you were not in the game for very long. That was brought home to him later in the season when he suffered an injury that put an end to his professional career even though he was able to play as a shamateur – oops, I mean amateur – for Manchester a long time afterwards.

Not surprisingly, the lads played like drains for much of the first half and leaked four tries in the first quarter of an hour. They finally hauled themselves into a contest they should have won easily and, in the end, were beaten 33-31. Mitch, who had had to withdraw from the side yet again because of the work permit problem, said in the media that there had been a good deal of contractual activity going on behind the scenes but the spectators had no idea as to what extent.

There were even repercussions at the Memorial Ground, where the second team was playing Bristol United. I think we travelled with just 15 players and the skipper, John Abe, took me on one side and said he needed a good game from me. I told him that I was sorry but was playing in a side that contained too many players who simply weren't up to the task. I was playing either wing or centre, was not getting any ball and was spending all my time tackling.

"I have just had a letter from the club trying to cut my contract so if you expect me to pull my guts out for the club today then you can think again," I added.

That attitude won't have gone down any better than John Fowler's but the scenario was a nightmare one for a professional. There was then, and still is to some extent, an attitude from the "suits" that we are all mercenary. Fair enough, they didn't get paid in their day, but the game has gone professional and they simply have to grin and bear it. After all, they all had secure jobs outside the game whereas a great many rugby union professionals today have only one career and that can be short-lived. I played for Cardiff without getting paid but, because I happened to be good at rugby, I turned professional. I thought that was the best way, at that time, to make a living and support my family. With hindsight I might have been better off looking for a career outside rugby.

The sad thing is that one thoughtless act by the management very nearly derailed what was a good side. The boys had some good results, team spirit between the players was was brilliant and there were no prima donnas. Andy Clarke, the brother of former Great Britain rugby league star Phil, was brought in to take charge of fitness and he did a very good job. He had already been involved with England, Ireland and the Liverpool soccer team so he certainly knew his stuff and the players respected him, even if he did work them hard.

The playing squad had been strengthened by the recruitment of the players I mentioned earlier, plus Phil Winstanley, a north of England prop from Orrell. Already there were the likes of full-back Jim Mallinder, wing David Rees, centres Jos Baxendell and Chris Yates, hooker Steve Diamond and the propping Smith twins, Andy and Paul, second rows Dave Baldwin and John Fowler and back rows of the calibre of Charlie Vyvyan and Andy Morris, along with Dylan O'Grady and Dave Erskine, who both went on to play for Ireland.

I'm not aware what the whole operation cost that season but I suspect it was one of the cheapest the club has had since it turned professional. For all that, Sale reached what was then the Pilkington Cup Final for the first time in its history and finished fifth in the league, just missing out on a European Cup spot the following season. Many believe they missed out when Leicester sneaked a draw at Heywood Road two weeks before the final but in my book the Euro disaster was entirely down to the letters that arrived on the doormat on the day of the home game against Bristol. The Leicester game was always going to be tough to extract two points from. The Bristol game had been eminently winnable.

My own senior debut had been held up by the injury to my finger but I finally made it into the side for an Anglo-Welsh Cup clash with old adversaries Llanelli. We won that game quite comfortably and Phil Winstanley had a memorable debut. He was brought on in the second half and stunned the crowd by chipping over the Llanelli full-back's head, racing around him, re-gathering and sprinting to the line. Not bad for a prop, but then he did start life in Orrell's back row and has obviously got slower as the years advanced.

I played on the wing but always thought my role at Sale would be in the centre and that's where I ended up, with Jos Baxendell as my regular partner. Centre was hardly a new position for me and it gave Sale extra experience in midfield whilst leaving the wing positions free for the quick youngsters, Tom Beim and David Rees. In fact they had been playing so well that I had to wait to get my chance on the wing in the first place. That came when Tom was injured and I found myself playing against Jim Fallon when we met Richmond in the Tetley's Bitter Cup.

I knew Jim from rugby league and, whilst a decent player, he wasn't as good as he thought he was. I had no problems with him, apart from the fact that we ended up having a couple of brawls. The second led to a penalty that Mannix kicked to put Sale in front; it was a little unfair on Jim, because I was the one who had started it. But that's rugby. Sometimes you get away with it and on other occasions you get penalised when you are the innocent party.

That cup-tie day was also memorable because that's when I met my partner Amanda Cheshire. It was Amanda's first day at Heywood Road, where she had arrived to look after corporate hospitality. We bumped into each other in the kitchen in the office block and were introduced but little did I realise then that it would be the start of long-term relationship.

It settled into a very good side and Sale attempted to play the type of rugby I have always enjoyed. They moved the ball about and, with wings like Tom and Dave, that certainly made sense. Reesy was a brilliant player with a solid defence and a good sidestep. He was also very difficult to haul down and, even when you succeeded in putting him on the deck, he had the determination to bounce up like a rubber ball and come at you again. I was sorry to lose him to Bristol after I had taken over as director of rugby, but that's another story.

Reesy was also a great lad off the pitch and it's a pity he suffered the injuries he did when he was playing so well for England. It's good to see him on his way back and I couldn't understand why England weren't playing him in the tests during the tour to Canada and the USA in the summer of 2001 because I watched the videos and he's a better player than the guys who did start in those games. Tommy was a different type of player to Reesy. He had a lot of good things in his armoury but, whilst he could tackle, he wasn't as aggressive defensively, nor had he Reesy's jink in attack. You could actually read which leg he was coming off and that made it easier to stop him but he was very quick and, with Jim Mallinder at full-back, Sale had a lot of attacking options in those days.

That season Jim was playing probably some of the best rugby of his career. He was another of those full-backs you could rely on to take the high ball under pressure and he was a long striding runner who was hard to stop and who had the ability to stay on his feet in the tackle and make the ball available. Both Reesy and Tommy took full advantage of some of Jim's surges downfield and it's ironic that, in some quarters, there were those who wanted to get rid of both Jim and myself at the end of that season. Jim, of course, played for England on the 1997 tour to Argentina and was on the reserve list for the British Lions' tour to South Africa. As I was also on the reserve list for the Lions, it makes you wonder why certain people at Sale wanted rid of the pair of us.

Mannix was brilliant at controlling things in midfield and I'm surprised that he didn't win more caps for New Zealand. Dewi, as was expected of him, controlled the pack and, considering Sale's problems at the lineout in more recent times, they had no problems in those days courtesy of Baldwin and Fowler. Although I didn't like the guy, I have to say that Baldwin was brilliant as a front of line jumper, especially when he was up against the likes of Martin Johnson, and Fowler was one of the best people I have seen at hitting rucks. He would also get around the park all day for you and had the sort of brain that Leicester players develop in terms of illegally slowing things down when necessary. He was sorely missed at the cup final after suffering a serious injury playing against Saracens.

The Smith twins were great lads who had grown up at the club and gave it everything. Both had to retire early through neck injuries and I feel sorry for the pair of them because they deserved more from the club. They had played for peanuts in comparison to players who were far less committed but far better remunerated. At least Paul was eventually offered a place in Brian Kennedy's organisation after he had taken over the club. They often formed a very competent front row with Steve Diamond, who was just the sort of hooker you needed. He was a complete nightmare to oppose on the pitch: a hard lad and would be constantly having a go at opponents, both on and off the ball.

So we had a far better season than pundits had predicted and we were always chasing a top spot in the league. Apart from the opening game against London Wasps, when we were pipped 33-31, the only game we lost at home was the Bristol debacle and even Francois Pienaar and his hotshots from Saracens were steamrollered by us one very enjoyable evening. Gloucester were stuffed by 30 points, along with London Irish and Leicester were very lucky to escape with a draw. The thing is that nobody looked forward to playing at Sale in those days. Heywood Road is a small ground and when it is full, which used to happen that season, the atmosphere is tremendous. The fans are very close to the playing area so it is fairly intimidating and just to make matters worse for opponents, the visiting dressing room is miniscule and split into two. Most unwelcoming. One or two people at the club wanted to christen it 'Fortress North' but others saw that as tempting fate.

Unfortunately, in more recent seasons, there hasn't been anything remotely intimidating about playing at Heywood Road and some of Sale's best results, under their new guise as Sharks, have been when playing away from home.

Sometimes we would win games purely through our defence; not because we had a defensive coach who used to try to organize us and teach us how to tackle, as is the vogue these days, but simply because everyone in the side wanted victory so badly. Defence is not just about organization, which seems to have become a job creation scheme for out of work coaches from rugby league, but about heart. You have to want to defend and you have to be prepared to put your body on the line time and time again. If you are not prepared to do that, both for yourself and your teammates, then you will still miss tackles even if you have the best defensive coach in the world.

That season we had Simon Mannix, whose defence was excellent, as Northampton's Tim Rodber discovered to his cost one afternoon when he never seemed to get the message and kept driving into our midfield only to be dumped on his backside time and again by Simon, and Jos Baxendell and myself were un-compromising in the centre. Both wings could tackle when they had to and, if anyone did get through, they had Jim Mallinder to deal with.

Things continued to go reasonably well in the league and, after we had chalked up the double over Harlequins, their then coach Dick Best gave us the tag of "Dark Destroyers." The victory at The Stoop was quite remarkable for its execution. It was nip and tuck throughout and Thierry Lacroix kept the scoreboard ticking over for Quins with a succession of penalties. They seemed to have it in the bag as the game entered the later stages but Dave Baldwin got over for a try and we sneaked a one point victory when Chris Yates, of all people, calmly dropped a goal. People standing behind the home posts said the ball went in every direction other the one in which it was meant to go until the very last second when it suddenly veered between the posts after looking all the world as though it might hit a corner flag!

"Kiwi" Yates dined out on that one for quite some time although we had trouble stopping him attempting them at every opportunity for weeks to come. It was an effort that Simon Mannix would have been proud of but that was the day he had pulled out of the side, publicly because of a bout of 'flu, but in reality because he was upset that his wife had flown back to New Zealand with his daughter. And he wasn't to know that she would have a change of heart halfway there and come back again.

Our meeting with Quins at home was staged as a night match and we ended their unbeaten run with a stunning performance in front of a capacity crowd. A lot had turned up to see England skipper Will Carling and the club's two temporary signings from rugby league, Gary Connolly and Robbie Paul. Quins had started as though they would take us apart but our defence was tremendous and we were probably helped by the fact that Carling was proving that he never was a fly-half. Gary got a consolation try towards the end but it was Dewi Morris who caught the eye that evening and we thoroughly deserved our 24-13 victory.

We then stuck 58 points on West Hartlepool to help their downward spiral and did the same to Sale's closest geographic rivals, Orrell.

Quite apart from pushing for a top four place in the table, there was a sudden realisation that it could be Sale's year in the cup too. After disposing of Newbury, we pulled off a last gasp win over Richmond at Heywood Road. Big spending Richmond were going well at the time and we trailed throughout the game. We started by giving Richmond scrum-half Andy Moore an interception try and Simon Mason, the young full-back who had joined the Londoners from Orrell and earned himself an Irish cap at full-back, started popping over the penalties. The cheeky devil even added a try from his repertoire and a cup exit was staring us in the face. We were helped by two crucial incidents: England hooker Brian Moore was sent off for stamping on Dave Baldwin and David Rees, who had been injured, was brought on when John Devereux succumbed to another injury.

With almost his first touch, Reesy tore through Richmond's defence to touch down by the posts and Mannix kicked the conversion to take us to within two points. Richmond infringed as we put them under pressure in the dying minutes and Mannix drilled over two more to give us a 34-30 win.

We dealt with Orrell in the next round and had to travel to face Northampton in the quarter-finals. We had lost in the league at Franklins Gardens so felt we had a score to settle. Mitch played in that game and it was the three Ms – Mitchell, Morris and Mannix – who controlled things for us. Paul Grayson and Mannix exchanged a couple of penalties apiece before Dewi scavenged a crucial try when Northampton tapped down at a lineout on their own line. Grayson managed another penalty but Mannix kept our noses in front until Dylan O'Grady followed up a Mallinder break and scored the try that put us in the semi-finals.

When we were drawn at home to Harlequins, a side we had already beaten twice in the league, we knew we could go all the way. And what a day it turned out to be. Another full house and the noise was incredible. The decibels went up when I broke down the middle and found Dylan O'Grady in support. He took my pass and scored a try that Mannix converted and Lady Luck was with us because Will Carling did all the running for a Quins response only to see Peter Mensah drop his pass with our line at his mercy.

Harlequins enjoyed their moments of pressure but one of those moments led to our next try. David Rees got his hands on the ball and wriggled his way out of defence to set up a ruck. Dewi Morris fired it out and I drew the cover before hurling a pass into the path of Jim Mallinder, who had already worked up quite a head of steam. There was no stopping big Jim and he powered his way past the cover in a 50-yard race to the line. You could tell then that Quins sensed it wasn't going to be either their day or their cup and, when they dropped the ball on our ten metre line, Tom Beim swept it up, forced his way out of a tackle and had a clear run to the line. We had done it. Cup finals were nothing new to me but I was looking forward to this one.

Two weeks before the final against Leicester, we had to face them in the league at Heywood Road. In some ways it wasn't the ideal scenario because the league points were vital to both clubs but I don't think either side really wanted to show all the cards they had in the deck so close to the Twickenham showdown. Not surprisingly, it was a fractious game and there was an incident that was very costly for Sale and sparked an unfair hate relationship between the Sale fans and Martin Johnson. Charlie Vyvyan, who was a vital component in our side at number eight, broke his leg at a ruck and the fans felt that Martin had been responsible. Video evidence showed that that wasn't the case at all, it was a pure accident and Martin had had nothing to do with it, but it soured the atmosphere and there was too much concentration on players having a go at one another rather than on the rugby.

At one stage Neil Back was fighting with one of our players and our baggage man, Robbie Dixon, ran on and joined in. I had hold of Austin Healey – unfortunately not by the gob – and suddenly noticed Robbie next to me. I asked him what the fuck he thought he was doing but he was just raving and two of our replacements had to run on to drag him off. Needless to say, Robbie, who has a great heart, got a serious bollocking for that.

I had taken over the role of team manager by that time, working in tandem with Mitch, and we got hold of some office notepaper and devised a letter to Robbie, purported to be from Howard Thomas, and saying that in view of his behaviour at the Leicester game he was being barred from any involvement with the team on cup final day and would not be permitted on the touchline. We handed Robbie the letter, saying it was from Howard, and he nearly burst into tears when he read it. He was really upset at the thought of not being involved in what was the biggest day in the club's history. We shouldn't have done it really but he took it well when he realised it was a spoof. Robbie is a great bloke who devotes a lot of time and energy to the side with little or no reward but he wasn't going to stand quietly by whilst one of his lads was getting the worst of it on the field!

Throughout that season I had continued to work on the commercial side for the club as well as having taken on the responsibility of team manager. Mitch, who had arrived at Sale to coach the side, had found himself effectively in the dual role of director of rugby as well and he was under a lot of pressure. Coaching is a full-time job at that level but he was having to involve himself in a lot of admin stuff as well. He said he needed a team manager and I suppose I was the obvious choice.

I settled into a player/manager role but still had some dealings with the commercial side because of the contacts I had established during my time at the club. Amanda had started working for me on the commercial side and, as my own marriage broke up, she became my partner. That caused a few problems and I wasn't happy with the way Amanda was treated by some of the wives and girlfriends of the players, who took a very dim view of our relationship. Amanda was given the cold shoulder, which made life uncomfortable socially. I was invited to a New Year's Eve party at Mitch's house but was told not to take Amanda with me. Naturally, I didn't attend. People in glass houses shouldn't throw stones, however, and I wondered what their attitude would have been if some had been aware of what their own better halves had been up to.

Talking of parties, Mitch organised a house-warming that he then decided to hold at the club because of the large number of people he had invited. He proceeded to arrange drinks and food and, when the party finished, he took the money for the food and drink out of the players' fines kitty, explaining that it was a players' function. Needless to say, that didn't go down too well with the players.

The cup final was clearly going to be Sale's big day but first we had the slight matter of a visit to Bath in the league. Having lost Charlie Vyvyan and John Fowler, two key forwards for us, we simply couldn't afford to lose any more. For that reason we sent a virtual second team to Bath. The news wasn't broadcast and I know a few of the boys made a lot of money by gambling on Bath's winning margin. Being a betting man myself I would, along with some of the other players, have a flutter occasionally on the outcome of Premiership matches. We all obviously had inside information about the Bath game.

I don't know about the bookies but I know the RFU weren't too happy about our sending a second string but the decision was taken to enhance our chances of winning the final, when we were always going to be underdogs, and the only involvement of most of the cup side at Bath was as spectators. Embarrassed spectators at that.

We got absolutely hammered at The Rec and a few fringe

players did their long-term cause no good that afternoon. Given their chance, I'm afraid they failed to take it. We knew they would lose heavily but the eventual 80-point margin was ridiculous. Adam Griffin, who had played at Salford Reds, was included in the side to do the goal kicking and he turned up with blue boots. Mitch told him that if he was thinking of running out in those at The Rec he had better make sure he had a bloody good game. It was so good, in fact, that he was brought off after about 20 minutes.

In the build-up to the cup final I had been very busy organising hotels, kit, transportation and, of course, our cup final outfits. We went to a local company, Corporate Couture, and were measured for jacket and trousers and I remember our initials were embroidered on an inside pocket. We deliberately went for an outfit that we would happily wear again socially but that didn't go down too well with the members, who were unhappy that there was no Sale emblem on the jacket. For our part we couldn't see the point in walking around in future wearing something that related to a rugby cup final we once played in. Perhaps as a result of that we were told there would be no cash bonus for having reached the final. The outfit would have to be in lieu of that. The players seemed content enough with that situation but then professional rugby union was in its infancy. When I played rugby league the first question for any important game related to what bonus we would receive.

Training was pretty relaxed in the build-up to the game but, as the time got closer, you could see that one or two of the less experienced players were getting a little excited about it all. I was pretty relaxed about the whole thing but, as an international who had also played in two World Cups and four Welsh Cup Finals, that was to be expected. Even so, it was quite something to play at Twickenham in front of what became a record crowd for a club match anywhere in the world. It was remarkable how the final caught the imagination of the public. More than 15,000 people travelled to Twickenham from the Manchester area and I'm told the M6 motorway was a sea of blue and white. People from pubs and clubs as far away as Cumbria gave us their support that day.

Yet in the end the game was disappointing. It rained when we wanted sunshine and dry conditions and that certainly answered Leicester's prayers. They had a lot more experience in their side and we knew our only realistic hope was to move the ball around as often as possible. The problem when you play Leicester, very often, is winning enough ball to do anything with. I recall one game at Welford Road when I don't think we touched the ball for 20 minutes, apart from kicking off at the start of the game and after every score.

It was obvious that their tactic would be to deny us the ball and it was no secret in the Premiership that Leicester were masters at stopping opponents playing. We knew they would kill the ball as often as the referee let them get away with it and that frustrated our planning because we weren't sure how we were going to deal with it. I had my own ideas of course and that almost resulted in me being sent off after just 20 seconds of the game. At just about the first ruck Neil Back went in and killed the ball and I was so frustrated that I ran in like a mad man, stamped all over him, and then ran back out of the way in the hope that nobody realised it was me.

Despite our dreams I'm afraid Leicester just had the edge on us all afternoon. Will Greenwood was playing in the centre for them and I had some good battles with him over the years. I think we had a fight that afternoon and I doubt there was any love lost because, Trevor Ringland apart, I tended not to mix with opponents off the pitch. I might say hello, how are you? and goodbye, but little more than that. Sometimes fans would ask what Will Carling was like, for instance, but I couldn't tell them because we met on the field and that was it. In Will's case he was a good, hard opponent and we would have digs at one another and try to wind each other up throughout a game. But we wouldn't have a laugh and a joke together afterwards. Now that we don't play any more I suppose that if we bumped into each other in a bar we would probably have a chat about past battles but it's different when you are still involved in the game and might meet up again in opposition a few days later. The thing that used to really piss me off at Sale was the way some of the players would have a laugh and a joke with opponents either on the pitch or in the dressing room corridor before a match.

I felt sorry for Dewi Morris that afternoon at Twickenham because he had made it pretty plain that it was going to be his swansong. He had come out of retirement to do a tremendous job for the club and it would had been marvellous if he could have gone out of the game on a real high. But it wasn't to be and maybe he tried too hard to make it special because he wasn't at his imperious best that afternoon. Like Dewi, John Mitchell and myself, Simon Mannix had big match experience yet even he lost a little of his composure by missing kicks that could have swung the game our way. I don't think the younger players froze on the day but I believe the size of the stadium and the crowd, along with the atmosphere, got to them a little bit. With more experience they could perhaps have come through but playing in big games at Twickenham was just bread and butter to the Leicester boys whereas to the majority of our players it was a once in a lifetime experience.

I have been in tears after losing cup finals but I didn't shed any after that defeat because Leicester were the better side on the day and we could have no complaints. We weren't expected to win, and we didn't. It was still a great experience and I hoped the young players would benefit from it. David Rees certainly did because, but for injury, Twickenham would have become almost his second home.

The aftermath of a final is a complete shambles if you have lost. You know you have a formal dinner to go to but, really, it's the last place you want to be. You just want to be with your mates having a quiet drink until the pain of defeat starts to abate somewhat. As soon as the formal bit was over we descended on the Orange Tree pub in Richmond and started to get shitfaced. Back at the hotel we were joined by our families and, the following morning, one of the players asked if the wives could travel back on the team bus. I put my foot down and said no way. My decision didn't go down too well in all quarters, especially among the ladies, but I have played in six or seven cup finals and wives have never travelled back with the players. The build-up, the game itself and the recovery in the cold light of day is strictly a team thing to my mind.

There was going to be a barbecue for players, families and fans back at Heywood Road anyway on the Sunday afternoon, so I was determined it should be a squad thing until then. In the event we left the hotel quite late because Marcus, our driver, didn't turn up on time. Hardly surprising considering his antics the previous evening when he got legless and ended up playing the piano stark naked until the wee small hours.

He was quite a lad was Marcus. The first time I went back to Cardiff in charge of Sale, to play an evening game in the Anglo-Welsh Cup, he was again our driver. I told him that, as we were staying overnight and could walk to the ground from our hotel, we wouldn't need the bus again. I told him he could go and get pissed if he wanted to. However, I didn't expect him to take me up on the offer quite as quickly as he did. I was in the changing room with the boys before the game when one of the Cardiff stewards walked in and said, "Adolf, there's someone in the bar who has had a few drinks, is getting a bit loud and says he's with you."

For those who may be wondering, Adolf is a nickname I acquired at school and it stuck with me. Some people at Sale Sharks thought I was called that because I was a stickler for discipline, which certainly wasn't the case; I was more easygoing than some. In fact, it came about because my initials are AH but I would like to think that is the only thing I share with the man responsible for the Second World War. Especially as they are now suggesting that he was gay!

I walked back with the official to the bar and there was Marcus in full voice. I apologised, told them that he was the bus driver and marched him out of there. I then gave him a ticket for the committee box, where I could keep an eye on him, and told him, "Stop fucking about and behave yourself."

Out on the pitch we were getting stuffed and at half time I went to get cups of tea for our replacements. When I got back I noticed that Marcus had gone missing but just assumed he'd gone for a pee. The game restarted, the referee awarded a penalty against us and the next thing Marcus clambers out of our dugout and starts running up and down the touchline berating the referee. I had to go down to pitch side to drag him out of there. When you're a team manager you don't just have to wet nurse your players, you have to act as a nanny to your bus driver as well!

CHAPTER TEN

Vote of No Confidence

THERE HAD BEEN a real buzz about Sale at the end of the 1996/97 season but the storm clouds were already gathering over Heywood Road. It was patently obvious that the club would struggle without an outside backer and they weren't exactly queuing up at the gates. When Brian Wilkinson had been chief executive he had courted boxing promoter Frank Warren and upset my old boss John Wilkinson by taking some of Warren's cohorts down to The Willows to have a look around. Apparently there had been some talk of Sale going to play there, a move that the fans didn't like the idea of. They had visions of having their BMW's nicked on match days.

I believe John let it be known that he wasn't getting involved in a Frank Warren venture, the whole deal collapsed and Bedford were the recipients of the boxing promoter's largesse. Brian also had talks with the developers of the Trafford Centre, the huge out of town shopping and leisure complex alongside the M60, Manchester's answer to the M25, and about a ten-minute drive from Heywood Road. The complex was scheduled to have a sports stadium and, for some time, it looked as though Sale might move in there. The upside of such a move would have been a new, purpose-built stadium and the fact that male fans could have used the shopping attractions as their excuse to sneak of for 80 minutes. The downside might have been actually getting to games, particularly in the pre-Christmas period when traffic would be backed up the motorway for miles at the weekend.

In the meantime Sale's overdraft was getting bigger and there were sighs of relief all round when Howard Thomas unveiled a mystery group of businessmen who were going to take over the club. I say mystery men because that's what they remained during their time at Heywood Road. Rumour had it that Mr Big was a businessman who also had links with Harlequins, and that may have been one reason why they eventually pulled out. The front man for the group, which originally operated under the name Tourney, an off-the-shelf company, was a chap called Patrick Austen, who was a former director of Liberty, the London store group, and was boss of Vax International. Vax makes vacuum cleaners but if he thought they were going to clean up in rugby, he was sadly mistaken.

The company's arrival on the scene put Howard Thomas in an unusual position. As chief executive of the members' club, he was dealing with John Devereux, who was trying to sue the club over his contract. Devs said the members club owed him money and the club claimed that it didn't. Howard then took over as chief executive of Tourney and one of his first tasks was to get Devs to sign a new contract with what was effectively a new company.

Patrick didn't give much away and in one newspaper interview described himself and his fellow backers as "pretty boring really." Boring or not, they did put their hands in their pockets and the rugby budget was something like £2.8 million. Before the end of the previous season the club had signed Pat Sanderson, a talented schoolboy back row, and Darren Wright, my old teammate from Widnes who we felt would give us extra strength in the centre.

With Dewi having gone into retirement for a second time, we needed a scrum-half and went for two Welshmen. One was Kevin

Ellis, who had got close to a full cap for Wales before switching to rugby union, and Richard Smith, who had impressed us by scoring two tries when he played against us for Newbridge in the European Shield. He had spent the previous season at Bristol but hadn't really settled. The major signing was former All Black Shane Howarth, who had the ability to play at full-back, centre or fly-half. We needed him in the last position initially because the authorities started to raise questions about the eligibility of Simon Mannix to play. The old problem arose of people running a new professional sport who weren't aware of all the requirements concerning work permits, *et al*. Shane was a good signing but he didn't come cheap.

As the season progressed we brought in Simon Raiwalui, a typically physical Fijian second row, South African back row Dion O'Cuinneagain and, when we realised we had little cover at hooker, the old England and Bath warrior Graham Dawe. Mitch had recommended a prop from New Zealand called Murray Driver but he didn't turn out to be one of Mitch's better ideas and it was soon fairly obvious he wasn't up to the task we were setting him. If nothing else it perhaps demonstrated that scrummaging was becoming big again in the northern hemisphere whereas, in the southern hemisphere, scrums were taking on more of a rugby league look: in other words, a means of restarting the game with nobody wanting to push and shove too much in case it tired them out for the amount of running about in the loose they would be required to do. The reality in the northern game was that packs like Leicester's, for instance, would ensure you were tested at the most basic stage, the scrum. If you couldn't hack it they would take great pleasure in making you do it all afternoon.

There were those at the club who thought they had pulled off a real coup by signing Chris Murphy. The young second row had captained the England U-21 side and had played for the North in the old divisional championship whilst still wet behind his ears. I did hear a story that someone who ought to have been listened to suggested an alternative second row but Murphy was the man those that mattered wanted. So Scott Murray did not end up as a Sale player and Murphy consistently failed to live up to his early promise.

After the split with my wife, I moved in with Chris and Tom Beim for a while. We got on well enough but Chris, for all his size and ability, lacked something. I remember watching a match video with Steve Diamond and Jim Mallinder during which a mass brawl had broken out at a lineout. All the forwards on both sides, and some of the backs, got stuck in but Chris was seen bending down and tying his bootlace. Just as the fight was coming to an end he jumped up and started pulling people out of it but we three had to question why you worry about your bootlaces when your mates are slugging it out toe-to-toe.

After I became director of rugby, following Mitch's well-publicized departure, I released Chris from his contract and he went to play for Rotherham before moving to join his brother at Leeds Tykes. He had been out with a broken leg and I had started to lose patience with him because, injured or not, players had responsibilities both on and off the field and he would consistently fail to turn up for commercial activities he had been scheduled to attend. It even got to the stage where he received written and verbal warnings because, on one occasion, he went to Newcastle with his girlfriend when he should have been working with the club's development side.

At the time we had to offload players and reduce salaries and it would have been wrong of the club to have kept Chris on the books when he wasn't doing all that was required of him. A pity really because I think he is a decent player but he doesn't accept responsibility too well and, for a big guy with the body of Tarzan, he played more like Jane.

Later that season we signed Duncan Bell, a prop from Ebbw Vale who had had spells with London Irish and Harlequins and had learned his rugby at Bath. Mitch had a fit when he saw him because he was overweight but he was a talented player who might have made it to the top with more hard work in the gym and a more single-minded approach to the job. Not that I'm one to talk because I wasn't exactly keen on training. He was one of a number of Sale players taken to the southern hemisphere by England during the summer of 1999 – a tour that had Mitch installed as forwards' coach – who came back with reputations damaged rather than enhanced.

The 1997/98 season should have started on a high note because of our high placing in the league the previous season and our cup final appearance. Incredibly, the club never tapped into the marvellous local support it had at the cup final and, just to make things worse, it had embarked on one of its most disastrous ventures – a new stand to replace the old wooden structure. Instead of building a proper one, however, the board went for one that could be dismantled and moved to a new location if required.

At that stage there was a good deal of talk about Sale moving to a new ground as a matter of necessity because of the limitations of homely Heywood Road; hence Brian Wilkinson's interest in Salford and the Trafford Centre. Perhaps because of his interest in cricket, Howard Thomas pushed hard for a move to the Lancashire county cricket ground at Old Trafford but it wasn't an idea that went down too well with the cricketing fraternity although Pete Marron, who was groundsman at both clubs, was confident it could work without destroying one of England's test venues.

Just when Sale should have been tapping into the sudden interest in the club because of its cup exploits, the already meagre crowd capacity was further reduced because the local authority wanted more exits from the ground. The club had already upset Scottish and Newcastle, the brewers, by putting up the new stand partially on the car park of their pub, The Little B, that the ground backs on to. So they were hardly inclined to help out by creating exits for the club and, instead, launched a legal battle over the issue. It wouldn't have been so bad if the stand had been a good one. It was anything but, and metal roof supports effectively made games unwatchable from too many of the seats.

As if that wasn't bad enough, everything was behind schedule, so we started the first season after our cup final appearance without a stand of any description. Where the old stand had been there was just a building site and Saracens, who had been defeated there just a few months earlier, gained their revenge with a victory that, I must confess, the Londoners deserved.

One or two high spots were to follow, however, and it was very satisfying to go to Loftus Road and beat Wasps 38-22 by outscoring them four tries to one. The star of the afternoon was David Rees who scored twice and, for one of them, ran straight through Lawrence Dallaglio, Rob Henderson and Gareth Rees, which took some doing. Mannix played in that game, so Shane partnered me in the centre.

Then there was the 76-0 destruction of Bristol at Heywood Road. Reesy and Tom Beim cut the West Country outfit to ribbons with a hat-trick from Dave and four coming from Tom. As a Gloucester boy he really enjoyed that one. We had a great battle with Harlequins at The Stoop, losing 52-41: clashes between the two sides were often high scoring affairs with both sides attempting to go out and play some rugby. I was paired with Chris Yates at centre, which may not have been the best balance, and Shane played at full-back after Mitch had decided to drop Jim Mallinder, something that had been almost unthinkable but, as I say, there was a campaign to get rid of both Jim and myself. Jim did get on as a replacement and played well.

It was that game when Mannix had been cleared to play by the immigration authorities but Mitch wanted to keep the news under wraps and surprise Harlequins at the last minute. Mitch was a great one for mind games and, if he could have got away with it, he would have kept our line-up secret until five minutes before kick-off. That didn't always endear us to opponents and we played one game at Leicester where the line-up contained 14 changes from the 15 originally given to the Welford Road club for use in their match day programme.

Mind you, if you want to keep your intentions secret then you need to have suitable security in place. There was a game at Heywood Road when I believe the opposition was Saracens. They travelled up on Friday, stayed overnight and asked if their kickers could have a little bit of a practice on the ground during the evening. Permission was granted, as one would expect, but nobody had thought to lock the Sale dressing room, which had our match plan written out on a blackboard. Come the game and nobody could understand how the opposition seemed to know everything we were about to do before we even did it. When Mitch found out that some of their players had been in the dressing room the night before, he hit the roof. And, believe me, when Mitch went ballistic he went into orbit.

He never got physical with the lads but he would shout and scream at them. The walls would rattle and he was a fearsome sight in full flow. Lads used to stand and take it; I can't think of many who would have had the bottle to have a real go back. The only time I saw him come to blows with a team member was not in the dressing room but during a "friendly" basketball match when he and second row John Fowler swapped a few punches before the lads broke it up. These things happen.

Although we started reasonably well in the Premiership that season there were one or two games we would like to forget. One was a Friday evening visit to Coundon Road to play Coventry in the Cheltenham and Gloucester Cup. The fixture came just days after we had demolished Bristol yet we succeeded in going down 24-8. The only blessing was that Mitch, who had been recruited by England by that time, was down at Twickenham with the England squad. It was one of those performances where, as a team manager, you just sit in the dugout and hold your head in your hands. Admittedly we rested a lot of players but I expected better from a squad of full time professionals and so did Mitch. Coventry wanted it more than we did and, not for the last time in Sale's recent history, we made a complete bollocks of the lineout. There was no understanding between hooker Graham Dawe and his jumpers, Chris Murphy and Sean Fletcher, and, as the game progressed, Coventry's confidence simply grew. When Murphy made a good break it was Graham who couldn't hold his pass so it seemed the poor telepathy between the two worked both ways.

It was during this season that the chinks started to appear in the relationship between Mitch and the players. There was also a slight change in our relationship, even though we worked very closely together and would always share a room when the team stayed away. I recall one day when we were playing Wasps and were in our bedroom getting dressed in readiness for our departure to Loftus Road. Out of the blue he said, "If you don't have a good game today mate, you're out next week."

He just carried on getting dressed while I was left pondering on just how erratic he could be. For a start I was his mate, secondly I was trying to concentrate, as a player, on the game in hand, thirdly I was the team manager who was also trying to organize everyone else for the game. Yet there he was telling me I would be out unless I had a good one. He didn't attempt to develop his comment and never mentioned it again but it was hardly a ploy to boost my morale.

Having said that, I think I had one of my best games for the club that day but twisted my knee just before the final whistle. We were then due to play at Welford Road but I told Mitch there was no way that I would be fit to play. He let it be known that he wanted me to play, told me not to do anything all week other than have treatment and to strap up the knee for the team run on the Friday morning. If I got through that I was playing. I got through the run but I wasn't happy with the knee even though Mitch said I would be all right.

I was in quite a bit of pain with the injury and travelling on the team coach, with the leg stuck in one position, didn't exactly help. Even doing the warm up I knew it wasn't right. The knee was all over the place and, after ten minutes of the game, I simply couldn't run. Chris "Kiwi" Yates took my place and I found out, following a scan, that I had ruptured the cruciate ligament. Mitch didn't say anything when I came off but he lost it in the dressing room after we had been hammered 55-15. I had been telling him all week that I wasn't fit but he rounded on me and said, "Don't you ever play for me again if you're not fit."

He could be contrary and there was one occasion, when we had been beaten heavily at Bristol and hadn't played at all well as a team, when he ordered everyone in for extra training the following morning. Unbeknown to the players he telephoned ahead to Tommy, the barman at the club, and told him to lay on three barrels of Stella in the downstairs bar. When the players turned up as ordered on the Sunday morning they were wetting themselves because they knew how hard some of Mitch's sessions could be and it didn't help when they saw the assistant coach, Mark Nelson, putting the cones out on the pitch.

Mitch let them all get changed and gathered them around him and outlined all the tough exercises they were about to start. Faces fell to the floor until he said, "Okay. I'm only joking. I want everyone in the downstairs bar, we are going to play some games and nobody is allowed to leave the room for any reason until all three barrels have been drunk."

That was all very well but nearly all the lads had driven to the ground and some had come from as far away as Wigan. As nobody was allowed to leave the room it wasn't long, bearing in mind that most hadn't eaten a thing since getting up that morning, before lads were being sick on the floor and pissing in pint pots which were just left on the side. It was a complete shambles and I felt sorry for Liz, the woman who had to clean it all up. We were there all afternoon and the thing ended with everybody out on the pitch, stark bollock naked, playing touch rugby. That didn't go down too well with neighbours whose apartments overlooked the pitch or with some of the older members who were having a quiet drink in the upstairs bar.

He tried it on other occasions and it had anything but the desired effect of pulling the players together. There was another game when he let it be known there would be a Sunday morning training session and they all groaned. Then he went down to the back of the team bus, where nobody was drinking because they didn't fancy training with a king-sized hangover. He sat down next to Steve Diamond and offered him a beer. Steve declined as well but Mitch winked and said, "Don't worry mate, we're going on the piss."

He asked other players if they were going to join him in a few beers at the Little B when the coach got back to the ground. They all declined again but he was winking at players so one or two, like "Dimes", were starting to get the message. The following morning I got a call at home. It was Mitch. "Adie, every fucker knows that it's not training this morning and that we're going on the piss," he moaned. "Cancel the beer."

The trouble was that all the lads, convinced it was going to be another mammoth drinking session, had gone out after all and got shitfaced. They staggered in with hangovers only to find that they were training after all. The session, as you can imagine, was a complete shambles and served no purpose whatsover except to make the lads angry.

The boys also weren't exactly enamoured of Mitch when we played Northampton in the Tetley's Bitter Cup at Heywood Road on January 2 one year. We would normally have a team run on the morning of the previous day and Mitch told everyone that, even though it was New Year's Day, there would be training as usual. That ruled out a wild night to see in the New Year and some of the boys reluctantly settled for a quiet evening at home. Mitch, meanwhile, went out for a meal with several players, including scrum-half Richard Smith, fly-half Shane Howarth and hooker Steve Diamond. I believe that Steve Smith went along as well. I gather that it turned into quite a session and it was obvious people were going to be in no fit state to train. As a result Mitch apparently said training would be called off. Unfortunately, that message wasn't conveyed to anyone else: all the players arrived and had to conduct the session without our coach and half-backs. To his credit, Steve Diamond still managed to turn up but the lads who were there were annoyed that they could be treated like that.

We got through the season but Mitch was already starting to lose his players. It was a natural progression, or rather a steady erosion. We had moved on somewhat from the time when the players fought to keep him when rumours circulated that he was leaving to join Northampton. The boys actually held a meeting – something they proved to be quite adept at as time went on and to the detriment of both Mitch and fellow Kiwi Glenn Ross – which ended with a plea to Mitch to stay. The management seemed anxious to hang on to his services and, as a consequence, offered him a lucrative long-term contract they were later to regret having signed.

So Mitch stayed and, as results became increasingly erratic, he would walk into a room and make statements that would have been better kept to himself or, at the very least, between the two of us, bearing in mind that I was effectively working alongside him. The Northampton interest got out when he walked into the office one day and announced that he had "been fishing". In other words he had been to Northampton to discuss a job at Franklins Gardens.

All the speculation about Mitch moving to Northampton sparked yet another bizarre episode in the club's history. Simon Mannix knew Mitch had been to Northampton and there is no doubt in my mind that the former New Zealand fly-half saw himself stepping into his shoes. Simon was a good player and a very strong character on the field. He knew what he wanted and Mitch had been on the verge of making him captain. Mitch walked into the office one day and told Jim Mallinder, Steve Diamond and myself that he was thinking of appointing Simon instead of Jim for the following season but we were horrified because we had all been getting the vibes that Simon was causing problems within the squad.

Whilst we were all trying to keep Mitch at Sale, Simon appeared to be doing his best to help him on his way. He was talking to players and telling some that Mitch didn't rate them, which was hardly conducive to those players having good feelings about their coach. Things came to a head when we travelled to play a game at West Hartlepool and some of the more senior players, who felt they had been duped by Simon, apologised to Jim and Steve. I believe one or two were ready to string Simon up by his short and curlies because they thought he was effectively turning one player against another. He had his favourites and that number included both Tom Beim and Chris Yates; it is interesting that both ended up with him at Gloucester.

Jim, Steve and I took Mitch to the Little B pub and told him what was going on behind his back. Mitch asked what the options were for dealing with the situation but we said there weren't many because Simon was causing a rift between the players and really had to go. We called him in for a meeting and I've never seen Mitch as nervous as he was that day because he had known Simon from their playing days in New Zealand and had recommended him to the club. But a tough and unpleasant job had to be done and we sat him down and told him that we knew what he was doing and that it was undermining the team. Some players had actually challenged us about comments we were supposed to have made about them, but hadn't. Obviously, Howard Thomas had to be consulted but he backed our decision and Simon found himself on the transfer list.

That shocked the fans but we could hardly explain to them what it was all about. One of the problems of running a professional club is that you can't always level with the fans, often for a variety of reasons.

Simon, of course, said he couldn't believe what we were doing to him and denied that he had done anything to undermine the team. He didn't really have a leg to stand on because it had become apparent that some players didn't even want him in the same dressing room. Simon spoke to me later and was pretty distraught but I said the evidence against him had been too strong and, as a management, we couldn't stand back and watch the squad fracture into groups. In many ways his departure was a blow because there was no question over his ability as a player although he seemed to have great difficulty in handling his private life.

The season started to fall away after a reasonable start and, in the end, we were quite lucky to stay away from the relegation zone. It has to be said that Sale benefited in recent seasons from one club, or another, wearing the mantle of fall guy throughout the campaign so it was a case of thank you very much to the likes of West Hartlepool, Bedford and Rotherham. Despite the backers spending a lot of money the investment simply wasn't being matched by results and it was clear that more money was going to be wasted when Howard Thomas called me into his office and told me he had a chance to sign Barrie-John Mather from rugby league. He had asked me what I thought.

"That will be the worst money you will ever spend," I said.

That wasn't a criticism of B-J, who is a nice lad and good luck to him if he can make good money out of playing rugby, but he wasn't the sort of player you were going to pay a massive salary to. Howard obviously disagreed, or at least his advisers disagreed, because Mitch and I were sent to meet B-J and his agent in a local Chinese restaurant. And the rumour factory started up straight away because several players just happened to walk past the restaurant, glanced at the four of us through the window and put two and two together.

I think they were initially asking for something like £150,000 and I told them they had to be joking. Joking or not a deal was done – not at that ridiculous figure but big enough – and it wasn't Mitch's decision, which it should have been because he was director of rugby. There were deficiencies in the squad but centre wasn't one of them and I think Mitch was wondering where on earth he was going to play this expensive new signing. I have my own suspicion as to who was behind the major interest in B-J. Fran Cotton and Clive Woodward had been talking about signing RL stars for the England team and it was obvious to us that B-J was a forerunner for Jason Robinson. Problem was that B-J was a decent player but he was a long, long way from being a Billy Whizz. Howard Thomas and Steve Smith were very pally at the time and I wondered if Smith, Cotton's partner, had influenced a signing that was destined to fall well short of expectations.

When I ended up as director I made some good signings but am the first to hold my hands up and admit that I also made some bad ones. Mine were usually made virtually blind when trying desperately to pull a squad together without either the necessary time or financial resource. But more of that later.

Having dropped from a top six finish to an unsatisfactory tenth spot, there was a lot of pressure on Mitch to improve things the following season. We had already recruited another back row in Pete Anglesea, who had been released by Bedford in a cost-cutting exercise, and he had slotted in very well. We also signed Springbok prop Dawie Theron to give our scrum a little more solidity, and a young man who briefly was to take the game by storm, Steve Hanley. Alex Sanderson arrived to join his elder brother Pat, and Mitch was a big fan of the younger Sanderson. He had also been a big fan of Pat and had been rewarded when Pat had been one of the few successes on the England tour to the southern hemisphere when Mitch travelled as forwards' coach.

But their relationship was to break down badly in the 1998/99 campaign and there were times when the player felt he couldn't do anything right for a coach he clearly respected and who even spent Christmas at the Sanderson family home because his wife Kay had returned with the children to New Zealand for a holiday.

The season wasn't very old when the club picked up Phil Greening, the former England hooker who had been put on the list by Gloucester because he was "too expensive" and they were well served in that area anyway. That was seen as a major signing by the club, even if he did look overweight, but, despite the fact that the player regained his place in the England side, one suspects with considerable help from Mitch, he was destined to crap on all of us from a great height before very long.

Another newcomer was Jan Machacek, the former captain of the Czech Republic, who had been playing number eight for Newport. We had been well stuffed by the Newport pack at Rodney Parade the previous season and Jan had twice picked up at scrums to drive over from close range. It was fairly impressive and Mitch recruited him with high hopes that he would give our forward effort some much needed whoomph. The problem was that we hadn't studied Jan going backwards and that, after all, had become a fairly common direction for our packs to move in. So Jan become one of a number of forward signings who never lived up to the high expectations of them.

Our results were patchy and it could be argued that the regular absences by Mitch with England didn't help the cause. I felt it was a bad move by the club to permit him to spend so much time away with the national side when we were struggling. It may not have helped psychologically that the side actually played some of its best rugby when he wasn't there because I am sure quite a few of the players felt the club no longer needed him. Maybe the body language on his return was indicative of the crumbling relationship between Mitch and the majority of the players. He would let fly on the training pitch and it was clear the pressure of the job was starting to get to him. I must confess that I hadn't been aware of just how strong the feeling had been, except that the atmosphere seemed to be lighter when Mitch wasn't around. The better results during his absences may have been down to players simply being more relaxed.

He took us to France for two weeks when we played in the European Shield and we stayed first of all in Montferrand before moving to a camp owned by Ged Glynn, part of the England coaching set up and assistant to Dick Best at London Irish before the axe fell. A week later we played Montpelier but neither game went well and there was a clear hint of Mitch's displeasure the morning after the final game. After a good drink following the match I arrived back at the hotel at 8am to find all the lads in their training gear in the lobby. Mitch had decided they were going for a run so I had to rush up to my room to get changed. The run nearly killed me and Andy Morris, a fluent French speaker, was in even bigger trouble because he didn't turn up at all. The atmosphere eased when Mitch had to dash back to London for an England session and most of us settled in Montpelier for a good drink.

You could never be sure whether or not Mitch would relax after a game and enjoy a drink or put you on the treadmill. He liked his little mind games and his sense of timing was absolutely marvellous when he announced before an important game at Bedford that there was a lack of money at the club and that the investors wouldn't be putting in as much money the following season, with the obvious implications in terms of wages and contracts.

Some may say I should have been aware of the antagonism towards Mitch but, by that stage, I was no longer a player and players tend to have a beef amongst themselves rather than in front of management. They would probably assume that anything said in front of myself would go straight back to Mitch.

Things came to a head when I was chatting with Steve Diamond in the office one day and Chris Murphy walked in, in a bit of a tizz. "Mitch has lost it again," he stormed.

He seemed to think I should do something about it but I was Mitch's right hand man, so to speak, and if the players had a problem with him then it was up to them to resolve their differences with him. The next thing I knew the players had held a meeting and effectively come up with a vote of no confidence in Mitch. I was shocked when I was told that the only person who didn't vote against him was Dion O'Cuinneagain but I wasn't at the meeting so can't verify the accuracy of that. But it was evident that things had reached a serious state and I found myself in a very difficult position.

I believe that when Mitch found out about the meeting he thought Steve Diamond had been the instigator but nothing could have been further from the truth. Steve did get involved in the end as a spokesman but that's only because he was a senior player and a natural intermediary on their behalf, especially as Jim Mallinder, as club captain, had rightly distanced himself from the meeting. I was told that the players had lost their respect for Mitch and didn't trust him any more, which left me with no alternative other than to report what had been going on to Howard Thomas.

There was then another players' meeting, one that Mitch knew about, and he and I stood outside chatting as it went on in the upstairs bar at the club. Not all the players were there because some had been advised by their agent that they could be in breach of their contract with the club for attending such a meeting. Whether all the players attended or not, it was still obvious that the problem wasn't going to go away.

The next thing I knew, the businessman Patrick Austen was in at the club and Mitch told me that they wanted rid of him. I assured Mitch that they couldn't do that because he had a lengthy contract, but the next meeting was more emotional and he told me he was on his way. He was very upset and I think his pride was badly hurt, even though I suspect he had already lined something up with Wasps, which is where he ended up until he returned to New Zealand. The whole incident had been a classic case of player power.

Mitch never accused me as such of having had a role in his dismissal, which I hadn't, but he came to our hotel for a beer when we played Harlequins in London some time later and said he was aware that I knew what had been going on. I told him that I was just the piggy in the middle who was involved with neither the players nor the board whilst the whole issue was thrashed out but I think I was wasting my breath. I'm convinced, however, that he knew who had been behind it.

It was sad that Mitch's reign ended as it did because he was a very good technical coach and an excellent player. Unfortunately, his playing involvement was seriously curtailed by bureaucracy and he found himself with the responsibility for everything to do with rugby at the club instead of being free simply to coach the side. Perhaps he was simply given too much rope and eventually hanged himself with it. He was, after all, new to the administrative side of the business but I believe the experience, unpleasant though it most certainly was, will have helped his development of man-management skills to serve him well in the future. I have no doubt that, if he reflects on the Sale experience and learns from it, he will go on to be very successful.

His departure left the club without a coach and we still weren't out of the wood so far as relegation was concerned. Jim, Steve and myself were summoned to a meeting, yes, you've guessed it, at Cotton Traders to discuss what was going to happen next. The outcome was that the three of us were put in charge of the rugby side of things for the remainder of the season. We finished on something of a high, which often happens in situations in which the club found itself. When a face goes out and new faces come into a club the result is very often a bit of a lift for everyone, even if it is only of a temporary nature. A board meeting decided that

I should become director of rugby, with Jim as head coach and Steve as his assistant. We were pretty close anyway, Jim was good with the backs and Steve worked well with the pack and I would help out where I could in a coaching sense as well as running the rest of the rugby operation.

I wonder if we realised what we were letting ourselves in for. Our mainly mystery backers had provided a rugby budget of £2.5 million for the season just finished but made it perfectly clear that only £800,000 would be available for players' wages in the 1999/ 2000 season. At the same time Howard Thomas had left the club, ostensibly to "pursue other interests", but it was fairly obvious that the backers had lost patience with the lack of return (in a success sense) on their investment and were getting ready to pull out. Graham Walker, who had been commercial manager at the new Millennium Stadium in Cardiff and had formerly worked for the Football League, replaced Howard. I suspect his brief was to find either a major sponsor or to wind down the operation to make it attractive to a potential new backer. What we were quite certain of was that the current backers weren't going to continue burning money at anything like the same rate.

Julian Pollard, who worked with Patrick Austen, had assumed the chief executive role in the period between Howard's departure and Graham's arrival. Not long after Graham had come on board he walked into my office with Julian, who told me what the playing budget was to be for the new season. Graham just said, "Look Adie, you're the director of rugby and I don't know anything about that side of the business. You do what you want," and walked out. I have no criticism of Graham because he was always up front with me and left me to get on with things. He admitted that he didn't know enough about the game to start interfering in playing matters. If only other chief executives and owners had been as sensible instead of trying to think they were experts on something about which they had very little knowledge, if, in some cases, any at all when it came to running a rugby club, signing the right players for the right money and picking the best playing combination. There was also a tendency to listen to people who had no experience at the coalface.

Naturally, in the incestuous environment of a rugby club, the players were fully aware of the financial difficulties and the possibility that the backers would pull out at the end of the 1999/2000 season. The club hadn't told them anything officially but rumours spread and they were in no doubt when we started sifting through the existing squad to reduce the monetary level of their contracts.

Not surprisingly, the quality players in particular were not overjoyed at having their income reduced although some accepted the situation more readily than others. The realists among the more journeymen players clearly took the view that some money was distinctly preferable to no money, providing they could remain as full-time professionals.

One of our biggest losses was Shane Howarth. We wanted to reduce his contract but he was being pursued by Newport and his former Auckland coach, Graham Henry, was keen to have him based in Wales where his international career had taken off again. At that stage nobody realised just how brief that new career would be although, even though I got on well with Shane and admired him as a player, it didn't sit too easily on my shoulders as a Welshman to see him pulling on the famous red jersey. Nothing personal but Shane wasn't Welsh by birth. It's as simple as that. It pisses me off that players can chop and change their allegiance to countries.

He was followed to Newport by Simon Raiwalui, so we had lost our fly-half and a key second row at a stroke. We also lost David Rees, who had struggled all year through injury. It was tough luck for Reesy because it meant he lost his England place but, in practical terms so far as the club was concerned, he was costing us a lot of money and we weren't, through no fault of his own, getting a return on that investment. His rugby future was very much in the balance and, whilst we didn't want to lose him, we weren't prepared to keep him on the same money. Correction, we couldn't afford to keep him on the same money.

I think that in many ways he would like to have stayed at Sale. He had practically grown up there, having come through the development side run by Richard Trickey, and was very popular with the fans. For good reason too, because he had the attitude on the field that any manager or coach wants from his players. He was a real battler who would never give you less than 100 per cent but I think I upset him with a comment I made at a press conference. He was so rarely fit enough to play that a question was asked about him, in relation to the club's obvious financial shortcomings, and I said that he was costing us about £10,000 an appearance. It was said with tongue in cheek, even though it was perfectly true from a purely accounting perspective, but I have a feeling that comment didn't help negotiations between us.

There were other departures too and, even though he had captained Ireland, we decided to release Dion O'Cuinneagain. A nice guy, who could look good going forward, but he was a luxury in a struggling Premiership side in winter conditions. Dion arrived at Heywood Road with a big reputation but that was built more around the fact that he had captained South Africa at sevens rather than putting pressure on the backs rows in South Africa's 15-a-side squad. Doing the sort of cleaning up work under pressure on a wet afternoon that someone like Alex Sanderson would take in his stride was not really Dion's forte and we had reached the stage, with an incredibly limited budget, of needing players who could dog it out for us in the hope that we could survive as a Premiership club long enough to attract a new backer with the sort of money that would be needed to turn Sale into a club capable of keeping its head above water, let alone win anything.

Not that we learned our lesson so far as South African players are concerned. We ended up with a few "pups" and please save me from Christians from that part of the world because they are full of bullshit. We shouldn't be too surprised considering that such a God-fearing race should find nothing wrong in oppression of the majority in their country simply because of their colour. And the prize pillock of all time was Jannie de Beer, much loved by the English for teaching them how to drop goals in the quarter-finals of the last World Cup.

With Shane gone, we needed a goal kicking fly-half and knew that De Beer was looking for a club following the demise of London Scottish. Ironically, he had kicked Sale to defeat at Heywood Road during the season just finished, which had given the Exiles a double that we certainly hadn't wanted to concede.

I travelled down to London to meet him and have a chat and he came across as a really nice bloke. There was one worrying aspect, however. First impressions count and I'm always wary of rugby people who don't drink. At that stage I knew nothing about his religious beliefs. I only wish I had.

He said he was keen to stay in the UK to play in the Premiership and just wanted assurances that he would be coming to a nice area. I assured him that Manchester was a veritable Garden of Eden, the deal was done and we paid him a signing-on fee. When Sale played Bristol in the following season we had a few problems coping with Henri Honiball. Yet they were nothing to the problems Henry caused us when he pulled out of South Africa's World Cup squad. Having been in the international wilderness, De Beer was suddenly needed as cover so we knew we wouldn't be able to call upon his services until after the tournament. That wasn't the ideal scenario from our point of view because our best chance of Premiership survival was to pick up as many points as possible during the World Cup, when England's top clubs would be without most of their key players. Apart from that minor irritation, however, we were confident we had signed a player who would do a good job for us in the crucial areas of goal kicking and midfield playmaker.

Whilst the South Africans were in Scotland, where they were playing their pool games, De Beer was suddenly projected into their first choice starting line-up and we started to hear rumours that he was planning to return to his homeland after the World Cup to play for Blue Bulls in Pretoria. We didn't worry unduly because he had signed a contract to play for us and had already had his signing-on fee. Not only that, when I had rung South Africa to clinch the deal following our meeting in London, his agent had told me that Jannie had just come out of a prayer meeting and was definitely joining Sale because God thought it was a good idea and the move would be the best thing for his family.

God, it seemed, had had a change of heart, however. You can imagine my anger when his agent rang during the World Cup to say that his player was going back to South Africa after all and would not be joining Sale. I went hotfoot up to Edinburgh to meet De Beer and his agent in their hotel when it was immediately obvious to me that he couldn't give a shit. I felt like knocking his head off his shoulders.

I said, "We have already informed the media that you have signed to play for us this season and you said God thought it was a good idea. So how come God has suddenly changed his mind."

I might as well have talked to a plank because there was no way he was going to change his mind. Nor was there any visible evidence that he felt any guilt about the un-Christian stunt he had pulled.

By that time we were several weeks into the season and, fortunately, we had picked up one or too crucial wins against clubs that had lost players to the World Cup squads. We had also, despite the De Beer debacle, signed several of his fellow country-men – admittedly prior to discovering that Christians can sometimes be Christians only when it suits them. The rest of the time they can lie and cheat with the best of them, as former Springbok cricket captain Hansie Cronje demonstrated so graphically recently.

And it came as no surprise to me when Cobus Visagie pulled out of his contract to play for Leeds Tykes and Joost van der Westhuizen pulled a similar stunt at Newport. As a Cardiff boy it isn't in my nature to feel sympathy for those at Rodney Parade but, on this issue, I find it hard not to. Stephen Jones, who writes for the *Sunday Times*, probably hit the nail on the head when he suggested that signing up with European clubs could simply be a ploy to screw a better deal out of the authorities back home in South Africa.

Both Kevin Ellis and Richard Smith had gone back to play in Wales and the latter even went on to win a cap for his country, so we needed another scrum-half and picked up Craig Turvey, who had been playing for South West Districts. He was a good lad and mixed in well with the rest of the squad, as did Guy Manson-Bishop, who we signed from London Scottish.

The problem with the position that Sale were in at that time – with no money and an uncertain future – was that you were hunting for players at the wrong time. In an ideal world you do your deals towards the end of the previous season. If you don't you are left looking at players who are out of contract and haven't been offered a new one, or at players from overseas who are invariably unknown to you and all you have to go on very often is video footage and the recommendation of the player's agent. No agent is going to paint a bad picture of his client and only an idiot would submit a video showing clippings of missed tackles and dropped passes. Instead you provide images of your, often occasional, brilliance.

With Dion O'Cuinneagain on his way to Ireland and Pat Sanderson having gone to Harlequins, we needed more back row cover and came up with another South African, Janneman Brand. We paid Janneman a reasonable amount of money and he also came with a big reputation. Despite his rather lean frame, we were quite excited when he made his debut as a replacement against London Wasps in our Premiership opener on a sunny afternoon at Heywood Road. He had only been on the field a couple of minutes when he took the ball and raced away from the cover from halfway to score what turned out to be the game's vital try.

Janneman, like Dion, looked great going forward on a dry track but you don't get that too often in December in the UK and he didn't do the job around the fringes that we needed him to do. In simple truth I wasn't at all happy with his defence. He was also a bit like a fish out of water off the field because he had difficulty adjusting to the culture of the game over here. In other words, he found the birds, booze and bawdy language a bit of a problem. Some people may say that rugby behaviour can be a bit childish but that's the way it's always been over here. It has always been my experience that rugby players, of whatever calibre or code, like to unwind with a few beers, the odd schoolboy prank, the songs and, of course, appreciation of the female form.

Janneman was another Christian who took his religion seriously and it was obvious he wasn't comfortable sitting with the rest of the boys when the talk was all about shagging or watching films like the Exorcist on away trips. Having said that, Jason Robinson isn't too keen on that sort of thing either these days but, as Jason knows from personal experience, birds and booze play a major role in the culture of both rugby codes and, on his own admission, he was no angel until "Inga" Tuigamala taught him that there is another way to conduct one's life. Perhaps because Jason falls into the category of "been there, done that", he can now cope with being in an environment that isn't always to his taste, morally, these days. I don't have a problem with people who take their religion seriously and don't want to drink a lot of beer, swear like a trooper and chase women. After all I am a Catholic who still went to Mass when I was playing top class rugby, although I doubt I would ever be put up as an example of a good Catholic boy.

I believe Janneman would have been better staying within a

culture he felt comfortable with and I suspect he had a fairly miserable time at Heywood Road. He certainly wasn't performing so far as I was concerned and eventually I agreed to release him, with the result that he went back to South Africa and played successfully in the Super 12s. Things came to a head after we had travelled to Bristol for an evening game. We hadn't named either the team or the replacements before we left Heywood Road by coach. It was clear that one or two travelling players weren't going to be involved in the game but we had left our options open. I announced the 22 in the dressing room when we arrived at Bristol's ground and Janneman was not included.

I noticed Janneman chatting to his countryman, Dawie Theron, who later followed me outside and asked to have a word with Jim Mallinder and myself. He said he couldn't believe that we had dragged Janneman all the way to Bristol when we weren't going to play him. He could, he said, have stayed at home with his wife.

"I don't know where you are coming from Dawie," I said. "We pay his wages, this is his job and when we say he travels with the squad then that's what he does. We're not leaving him at home just because his wife happens to be a little homesick."

"Well, I think that's disgraceful," said Dawie.

"Dawie, he's a professional and he goes where we say. As for you, get this out of your mind and get out there and play," was my response.

When Janneman left he called in to say goodbye and said, "I have seen you with your children Adie. You love them, and this club, very much. You think some people are trying to destroy the club and don't want it to be successful but you just need to look deeper into their eyes to see where their heart lies."

I didn't know what the fuck he was on about.

So, what with one thing and another, the 1999/2000 season was interesting to say the least and it is a miracle I have any hair left. The three of us, Jim Mallinder, Steve Diamond and myself, really had our backs to the wall but we sat down with the fixture list and targeted certain games. As I said earlier, we felt the World Cup would be our salvation and so it turned out. We all agreed we needed to beat Bedford home and away regardless of anything else, as we saw that side as the weakest link and the one most likely to end up in the end of season play-off. We had to pick up ten points by the end of the World Cup or finish up shit creek without a paddle. We were still without a fly-half so centre Jos Baxendell had to be drafted in at 10 and it wasn't until the end of the World Cup that we resolved that particular problem.

Once we knew De Beer was definitely out of the frame we started to trawl the world for a replacement. I ended up speaking to Bart Campbell, an agent I knew quite well, and he recommended a young Fijian called Niki Little. Niki was actually playing for Fiji in the World Cup so we had him watched and felt he could do a job for us, if he was willing to join us from North Harbour in New Zealand. Niki had a very solid defence, was a good goal kicker and, thank God, wasn't going to rely on the Almighty to make his decision for him.

Not that it was all plain sailing, however. Jim and I travelled down to London to meet Bart and Niki at a pre-determined restaurant. The only problem was that Niki wasn't there and Bart hadn't a clue where he was. Until he got a telephone call to say that Niki wouldn't be joining us for dinner after all because he had got on a train going the wrong way. Instead of heading towards London, he was speeding away from the capital with no means of getting off the train, other than by pulling the communicating cord.

Not an auspicious start, but it was to get worse. We carried on eating and discussing the terms of the contract when Bart suddenly announced that Niki had signed to play for a French club. However, he said he didn't see any problem in getting him out of it. Jim looked at me across the table with his eyebrows raised and I said, "Bart, what the fuck's going on? You said he was free to join us and we need him now, not at the end of a lengthy contractual row with a French club. Is there anything else we should know?"

When Bart told us that there was just one other little problem, in the shape of a fee that would have to be paid to North Harbour, I moved up into the stratosphere. I couldn't believe what I was hearing so Jim and I travelled back to Sale considerably deflated. Bart felt the New Zealand outfit would release him without difficulty because they would see a spell in England as being good for his game, and so it turned out, with payment of a small fee. We went ahead and announced Niki's signing, with the result that a French club that we had never heard of then tried to sue Sale for about £70,000. Fortunately, the whole thing was resolved but that wasn't the end of the Niki saga.

We had still not met the player but had his travel arrangements confirmed to us and Jim and I turned up at Manchester Airport early one November morning to welcome our new signing. The flight arrived and the passengers started to pour out through customs and we waited, and waited, and waited. We had the media standing by ready to interview him and take his photograph but there was no Niki.

I got that sinking feeling in my stomach when I heard a voice on the tannoy requesting me to attend the information desk. I was handed a telephone and someone in immigration was telling me that a Mr Little had arrived saying that he was going to play rugby for Sale but didn't have a work permit and wouldn't be allowed in.

Here we go again, I thought. After all the fuss over Mitch and Simon Mannix, our latest acquisition was about to be embroiled in the same bureaucratic mess. Thankfully, the matter was resolved and a somewhat weary Niki eventually shuffled out all by himself with bags in each hand and a guitar flung over his shoulder.

By the end of the first month we were top of the Premiership, having beaten London Wasps and Bath at home and Harlequins in an eminently forgettable game at The Stoop. The only defeat was at Welford Road where we played poorly against a seriously weakened Leicester. Perhaps we were a bit overconfident whereas the Leicester understudies were in no mood to relinquish the club record of being virtually unbeatable at home. What really annoyed me was the fact that we still couldn't get a result when Leicester were reduced to 14 players after their second row, Neil Fletcher, had been sent off following a fracas in what was an ill-tempered game. Later in the season, when we were struggling for numbers, we took Neil on loan. At least we knew he was prepared to get stuck in if necessary!

After all the predictions of doom and gloom, one or two people were getting excited about our league position but Jim, Steve and myself were under no illusions. According to the timetable we had set ourselves, the Leicester defeat meant that we had to win two of our remaining games during the World Cup. We lost the lot. By our reckoning we felt we were in with a chance at home against Northampton and Saracens but lost the first by four points and then, on a Friday evening, we were absolutely destroyed 58-12 by Sarries. We were so bad on that occasion that our match day sponsor, who traditionally picks a man of the match from the Sale side, felt that none were worthy of the honour and a somewhat surprised Tony Diprose was led into the hospitality suite to be presented with a crate of beer.

The following Friday we were at Kingsholm on the eve of the World Cup Final between Australia and France in Cardiff, and another defeat sent us further down the Premiership table. A week later we were beaten 40-15 by Bristol at Heywood Road. It would be December before we enjoyed the sweet taste of victory again. Perpignan beat us 31-16 in the European Shield on our ground – no longer fearsome territory for opponents – and we made a complete mess of our performance at Pau at the end of November to ensure that there would be no pickings from that competition either. Pau went on to win the competition.

There was an element of farce about that trip, which set the pattern for that season. We flew to Biarritz from Stansted Airport, which meant a four-hour drive and seemed ridiculous when Heywood Road is a mere ten minutes drive from Manchester Airport. But then, considering the financial plight the club was in, we were forced into looking for the cheapest deals all the time. Everything was fine at the check-in desk until Guy Manson-Bishop, Janneman Brand, Dawie Theron and Craig Turvey handed in their South African passports. The airline was disinclined to accept them, saying it would have the expense of flying them back if they were refused admission by French immigration authorities. It seemed that South Africans were not top of the popularity list with some European nations and their nationals needed a special visa.

Right up until the last minute it looked as though they wouldn't be allowed to travel but, at our insistence, calls were made to French immigration authorities in Biarritz and, perhaps because south-west France is something of a rugby hot bed, they assured the airline that our South Africans would be let in. We were left pondering how we would have coped without that quartet; we were to find out in due course.

In January we had to travel to Perpignan, so got in touch with the European competition authorities to find out what the situation was regarding our South Africans, because we didn't want to have to go through the same nonsense a second time. We received a letter back saying that no special permits were needed for players who had been named in the club squads when they had been declared earlier in the season, because all the governments in the EEC had agreed to the competition going ahead. The inference was that if the four wanted to take a holiday in another EEC country they would require a special visa but not for a short trip purely to play in a rugby match.

David Swift, who was the club's financial director at the time, made the travel arrangements within the usual financial constraints and that meant flying from Liverpool to Barcelona on Easyjet and then travelling by coach over the Spanish border to Perpignan. When we arrived at the check-in desk everything went smoothly until our four South Africans produced their passports. No, they weren't travelling, we were told. Once again it was a case of telephone calls to all and sundry and, in the space of an hour, Swifty, who then earned the nickname "ABTA", aged about 20 years. It was the now old, old story of the airline not wishing to be left with the responsibility of bringing back passengers turned away by immigration officials at the destination airport. Mind you, knowing Spanish airports, the chance of anybody actually asking to see their passports would have been pretty remote. We were prepared to take our chances, armed with the letter from European Cup Ltd, but the airline have the final word and that was "NO".

As we piled the disconsolate and, by that time, totally bemused quartet into a taxi to take them back to Sale, we boarded the aircraft four players short and with a lot of serious juggling to do in order to field a team, let alone pack a replacements' bench. It had already been determined that Jim Mallinder wouldn't play but that option seemed to have gone out of the window. As I sat on the aircraft a good deal of my anger was directed at Dave Baldwin.

We had already had a big bust-up that week because he knew we were struggling for second rows but wasn't prepared to give it a go, claiming injury. The medics felt he would be all right but old "Stinker" Baldwin didn't. I had pleaded with him to travel with us and said it would help if he could just give us half a game but he wasn't having it. If the medics had said he hadn't been fit enough to risk it then I wouldn't have asked but they didn't have a problem with him playing; it was just the player being selfish, in my opinion. He knew our situation but wasn't even prepared to give it a go. Yet he's the only player at Sale to have been awarded a testimonial year and even that seemed to have stretched into more than twelve months. It was set up in Howard Thomas's time but Peter Deakin agreed he could have a testimonial match at the start of the 2001/2 season.

Crazy when you consider that Jim Mallinder and Steve Diamond, and the Smith twins, Andy and Paul, who had done far more for the club than Stinker, have never been offered a testimonial to my knowledge. He certainly didn't like his nick-name, which I think came about because he once complained that his son had been called Stinker at school. Rugby players are notorious at latching on to the slightest thing and the obvious happened but Dave got so worked up about it that he walked into the dressing room one day and told everyone they had to stop calling him Stinker. His name was David. He should have been thankful that teammates didn't latch on to the fact that he wasn't averse to colouring his hair.

We knew that Perpignan would be no picnic, even with a full strength side, but it was going to be a nightmare with our ranks so badly reduced. In the end we did well to only lose 46-23 but the team spirit was tremendous. It had been all season and probably had a lot to do with having our backs to the wall. Reserve scrum-half Paul Knight had to play in the centre and prop Phil Winstanley was drafted into the second row. Phil wasn't fully fit but, unlike Stinker, he was prepared to grit his teeth and get on with it. When he had to go off in the end we had to send on Jim Mallinder. The idea was that he would go into the back row with Pete Anglesea at lock but crafty Pete told him he would be all right in the second row because the Perpignan pack had stopped pushing at the scrums. So Jim popped his head into the first scrum and ended up going back about 30 metres!

Although we needed all available bodies for our survival battle, we were very good to Phil Greening by resting him when we could and we excused him from our European Shield trips to France. He had got back into the England side and we wanted to do everything possible to help him stay in the team. So you can imagine the bombshell on the day we entertained his old club Gloucester at Heywood Road when the *Daily Express* carried a full-page article in which the player slagged off the club. We had picked him up when Gloucester hadn't wanted him, provided him with a platform, however rickety, to re-establish himself in the England camp and then he was prepared to kick us in the teeth when we were pretty much on our knees anyway.

I just couldn't believe what I was reading. He said the club had been a shambles since the departure of John Mitchell, conveniently forgetting that he had done nothing to fight Mitch's corner when the players held their vote of no confidence in him. Phil also made it perfectly plain that he didn't want to be at Heywood Road and was extolling the virtues of Gloucester on the day we were due to play against them.

The reaction was total shock in our camp. It is fortunate that not many players had read the *Express* that morning and didn't know anything about what he had said. I held a hurried meeting with Jim, Steve and Graham Walker. We were faced with a dilemma: Did we play him anyway, in the expectation that he would hardly want to play badly and look an idiot against his former teammates and in front of our own fans? Or did we leave him out of the side, even though it put us under even greater pressure from a personnel point of view?

We decided to play him in the game on the basis that he was hardly likely to play like a complete idiot against his former teammates. I told him I wanted to see him after the game but he cleared off more or less straight away. After that he went to ground, I suppose partly because the media quite rightly rounded on him, and attempts to contact him fell on deaf ears, even though we left messages ordering him to report for training. In the end we unloaded him to Wasps, where Mitch had been involved in helping Nigel Melville with the coaching, and it was good riddance so far was we were concerned.

Earlier, Sale had gone from October 10 until December 11 without a win and then had won four of the next five. We beat Caerphilly comfortably enough home and away, although I have never seen anyone look colder than Niki Little as the snow swept down off the Welsh hills. We only just escaped in time after the game before snow made it impossible to drive in the area. So far as the competition went the victories over Caerphilly meant very little but they were useful in giving the boys a bit of confidence for the challenges ahead. The main challenge was the Boxing Day game against fellow strugglers Bedford at Heywood Road. That really was a must-win game and, despite some resistance in patches, we won 22-3.

The following Wednesday we were due to play Newcastle Falcons at Kingston Park but the weather had closed in and I was convinced the game would be called off when we arrived at the ground. Parts of the pitch were frozen solid and, as this was an evening game, conditions were only going to get worse rather than better. We couldn't even believe they had let us get to the ground but Rob Andrew seemed determined to play the game no matter what and, despite the fact that we thought it would be dangerous, the referee, Geraint Ashton Jones, agreed with Rob that the game should go ahead. He was a naval gentleman and I suppose he was hardly likely to go along with me considering that I had told him after one game that he should stick to sailing boats. I think people are influenced by Rob because of who he is and what he has achieved. It may be an over-simplification but I saw it as a case of Rob, the squeaky-clean former England and British Lions fly-half, saying a pitch was playable so what did it matter what Hadley, a working class lad from Wales, thought about it?

It nearly rebounded on Rob because Newcastle only managed to beat us 12-6 but it was costly for us because Steve Hanley went down on a hard patch and injured himself. Niki Little also missed several kicks at goal and we had a try disallowed.

The new millennium dawned with a visit to see my old pal Phil Davies at Leeds Tykes. That was a Tetley's Bitter Cup clash at Headingley we desperately needed to win if for no other reason than to give ourselves another focus. We managed, 13-3, but it was a poor game and we went out at the next stage of the competition at Bristol. Although our threadbare squad battled manfully for the remainder of the season, we only managed one more victory before the end of April and that was a home win, 36-20, against Harlequins.

There were two more games to play during the first two weeks of May, at home to Newcastle and away to Bedford. By then, however, things had changed at the club. After months of speculation a new owner had arrived in the shape of rugby-playing millionaire businessman Brian Kennedy.

CHAPTER ELEVEN

Double Glazing Salesmen

I WAS FIRST made aware of Brian Kennedy's existence by Geoff Green, rugby correspondent of the *Manchester Evening News*, with whom I had established a close working relationship. Some players and officials distrust the media but I have always got on well with journalists and that may be due to the fact that I have always been prepared to level with them. Back in Wales I was on good terms with rugby writers like John Kennedy and Rob Cole and, in Manchester, I could always trust Geoff to honour a confidence. I find media relations to be a two-way thing. Do right by them and they will invariably do right by you.

Even before the season had started it was no secret that the club was looking for a new backer and Geoff walked into my office one morning and dropped Brian Kennedy's name onto my desk. He had interviewed Brian for the *Manchester Evening News* about his attempt to take over London Scottish. A rugby-playing Scot, he had appeared in the back row for Wilmslow and was said to be keen to "save" a famous club from extinction. He had also, it transpired, unsuccessfully attempted to buy the Hibernian soccer club in Edinburgh.

Geoff thought he would be worth a shot with a view to buying Sale and I wasted no time in making contact with him. Initially I wrote to him and then spoke to him on the telephone. He said he would think about it but, apparently, started almost immediately investigating how much money we were losing, what revenue was coming into the club and where from, and who was involved in running the club at that time. I spoke to Brian on a number of occasions and he had a number of meetings with Graham Walker, who was a fellow Scot.

Graham was in a funny position because he wasn't popular with the members, those who had run the club before our mystery businessmen stepped in, and there had been something of a furore when news leaked out that talks had taken place with Stockport County about Sale possibly using the soccer club's Edgeley Park ground. The idea was that we would play there on a Friday evening and the reason Graham had got involved in talks was the inadequacy of the Heywood Road ground in the light of moves by the leading clubs, under the umbrella of EFDR (English First Division Rugby), to make an 8,000-seater stadium a pre-requisite for a place in the top division.

At the time there were plans to divide England into four distinct regions – North, South West, London and Midlands – with three professional clubs in each. The 12 places were to be offered on a franchise basis so it was important that Sale, even though at that stage the club seemed more likely to go down the pan than anything else, had a contingency plan in place to qualify from a stadia standpoint. In all other aspects there was no other north-west club even remotely in a position to bid for a franchise. All right, Orrell, Waterloo, Manchester and a number of other clubs could have leased a stadium but only Sale had a full-time squad of professional players and the necessary back-up off the field.

The members' attitude towards Graham veered from seeing him as a man who wanted to take rugby away from Heywood Road to some Godforsaken soccer stadium to a man who was intent on simply running the club down so that the backers could more readily extricate themselves at the end of the season. Graham had also had the temerity to suggest that the members' club, that was in the process of selling some pitches a short distance away from Heywood Road (for millions as things turned out), might like to make a substantial contribution to the money pot in the hope of making the club more successful. Having run up a sizeable overdraft trying to run a professional rugby club in pre-Tourney days, there seemed to be no way they were going to risk any more of their cash, however.

They did agree to fund the development of young players but the anticipated money took a long time to arrive and attitudes between the professional club and the members started to harden considerably. I know that Graham used to get very frustrated and the members made much of the fact that he still lived in Bath and, rather than uproot his family, rented a small flat close to Heywood Road. The members saw this as a lack of commitment and believed it supported their view that he had only been put in place to wind things down. Even we started to get that idea when you went to him for any money and he told us repeatedly that "there isn't any money."

He certainly wasn't telling any porkies because there wasn't any money and we were literally limping from match to match. All that time Brian Kennedy's accountants were in and out but the prospect of him taking over seemed to diminish rather than grow and those of us who knew the financial score were all pretty depressed about our future prospects. I had stopped playing because of injury so my career was at an end in that sense and, if Sale went to the wall, I would be in the dole queue. Jim Mallinder was in a similar position. He was still playing but was in the twilight of his playing career and wasn't sufficiently established as a coach at that time to feel confident of walking into a full time coaching job elsewhere. And, when you are looking for employment in sport, having been at an unsuccessful club, even though through no fault of your own, it doesn't exactly look great on your CV.

Steve Diamond was in a similar position to Jim with regard to his playing career and he had less coaching experience. But he had fingers in many pies, owning a number of houses and having a share in a printing business. He was better placed to put bread on the table than either Jim or I and the only downside for him if the club did go belly up would be the loss of rental income because quite a few players rented property from him. Steve's business interests had also become a bit of a bone of contention because he would often be late for meetings due to other demands upon his time. It wasn't a case of all or nothing as it was for the two remaining members of the trio running the playing side of the club.

Although the three of us were very close and worked well together in adversity, relations with Steve started to change as problems mounted and Sale's future looked bleak. The patience of the backers had run out and they set a deadline at the beginning of May for an end to their involvement. There was even the possibility that they would put the club into receivership, as had happened elsewhere in the game.

That galvanised the members' club and, as always happened in any sort of situation at Sale, they turned to Steve Smith and Fran Cotton. The outcome was that the members called a meeting at which they had various choices put to them. One was be to re-take control of the club when the backers pulled out and I know that appealed to some of the suits, who didn't like being in a position where they no longer had any say in the running of the professional team. They held a meeting at the Cresta Court hotel in Altrincham and I had no doubt that Steve Smith would carry the day. When Howard Thomas was in charge there had been a similar meeting at Sale Town Hall to debate a major issue and when Smithy stood up to speak you could see the members uniting behind him.

That happened again and, even though nobody said where the money was coming from, the membership followed Smithy's lead and voted to re-take the club. My own feeling is that they would then have got rid of all the professional staff and reverted to being an amateur club. Unless, of course, they were relying on assurances from Fran Cotton about future funding from Twickenham.

Whilst Graham, Jim, myself and most of the office staff were all doom and gloom, Diamond was very buoyant and telling players that they would be all right and assuring Jim and myself that we would be okay if the members took charge again. He walked in one day and said he had been talking to Smithy and it had been agreed that the three of us would stay under the new regime but that Graham would be shown the door. Graham knew that and was fairly philosophical about it all, especially as he knew the members wouldn't want to spend their millions on players. Instead it would be the end of top class rugby at Heywood Road, something that would have upset the fans but delighted those members who wanted to go back to the days of being in control of an amateur club.

It would have helped if we had known Brian Kennedy's intentions but he was playing his cards close to his chest. He did turn up at the Gloucester match in February, however, along with his business partner Ian Blackhurst. The pair had met at Holmes Chapel rugby club in Cheshire and then switched to Wilmslow where Kennedy sponsored the club through one of his companies, Weatherseal Windows. He also established the offices of his Latium Group in that town and set up a mobile communications company called Genesis with Ian, based close to the Lancashire cricket ground at Old Trafford. It was that company that would eventually bale out Sale.

He chose well attending the Gloucester game because that was the day that Phil Greening had his public spat. After the game Brian and Ian walked into the dressing rooms and then followed me into the press conference. They were supposed to be incognito but several journalists guessed who they were and that started the speculation of a takeover once more. All the questioning by the media at the conference, however, concerned Greening's outrageous outburst. I gave them both barrels and the next thing I knew I was being sued for defamation by John Mitchell.

Apparently, he took strong exception to something I said in response to a question about Greening's comment that the club had become a shambles after Mitch's departure. At the conference I simply made the point that we were currently tenth in the Premiership on a playing budget of £800,000 whereas the previous season, when Mitch had been there, the budget had been more like £2.5 million and we had also finished in tenth place. Mitch's retort was that he hadn't been in charge of the budget the previous year but then I never said that he had. I simply used the financial comparison to provide a logical reason why Greening may have thought things more shambolic than they had been. But I also pointed out that, shambolic or not, our position in the Premiership was no different from what it had been the previous season.

After Kennedy's visit, things started to go a little cold and I for one felt my days were numbered. Despite what Steve Diamond had said I didn't think for one minute that Smithy would want me around if the members were back in charge. I was also under no illusions as to who would be pulling the strings, whoever the members installed in key positions in the administration block.

Having cut his teeth on selling kitchens and double glazing, I had no doubt that Kennedy would be a master at closing deals and displaying brinkmanship if he so wished. Just when the members were starting to plot their campaign for running the club again, Graham and myself were called to the Latium headquarters in the first week in May, days before our home game against Newcastle, and Brian signed up to buy the club. We set up a press conference and there was a good media response because Brian was seriously wealthy and they could perhaps see the little club in the Manchester suburbs turning the corner.

He was fine in the build up to the Newcastle game, asked questions about what we were hoping to achieve and then offered the players a £500 bonus to win. As often happens when there is a new face in charge there is a sudden uplifting of spirits and he went to give the boys a little pep talk. Fine at the time but Brian's dressing room appearances and little pep talks started to become counter productive as the following season wore on.

Still, this was a new beginning, Brian waved to the crowds and the players turned it on to win.

A week later we finished our season at Bedford and beat them even though they had been abroad to prepare for the play-offs against National One champions Rotherham. I believe they made a mistake putting out their strongest side against us because victory woudn't have improved their league situation. I suspect they were hoping for a confidence boosting victory on their own patch to get themselves into the right frame of mind to play Rotherham but it all went horribly wrong because they lost two key players, Andy Gomarsall and centre Dan Harris, through injury. Gomarsall's absence was a crucial factor to my mind. With Andy's leadership they would probably have reduced Rotherham's winning margin at Clifton Lane and then outscored the Yorkshire outfit sufficiently well at Goldington Road to win on aggregate and retain a Premiership place.

That wasn't our worry, of course, and we started to look forward to a season backed by financial security. Little did I know how difficult a season it would be and just how disappointingly it would end for me.

The first problem concerned coaching. At his first press conference, Brian announced that his first task would be to appoint a new head coach. That left Jim Mallinder in an awkward position and I told Brian that I didn't see any reason to go spending money on coaches when Jim and Steve Diamond had done a good job under very trying circumstances. I suggested we should save the money and just see how things went. Brian wouldn't have it.

I said, "I disagree."

I don't think Brian is used to losing arguments and, as he was the paymaster, he had his way and we started the process of searching for a new coach following a board meeting at which he and his partner said they felt a "top" coach was required. I agreed to identify possible candidates and came up with a list that included, in no particular order, Clive Griffiths, Timothy Lane, Andy Leslie, Phil Davies, Brendan Venter, Alan Zondagh, Christian Stewart, Graham Taylor, Ian McIntosh, Andre Markgraaff, Rudi Streuli, Lloyd Walker, Adrian Thompson, Philippe Berbizier, Andy Keast and Glenn Ross.

We interviewed several candidates including Rudi Streuli, who had done a difficult job at Bedford, and Phil Davies, who was coaching Leeds Tykes. Next up was Andy Keast, who had been released by London Irish. We met Andy at the headquarters of Weatherseal and, as we were leaving, Brian said to me, "Yes. He's got the job. He's brilliant."

I said, "You can't appoint him yet, we've arranged for Glenn Ross to come over from New Zealand to be interviewed for the job."

"Ring him up and tell him not to bother coming over," was the response.

I then had the embarrassing task of ringing Glenn in New Zealand to say that we had changed our minds and didn't want to interview him after all. The trouble was that when I got through to his home his wife said he had already left. Of course, I didn't reveal the purpose of my call!

There was no alternative, we had to go through with the interview but I suspected that Brian was sold on Andy Keast. It was at the back of my mind that, if he had taken any advice from Steve Smith, it was worth remembering that Andy had been part of the coaching staff when Fran Cotton took the British Lions to South Africa in 1997. We met Glenn at his Genesis headquarters in Old Trafford and I have to say he interviewed very well. When it was over, Brian said, "He's brilliant. I'll ring Andy to tell him he hasn't got the job."

The feeling then was that we wouldn't need a backs coach because that's where Glenn had played but he insisted that he preferred to work with the forwards. So Jim was retained as backs coach, with Glenn looking after the forwards. Glenn said he didn't need anyone else working with the forwards so that left Steve Diamond, of all people, in the firing line.

Needless to say, Steve wasn't a happy bunny and wanted a playing contract. We had young Joe Clark on the books and we had signed Bernard Jackman, who had played for Glenn at Connacht, where he had been coaching for the previous two seasons. I went to a board meeting in June, said we needed another hooker and suggested Steve. Quinten Smith, a solicitor on the board, said that he felt Steve had made unprofessional comments at the members' club dinner. I didn't see how that would be a problem because Steve had launched himself on to the after dinner speaking circuit and it is normal practice to take the mickey out of teammates on these occasions. Kennedy joined in to say that he was taking the decision about Steve out of my hands and said Steve was not to be offered a new contract.

That put me in a very difficult position because Steve and I were mates and I am convinced he thought it had been my decision. I told him I was sorry about the situation but was powerless to change anything. He was so annoyed he used to leave messages on my telephone telling me what a twat I was. When Dimes is unhappy you get to know about it.

So, we had a new head coach and a new chief executive because Graham Walker departed and Peter Deakin was suddenly brought in from Warrington Wolves. One of his first public pronouncements was to promote the idea of Sale moving to Warrington to play in a new stadium he had been planning for the rugby league side. Sale fans greeted that suggestion as enthusiastically as they had the idea of moving to Stockport County's ground and I'm not sure Kennedy was entirely in favour of such a move anyway. He had attended games at Warrington and there had been speculation that he might take over that club too and run the two teams in tandem but trying to move Sale's admittedly limited fan base to Warrington would have carried an element of risk. The fans weren't too impressed either when Brian suddenly announced that he was considering taking the side to play at Maine Road, Manchester City's ground.

"Deaks" had acquired a reputation that clearly impressed Kennedy. He had drummed up crowd support at Bradford Bulls and had indulged in a similar exercise for Saracens, so was being regarded as some sort of miracle worker. If that was going to be his role at Heywood Road then fine but it was soon apparent to me that he wanted to run the whole shooting match – which included the rugby side of things, even though he was hardly qualified. Apart from a handful of games for Oldham, his only experience as a player was amateur rugby league. He certainly had no hands-on knowledge of top class rugby union but it didn't take me too long to work out that he wanted to deal with playing contracts. So far as I was concerned he was a frustrated director of rugby.

His arrival was the beginning of the end for me because I didn't have a new contract and I think he saw a way of saving money. Not that Kennedy seemed to go along with that line of thinking because he told me he didn't want "Deaks" having anything to do with the rugby section. Having spoken to a couple of Warrington players, my feeling was that he had probably interfered on the playing side and his efforts had been counter productive. Kennedy told me that I was responsible for points and Deakin for bums on seats. Well, I reckon I pulled in more points than he did punters because gates were poor all season. But I couldn't tell him not to get involved in rugby matters because he was effectively my boss, so I told Kennedy that he would have to speak to him if that was how he wanted to run things.

I don't know if he did speak to him but, if he did, it didn't seem to make any difference. In any case Sale was quickly turning towards rugby league in a number of areas. Dave Swanton was recruited from Warrington Wolves to act as media manager and Allan Rowley, whose son Paul played for Great Britain, joined from St Helens as special projects manager. We signed Apollo Perelini from St Helens and, of course, the major signing was Jason Robinson from Wigan Warriors. Jason's signing prompted massive publicity but, because the RFU deal, under which the governing body would pay half Jason's salary, never materialized, a big hole was left in the playing budget.

Apollo, at the end of a very hard rugby league season, had difficulty adjusting to a game that had changed considerably since he last played it, and we only saw him at his best in flashes. That wasn't his fault and I am sure Sale will see a different animal after a good rest. Jason, of course, did what we all knew Jason could do. He is a master line-breaker and a great crowd pleaser.

The signing from rugby league that really got up my nose was Marty Hulme, the Aussie who was fitness and conditioning coach at Wigan Warriors. We didn't need a new coach in that area because we had Andy Clarke, who had vast experience, having worked for England, Ireland and Liverpool football club. He had been with us for a number of years and was helped by Steve Hampson, the former Wigan and Great Britain full-back.

You can imagine my surprise when I got a telephone call from Kennedy's partner, Ian Blackhurst, saying that Jason Robinson had told him that Marty Hulme was the best fitness coach he had ever worked with and that we needed to get him on board. When I sat down later with Ian and he told me of the financial package they were planning to pay the Aussie I told him the figure was ridiculous. They could have Clarkey and Hampo for a third of that and the money would make Marty one of the highest paid people at the club, earning far more than myself, the coaches and all but two or three of the players.

Ian said we still had to have him. I said I had already agreed with Clarkey for the new season. At that Ian said it was my decision and I replied that I preferred to go with Andy. Then, just a week before the start of pre-season training, Ian telephoned to say they had agreed a contract with Marty. I said they couldn't do that because I had already agreed one with Andy. The upshot of it all was that both turned up for the first fitness session at Total Fitness on the outskirts of Wilmslow. At the time Andy was working with the players and they all wondered who this other guy was. That was professionalism out of the window so far as I was concerned and I immediately rang Ian to tell him that we had a problem.

I was told to leave Marty at the gym and he arranged to see Clarkey right away. Apparently he told him that if I wanted him to do the job then he did the job, but it didn't work out like that. The last I heard, Andy was taking the club to court. Marty couldn't do it all on is own anyway because he still had his job to do at Wigan until after the Super League play-off match against St Helens at Old Trafford, a game in which Apollo and Jason bowed out of rugby league on opposing sides. So they still needed to employ Hampo, who worked well with the lads, and, later in the season, it was agreed that Marty could take time out to work with the Scottish international squad. I thought the club would have learned from the mistake of releasing Mitch to England.

They were always telling me that I was the director of rugby and that I would make all the decisions relating to rugby matters, but, when push came to shove, it was they who called the tune.

Marty, of course, was out for himself and he and our new coach, Glenn Ross, were hardly bosom buddies. He didn't get on with our physio, Ryan McDermott, either – in fairness we did have a few problems with him – and it wasn't long before there were changes in that department too.

Meanwhile Glenn Ross had arrived and we started to plan the season ahead. As, by that time, it was July, it was hardly the best time to start looking for players. We had released quite a few players and needed to rebuild but decided to do it around Alex Sanderson, who we appointed as captain to make him the youngest skipper in the Premiership at a mere 20 years of age. Alex is mature beyond his years, handles responsibility well and is a born leader. Surprisingly, he had the captaincy taken from him at the start of the 2001/2 season.

We strengthened our back line by signing three new centres in Mel Deane, Dan Harris and Martin Shaw, who had impressed me when I managed a North All Stars team in a World Cup warm-up match against England. Jim Mallinder felt he was good for another season at full-back and we hoped that Steve Hanley would rediscover both form and confidence on the wing. The youngster had struggled following his sensational first season and we were hoping for big things from him.

Scrum-half was a problem area but that was solved when Brian Kennedy snatched Scottish international Bryan Redpath from under the nose of Harlequins. Bryan had been set to join Quins but his fellow Scot, who was good at selling double glazing, sold him his dream of Sale's future. By that time the club had become known as Sharks but, thus far, we had tended to be of the basking, rather than great white, variety.

Former Welsh international Rob Appleyard had performed well for us on loan from Swansea so we took him on board to bolster our back row and, rather than bring back Dawie Theron from South Africa, we signed Jon Thiel, the Canadian prop, who had been playing with Bryan Redpath at Narbonne, and Adam Black, who had played for Bedford and London Wasps. We needed another hooker and that's when I suggested Steve Diamond. But the answer was still no so we took a gamble on Norm Rusk, a New Zealander who had been with Waikato. He had a good CV but, because we had to sign him without being able to have a look at him in action – he arrived on the day we played Bridgend in a pre-season game – we had no idea just how good he was. Well, he wasn't a bad rugby player but he couldn't hit a barn door, which was no recommendation for a hooker. I hold up my hands and say that wasn't one of my better decisions.

As had happened during World Cup year, we got the season off to a good start, opening with a home victory against Bath. The downside was that Brian Kennedy started thinking that we were going to win the league. The following week we travelled to Kingsholm and sneaked a win but our weakness at the lineout was demonstrated that afternoon by Gloucester. It was almost as though our hookers were put off by the presence in the Gloucester line of All Black Ian Jones and even before the lads had had a chance to get off the pitch at the end Brian was dragging me back on to it.

"That was a load of shit," he said. "Get Glenn out of the dressing room and out here now."

Whatever he thought about our performance, that was not the moment to discuss it. At the end of the day we had picked up another victory and they don't come cheaply at Kingsholm. But that was to become the pattern, if you could call it that. It wasn't long before Kennedy, Peter Deakin and Marty Hulme were interfering and team spirit was eroded as the season progressed because there were so many different messages coming through. A case of too many cooks spoiling the broth.

I remember an evening match at Bristol, which we won. Kennedy telephoned me on the team bus as we were driving home to say that Marty Hulme had told him the players didn't normally get fed after training. I said they didn't because it cost about £40,000 a season to provide that service.

"Get them fed," was the response. When I next saw Deakin I told him that Brian wanted the players fed after training. When I told him how much it would cost he told me to forget it.

Brian had these little fads but he was right about the lineout. It was a mess and our early season success rate started to drop. So too did our placing in the Premiership and it was going to be touch and go whether or not we reached the top eight to clinch a place in the end of season play-offs that had been masterminded for the league by Deakin. Even when Jason was available it was going to take rather more than a little of his magic to help us to beat the better sides and another heavy defeat by Saracens at Heywood Road did nothing for our confidence. On that occasion it was Scott Murray causing us all manner of problems at the lineout.

The most encouraging aspect at Heywood Road was the success of the development side that I set up. I appointed James Wade, an RFU development officer in the region, to manage the Under-21 side that became known as the Jets. The pair of us covered the north-west in search of talent and built a squad that for much of the season challenged for the title. We were to give three players their chance in the senior side rather sooner than we might have in an ideal world. We had such a problem with the lineout that we gave young England Under-21 hooker Andy Titterrell his chance along with Anthony Elliott on the wing. The player who did make a difference, however, was Charlie Hodgson at fly-half. Long before the end of the season the 20-year-old had established himself as first choice goal kicker as well as fly-half. We tended to bring on Niki Little in the second half so as not to overexpose Charlie but, whilst he still had a lot of learning to do, especially in defence, he did have the ability to get the line moving, was better than Niki at engineering gaps both for himself and others and his tactical kicking was of a higher order.

Jim Mallinder broke his jaw playing against Agen in the European Shield and we experimented by playing Jason at full-back, a position I always felt he was highly suited to. He had had few chances on the wing because we simply weren't winning enough good quality ball but moving position gave him many more options. He made his debut there against Northampton at Franklins Gardens and he was sensational, dancing over for a try as we scored twice to take a 14-point lead in the opening minutes of the game. That stunned the home crowd and with 50-50 possession we would have skinned them that day . But Northampton got their act together, knew they could beat us up front and proceeded to win courtesy of a pack that we were unable to contain.

By Christmas, however, things were starting to unravel and I had lost confidence in everything. We were getting stuffed up front and the hookers weren't hitting our jumpers at the lineout. After we had beaten Rotherham the week before Christmas, largely due to some good work by Charlie Hodgson in the first half and some fabulous breaks by Jason after the interval – he pulled so many players out of position he was leaving holes everywhere in the Rotherham defence – Kennedy told Glenn he couldn't coach the forwards. The club needed a specialist forwards' coach, he said.

There was a board meeting in the November when we played Coventry in the Tetley's Bitter Cup. We won the game but had trailed at half time and weren't what you would call convincing. There was none of the domination up front that you would expect in games between sides from the Premiership and National One and, at the meeting, Richard Trickey was asked for his views. "Tricks" was the members' club representative on the board and he had been a very experienced second row whose Sale career had spanned two decades and who had played in the

North West Counties side that had been the first English provincial side to beat the All Blacks back in 1972.

Richard highlighted the poor performance of the props and the second rows and said he felt that Glenn, as a former back, shouldn't be coaching the forwards. He said they needed a specialist forwards' coach and Kennedy said he felt the same way. I said our coaching drills did work but added that some players weren't mentally tuned in when we played lesser opposition. The quality of some players was also debatable. At that Kennedy reiterated that we had to make the best of what we had and to make the players as good as possible. All were agreed that that wasn't the time to sign either players or coaches but to concentrate on identifying the right people for the following season. And it was pretty obvious, even at that stage, that there would be changes before long.

With Jim working with the backs it was pretty clear where the decision to seek a new forwards' coach left Glenn, but the problem was finding one, especially, one who could redress the problems at the lineout. When we played Newcastle in the cup at Kingston Park we lost so many lineouts on our own throw that Jonny Wilkinson was able to kick the ball off the park as often as he liked in the almost certain knowledge that the Falcons would get it back again.

It was fairly clear, even before the demand for a new forwards' coach, that Brian was being pressed to bring back Steve Diamond, who by that stage was player-coach at Macclesfield. Steve had clearly been doing his lobbying and he had Steve Smith as a very influential ally. Brian said he made his own decisions but he certainly listened to Steve Smith and Fran Cotton and even met Diamond, at the player's request, at Mere Golf and Country Club. After that meeting Brian rang me to say that he thought "Dimes" wasn't such a bad bloke after all and that perhaps we should get him involved again.

I told Brian that we already had three hookers in Bernard

Jackman, Joe Clark and Norm Rusk. He then said it was my decision as to whether or not we brought in Steve as a fourth senior hooker.

"No, it's not my decision Brian. It's your money and you can have what you want," I said. "Do you want to spend another £40,000?"

No, he didn't, so the decision, or so I thought, had been made.

The decision to relieve Glenn of responsibility for the forwards was, ultimately, to open the door for Steve's return. Glenn was adamant that he didn't want Dimes involved as forwards' coach. Deakin wasn't keen either because he said he didn't trust him but soon changed his stance when he did return later. I said that I thought we should give him the job. I didn't think they would get anyone better qualified and, although he had proven to be a political animal, I felt that, if he was in our little circle, we could manage him. I was going to be outvoted on this issue so left it. Jim telephoned me and suggested Dave Baldwin and my response was "over my dead body" and it was at that stage that Phil Winstanley's name came up. Phil was getting towards the end as a Premiership player but he was a key part of the staff at Heywood Road because, with his legal background, he acted as ground operations manager.

The concern was whether or not Phil wanted to take on what many saw as a poisoned chalice and whether or not the players would accept him. It doesn't always work out when a teammate suddenly takes charge of you but we tested the water with a couple of senior forwards and they said they would have no problem with Phil in the hot seat. For his part, Phil ducked and dived a little at first, and who could blame him for being wary about putting his head on the chopping block, but he gradually warmed to the idea and joined the coaching panel.

Our problems at the lineout continued, however, and it was obvious to me that they were unlikely to get much better in that department. The hookers still couldn't find their targets despite extra throwing-in sessions, plus the coaching of England's throwing-in coach. And we weren't exactly blessed with natural jumpers like a young Dave Baldwin. Neil Fletcher had a long-term injury, as did Andy Whittle. Guy Manson-Bishop, in fairness to the lad, was a converted number eight, New Zealander Scott Lines was happier in the back row too and our most effective jumper on many occasions was flanker Pete Anglesea. We didn't even have the option of Alex Sanderson at the back of the line because he was out of action with a neck injury that could have finished his career almost before it had started.

So, with things going from bad to worse and a top eight place suddenly looking a much harder target to attain, Diamond's name cropped up yet again. Kennedy said he wanted him brought in as a throwing-in coach for the hookers. Glenn and Deakin weren't happy about it and Phil was totally opposed to the idea but it wasn't going to be their decision, as Kennedy graphically emphasised when I attended a meeting with several members of the board, including Blackhurst and Deakin. He walked in and said, "I want Diamond in as throwing-in coach, just to work initially with the hookers and then later with the full lineout, and if any of your management don't like it then they know where the door is."

I could see trouble ahead. Phil didn't want Dimes involved and I could understand that. He was adamant that he would only allow him to work with the hookers but I knew that wasn't going to work. If Dimes was back then it was logical that he would work with all the forwards in developing a lineout strategy. In the end Phil went to see Deakin, who promised to speak to Kennedy about the situation. Two hours later Deakin called Phil into his office and said he wasn't going to approach Kennedy on the issue because he didn't think it was good for the club. Phil, who had steam coming out of his ears by that time, said that if Deaks wouldn't speak to him then he would go to speak to the man himself.

Deaks told him he couldn't do that but Phil went ahead anyway, telephoned Kennedy and was immediately invited round to the majestic Swettenham Hall for a chat. Phil told him he wasn't happy about the Diamond situation and Kennedy assured him he just wanted him involved at the lineouts and said Phil should manage him as he saw fit. He looked Phil in the eye and gave him his word that Diamond wouldn't take over his role unless Phil promoted him into it. Not long after that Phil resigned and Diamond stepped straight into his shoes.

That wasn't the end of it so far as Phil was concerned. When he agreed to take the job in the first place he had been given an assurance by Deakin that, if it didn't work out, he would continue in his ground operations role whilst being free to go back to playing junior rugby at the weekend. He thought they could manage without Phil on match days, which they had been doing throughout anyway because he was invariably involved with the playing squad and you can't play or sit on the bench and have people coming up to you with ground operational problems. Initially they reneged on that arrangement but relented later and Phil went back to Orrell as player-coach. I find it quite amazing that James Wade was forced to give up his playing career because Kennedy wanted him at games but the ground operations manager and Wayne Morris, the community development manager, were free to play for other clubs at the weekend.

Although Glenn was still technically the head coach, Jim was working with the backs whilst Phil, and later Steve Diamond, worked with the forwards. That left Glenn hanging around in the middle of the field holding a clipboard and making notes. It was difficult for the players. They were struggling on the pitch after a season that had started so promisingly and had gradually lost all confidence in Glenn as a coach. It was a case of *deja vu* when Bryan Redpath, the most senior player, came to see me to say there was a problem. The players had held a meeting that resulted in a vote of no confidence in the coach.

I said I needed to know what was going on and attended a meeting with them at Cottons Hotel, near my home at Knutsford – no, the hotel is not part of the Cotton-Smith empire – and had also told Deakin that we had a problem which, with hindsight, I perhaps shouldn't have done, just to keep it amongst the playing side of the club. The complaints were that Glenn was never about the club and never spoke to players individually. They said he just came up with excuses when they were dropped and the players had to go to either Jim or myself for a straight answer as to why they had been left out. Jim was well respected by the players and they knew that I wasn't one for mincing my words and wouldn't duck an issue.

Word got back to Kennedy who decided that Glenn should speak to each player individually every week. It was rumoured that Marty Hulme had told Ian Blackhurst and Deakin that Glenn wasn't spending enough time with the players and Marty and Glenn had something of a heart-to-heart whilst the rest of us left the office.

Deakin and I had a meeting with Glenn and Deakin told him that he was a good coach and that he would back him to the hilt. When Glenn left the room, Kennedy walked in and said, "Right Adie, what do we do. Do we get rid of him?"

Kennedy acts as though he is running a double glazing company, which is more his forte. If your salesman isn't selling many windows then you get rid of him but running a sports company is different and you simply can't get rid of a hooker, for instance, just because he isn't playing well when he has a three-year contract. I asked what the point of that would be and Deakin reminded him that it would cost a fortune to pay him off. At that point Kennedy said he wanted Glenn in the office every day from 8am until 6pm. To what purpose he never said.

Glenn was also removed from his post as head coach and put in charge of recruitment. The good old sideways promotion to a virtually non-existent job. I suppose the hope was that he would be so pissed off that he would simply walk away from the club. But would you, if you were involved in a classic case of constructive dismissal?

By that stage I had lost all faith in the club. When Kennedy arrived I really did believe the club had a chance of a new beginning. It would take a few years to achieve what everyone wanted but Kennedy was used to quick results. He wasn't getting them, he was spending rather more money than he had bargained for and he wasn't a happy bunny. There was no stability and, so far as I was concerned, I was merely doing as I was told. I was under no illusions as to what lay ahead for me. You didn't have to be a space scientist to work out that heads would roll. Mine, I knew, would be one of the first on to the block. I had already had a call from someone in the know telling me to watch my back. He had heard on the network that Deakin had said he didn't think he needed either a full-time director of rugby or rugby manager.

If I had any doubts they were confirmed when I had a meeting with Deakin in his office. Darren Cornwell, the finance director, was also present and we were talking about how much money Marty Hulme was on and what perks he was getting. When Darren said he would like a cup of tea, I offered to make it. See what we had been reduced to. Glenn was sitting looking at the wall from 8-6 and I was the tea boy!

As I left the room I didn't close the door behind me properly and heard Deakin say that I was on far too much money for managing the team. It wasn't long after that that I had a telephone call at training to say that Ian Blackhurst wanted to see myself, Glenn and Marty in the office. As we sat awaiting our fate I told the other two that I knew exactly what was about to happen. "He is sacking me first, then Glenn and then he will make you director of rugby, Marty," I said.

Marty went beetroot red, told me not to be so stupid, and walked out of the office. Glenn asked me if I was being serious and I said the scenario, if it turned out like that, wouldn't surprise me one little bit.

That hadn't been the first time I had got a blush of embarrassment out of Marty. When he arrived at the club Ryan McDermott was the physio but we had a problem and he was relieved of his services. Marty said he would bring in a girl from Wigan called Andrea on a temporary basis but he had another girl in mind for the job, called Michelle. Obviously Andrea was hoping to impress sufficiently to be offered the job on a full-time basis and it was decided not to tell her that she wouldn't be getting the job until a week before her temporary contract was due to expire. The job of telling her was going to be down to me, even though the decision of who to appoint was very much Marty's baby. We were relying on his recommendation so you can imagine my surprise when Andrea suddenly burst into my office in tears and accused me of appointing Michelle without telling her.

Later, when she was treating players, they told her it would have been Marty's decision, rather than mine, because he had been on about Michelle for weeks. Andrea came back to apologise because she knew then that it hadn't been my decision. A few minutes later I walked into the kitchen and Marty was there, with Andrea, and was in the process of telling her he had had nothing to do with the decision and it had all been down to me. I just looked at him and he went that funny colour again. I tell you, I wouldn't trust that bloke as far as I could throw him.

I was summoned down the corridor to Deakin's office and Peter was coming out through the door. He saw me and, without looking up, ducked into the marketing office. He certainly wouldn't look me in the eye. Once in the office I sat down opposite Ian and the situation was slightly unreal because, not many days earlier, he had telephoned me at home to see if he could pop round to watch the England v Scotland match on Sky television with Apollo Perelini and another friend. We all watched the match, had a few beers and now here we were facing each other across a desk. I was waiting for him to put on his little black cap before pronouncing sentence.

"How do you think things are going," he asked?

"Not very well. The players say they have no confidence in the coach, as you are aware of. We are losing games and confidence is low."

"So," he said, "I need to make some changes. It's not personal. It was a difficult decision but I think it's best if you resign."

"Do you want me to do it now?"

"Were you expecting this?"

"I have been expecting it for some time."

"We'll make sure you get your month's salary."

"Hang on," I said. "Under the terms of my old contract, which still applies because you have never given me a new one, I am due six months."

"Well, if that's what your contract says, we will honour it."

I was reminded of the day Brian Kennedy treated me rather like a schoolboy by summoning me to his office to be presented with an office diary. He even wrote a message in it that read, "Adrian, You have great potential as a director of Sale and, like us all, you need to personally develop your managerial skill.

"One such skill is diligent follow through and organization. The greatest tool for this is a diary. All contacts, appointments and tasks recorded in one book. It's your corporate Bible! Set the task of the day and, before you leave the office, cross out all tasks completed and carry forward to the next day all outstanding tasks. This, you will find, will improve your efficiencies by 80 per cent plus. Use it and keep it with you at all times.

"You're a great lad and a real grafter. You deserve great success. Thanks for your hard work over the last few months. Build the foundation of the business – our second to none Academy."

I wasn't too sure how to take it. Perhaps he intended it as a job reference.

I had always got on well with Ian and I don't know whether he relished the role of hatchet man. He said it was a purely business decision and added that they had to be seen to be doing something in view of the season's results. I was tempted to say that if they had left things as they had been then none of this may have been necessary. It was ironic that Kennedy, who had been so determined to bring in a head coach despite my asking him to give Jim Mallinder and Steve Diamond a chance, had now ended up in exactly the position he had started out from, with Jim and Steve in charge.

And that was it. I walked out of the office and Deakin was coming the other way down the corridor. He just put his head down and didn't speak as he hurried past me. I went into my office, where Glenn was chatting to Alex Sanderson, and I picked up my keys, told the guys I was popping out, and cleared off. In some ways it was a relief because the whole place was such a shambles that it had become difficult doing the job I was paid to do. There were too many people dipping fingers into the pie instead of leaving people to get on with their jobs. There were also too many people who felt they were qualified to do your job for you and I had had enough of it.

After I had left the ground, Ian called a meeting of all the players to tell them what had happened. That's when it was announced that Jim and Steve would be in charge of the team with Glenn concentrating on recruitment. Pete Anglesea had the bottle to pose the question, "Was Adie pushed?" The answer was that I had been man enough to resign because things hadn't been going well and thought it was best for both myself and the club if I went. Which, of course, was a load of old bollocks.

My departure and the metaphorical castration of Glenn left Deakin where he wanted to be. Firmly in charge of just about everything at Heywood Road except, when you are dealing with Kennedy, you are never really in charge.

Glenn's world had been torn apart. He put a brave face on it but he knew it was all over too. He went back to New Zealand on holiday and the date of his return was agreed with Deakin. He was going back for a lengthy spell but the idea was that he would do some recruiting. He lined up Brendan Laney, a centre who would have been available once the season had finished in New Zealand, and was also targeting former All Blacks skipper Todd Blackadder. I don't know how those negotiations were going but it didn't matter anyway because the tone of the e-mails from Deakin started to change and he was eventually ordered back to Heywood Road.

Ordered back to do what? Clear his desk. The club had a problem because Glenn had the same agent that John Mitchell had used, Manchester lawyer Simon Cohen, who knew how to look after his clients. Sale did make an offer that wasn't far from what Glenn would have been prepared to accept but that was then taken off the table and, at the time of writing, I gather it was a case of, "See you in court."

Before I left Sale the club had got itself into a terrible mess over player contracts. I was told to tell players whose contracts were due to run out that they were playing for their contracts but it was then decided to start telling players they wouldn't be offered a new contract. The time to do that is at the end of the season, not when there are weeks still to go. The result was that some players like Guy Manson-Bishop and Matt Moore played no part in the last weeks of the season when their presence could have been useful. What made it worse was that Deakin was getting himself involved.

I recall seeing Steve Davidson. He had been told he was playing for a new contract. No decision had been made as to whether or not Steve would be offered one but when we had the meeting with him Deaks told him not to worry as he would get a contract. He had also told Guy that he would get a contract . The night before we played Saracens at Vicarage Road he told Guy that they wanted him to stay at the club and that he wasn't playing for a contract. Instead, he was playing to see how much they were going to pay him.

Then, two weeks later, he called Guy into his office and told him that his contract wasn't going to be renewed. He was one of a number given false promises and told me that rather than help him find another club, he was given bad references and it was suggested that he was a bad influence. Guy was released and told that they didn't want him around any more. "I don't know why but I was the only one to be given a formal letter telling me that," he told me at the time.

Rob Appleyard was another eased out, together with Andy Morris, who was also strung along by Deakin. "Mozzer" had a whole series of meetings with Deakin and was also told he was playing well and brought a lot to the team. Deaks said they didn't want to let guys like Mozzer go, which left him feeling that, as one of the longest serving players in the side, he had a future at the club. He was to discover that that wasn't the case at all.

Deakin kept telling him that he would "sort it" but, when the offer was finally made, it was derisory. Mozzer is a very successful businessman and said that if he had treated his company's employees like that then all hell would have broken loose.

Many players were moaning that they didn't know where they stood. That's hardly conducive to getting the best out of them. And when you know there is no place for you the following season, where is the incentive to pull out all the stops?

I was in negotiations with an agent regarding a player we wanted to sign for the new season. I agreed a figure with the agent to sign the player but Deaks said he wanted to be involved in the contract negotiations, something Brian Kennedy reiterated to me at a meeting at his Latium HQ. Brian's reasoning was that Peter could sell the club better than I could. That was another indication that I was on the way out but the irony is that the player ended up with a better offer from Deakin. So smart arse ended up costing the club more than necessary but good luck to the player and his agent on that one. No wonder his agent left Deakin's office with a broad smile on his face. By that stage I simply couldn't be arsed any more and I know Deaks was so worried at the prospect of losing Alex Sanderson that he tied him up with what was a fantastic offer for a young player who had yet to win a cap and had a question mark over his fitness following the operation to repair a neck injury.

The other aspect about Deakin is that he wasn't popular with the players. Many didn't like his style and he was probably wise to surround himself with former buddies from rugby league. Like a lot of bullshitters, what you see isn't necessarily what you get. Jean Swales, who had run the office since before the game went professional and was the one person who really did have her finger on the pulse of the club, quit because of the way he spoke to her. So he wasn't all charm and bonhomie.

I may not have much regard for the man but I was still sorry to hear of his recent illness, a brain tumour, which must be a great concern for himself and his family. You don't wish that sort of thing on anyone and I hope he makes a full recovery. But the fact is that he was one of those instrumental in putting me out of work and, because of his illness and with a certain irony, the club was left without an experienced full-time rugby club administrator at a time when a lot of contractual work still had to be done and when a fan recruitment drive, an area where Deakin is supposedly a master, was desperately needed.

Peter certainly had a panic when, soon after I had been shown the door, Sky TV asked me to do an interview with them prior to Sale's match against London Irish at Heywood Road. He telephoned Sky demanding to know why they were interviewing me and the producer reminded him that they interviewed who the hell they liked.

Maybe, but Deaks wasn't going to let them interview me at Heywood Road, which was irrelevant because they did the filming at my home. I suspect he was panicking about what I might say but that's not surprising. Having been on the inside I was in the right position to ruffle a few feathers.

I could have been very mischievous but have settled instead for simply telling what I felt was relevant to my story.

Epilogue

AT THE TIME of writing, my own future is still undecided. I have been looking at a few options and have acted as an agent for a number of players as well as establishing a recruitment agency that specializes in finding staff for sporting clubs, whether involved in the playing of the game or in its administration. Deep down, and despite all that has happened to me, I still have a desire for a hands-on involvement in rugby. I could hardly go back to the Inland Revenue: in any case, I'm not as fit as I once was and doubt if I could stand the pace of all the office parties.

Whether or not I will continue to have an involvement in rugby remains to be seen but I hope that, so far as union is concerned, we may now have a stabilizing period of peace between the Premiership clubs and the RFU. The game certainly couldn't have carried on as it had since going open when progress was repeatedly impeded by too many powerful people championing their own separate agendas.

Hopefully, clubs will concentrate rather more on player development than overseas recruitment although, whilst promotion and relegation remain on the agenda at professional level, the effects of that may be felt later rather than sooner. I don't know how the authorities will find a long-term solution to the thorny promotion and relegation issue but I campaigned during my time at Sale for the scrapping of movement between National One and the Premiership. That may seem tough on aspiring National One sides but it is patently obvious that few will ever be strong enough, either financially or in terms of playing power, to realistically take the step up. Cecil Duckworth has invested millions in Worcester, providing a fine stadium in the process. But, despite those millions, the Midlands' club has never risen above the also-ran stage, having to watch sides like Bedford, Rotherham and Leeds Tykes beat them to the promotion punch. Both Bedford and Rotherham have already sampled the yo-yo reward for winning promotion one year and suffering relegation 12 months later and I just hope my old pal Phil Davies doesn't experience the same fate with Leeds in their first year in the Premiership.

A period of stability at the top end of the game would enable clubs to take the long view and bring on their own players. Thankfully, there are signs now that young British players are starting to emerge in numbers in the Premiership and some have already gone on to play for England and the British Lions. There are many more very exciting young players currently working their way through the ranks, so it would be a shame if their progress was impeded by more of our commonwealth cousins seeking a pension.

Some people say that, if you take away promotion and relegation, you rob ambitious clubs of motivation and leave Premiership players in a comfort zone. I don't buy that argument because most of the so called ambitious clubs don't have the playing arsenal or the finances to survive with the Leicesters of this world and I don't know of any Premiership club owners who would settle for being rubbished by the rest every season. If you haven't picked up the message already, we are dealing with serious egos. But those with intelligence would see the wisdom in building a team on the Busby Babes principle. There might be a few bumpy years but, once youngsters who have been together since their teens start to gain real experience, there is the very good chance that they will provide the backbone of a successful side with enough gas in the tank to last for several seasons. But, whilst we have been trying to achieve this situation, money has been wasted at a frightening rate as clubs, backed by wealthy owners, have tried to buy their way to success.

Nigel Wray must have thought he had scooped the big one when he landed Francois Pienaar for Saracens, fresh from his triumph in leading South Africa to the World title. But, apart from a national cup win, we are still waiting for high spending Sarries to start dominating the English scene. That role has been left to Leicester, who soon decided that former Australian World Cup winning coach Bob Dwyer wasn't the man for them and haven't looked back since replacing him with Dean Richards. There is a culture about Leicester rugby club and "Deano" has been as big a part of that as you are likely to get. And his first lieutenant has been John Wells, his former back row colleague and one of the game's quiet guys who just gets on with the job of ensuring the club he played for stays at the top. Two guys who fully understand what makes Leicester tick.

Pity that their colleague Peter Wheeler can't see where rugby union's strength lies. Instead he, who knows as much about rugby league as my Aunt Fanny, thought it would be a great idea to invite some of the top 13-a-side clubs to play in the Premiership. He clearly learned no lessons from the cross-code games between Bath and Wigan Warriors that, despite Bath's limitations in a rugby league environment, proved conclusively that rugby league forwards are totally ill-equipped to play the 15-a-side game. The same could also be said for a lot of half-backs because the two games are so very different. Unlike "Wheelbrace", I know because I have played both games.

Wheeler's ramblings apart, the only real concession to outside influences (with the exception of a high-earning "Freddie" Tuilagi from rugby league) at Welford Road last season, when the Tigers copped the lot, was versatile Aussie Pat Howard, one of the few from the southern hemisphere to have been worth every penny. Joel Stransky did a reasonable job too when the game went open but whether or not fellow countryman Tim Horan will prove as valuable to Saracens remains to be seen. Reading between the lines, the Watford-based club has hardly been a happy ship in the Leicester mould and one hears rumours of Pienaar's clashes with both senior players and administrators like Mark Evans, who took himself off to struggling Harlequins and ended up with the European Shield, thus more silverware in the cabinet than Francois achieved last season. Again, I believe much of the difficulty comes down to the old culture question and I suspect that Pienaar is a very driven man who had a problem coping with the realisation that not everyone in his squad was motivated in quite the same way.

We had that scenario at Sale Sharks when I was there. New Zealander John Mitchell was, technically, an excellent coach and a major influence on the field – when he was allowed to play by the Home Office. But once he was confined to managing and coaching, and when things started to go wrong, his man-management skills, in an environment that was very different to the one he was used to back home, let him down. I suspect Pienaar fell down in that same area and one hears that, like my good friend Peter Deakin, he thinks he can do everyone else's job as well as his own.

Those great All Blacks John Gallagher and Zinzan Brooke arrived at Harlequins with trumpets blaring but the club struggled. A bloody good job too because, at the time, it took some of the pressure off my own club, Sale Sharks. In the end Zinzan, an undoubted rugby talent, couldn't do it as a player any more and it will be interesting to see who will claim credit for the sudden revival, once he had gone, that resulted in Quins winning the European Shield and clinching a place in the more prestigious

European Cup. Was that a case of Zinzan's efforts finally bearing fruit? Or merely the influence of Mark Evans following his move from Saracens, where he had overseen that club's rise to the Premiership in the days before Pienaar, his fellow South African Alan Zondagh, Aussies Tim Horan and Michael Lynagh and French stars Alain Penaud, Thomas Casteignede and Philippe Sella climbed on board the Wraymobile?

All this time, Bath were continuing to make an impression but under the guiding hand of Andy Robinson, in his pre-England coaching days, and later Jon Callard: both good blokes who had more than served their time at The Rec as players. The club came through a difficult period when they started to fray at the edges and made life even more difficult for themselves by agreeing to a fly-on-the-wall documentary. They emerged as one of England's genuinely strong clubs without too much help from outsiders even though they looked extremely wobbly at the start of the current campaign.

The problem, of course, is that the game is bedevilled by owners who often know little about the top end of the game, but think they do, and who seem to be mesmerised by any well known name from overseas. Tom Walkinshaw, who tried to lead a breakaway of the top clubs not long ago, brought in Frenchman Philippe St Andre to run the rugby at Kingsholm. No disrespect to Philippe but, if one club has a culture that is worth points on the board, it has to be Gloucester, and, when it gets to the stage that the locals have to start learning French in order to communicate, you have to worry where it might all end.

Yet local boys who would die to pull on the cherry-and-white shirt have found themselves playing second fiddle to big names from outside and Philippe's scouting sorties invariably involve a cross Channel trip. Having played at Gloucester for both Cardiff and Sale Sharks, I believe you mess with the peculiar Gloucester culture at your peril.

I have to come clean, of course, and admit that I can't stand the

French. I hate the place, the people and, most of all, the food. We put pellets down in the garden to kill the things they seem to think is a delicacy. Yuk.

Brian Kennedy, the Scottish window magnate whose rugby claim to fame is that he rescued Sale Sharks from oblivion, is another owner who thought he knew all about the game. When he arrived at Heywood Road his stated priority was to find a new head coach because he didn't feel that the two coaches who had kept Sale in the Premiership, Jim Mallinder and Steve Diamond, were up to the job. With a certain irony, he went out and brought in yet another New Zealander, Glenn Ross. After less than a year he wanted him out and, guess what, as I outlined in a previous chapter, Jim and Steve were back in harness, the latter having been discarded by Kennedy months earlier.

Bristol dallied with Bob Dwyer for a time, as did Leicester; Dick Best and Ged Glynn were ousted at London Irish to make way for South African Brendan Venter; Ireland, like Wales, decided they needed a New Zealander, Warren Gartland, to coach their national side; and my first senior club, Cardiff, overlooked the claims of Welsh coaches to bring in a South African.

At the same time clubs have brought in average players from the southern hemisphere and, having got them here, have often used them at the expense of homegrown talent that would have cost considerably less. I know because, for a variety of reasons that I explained earlier in this epistle, I went down that road as a director of rugby. The simple truth is that local talent wasn't always being given the chance it deserves because the structure of the game meant that less well established clubs like Sale Sharks had to put Premiership survival ahead of longer term success. It's no good developing a great nursery if, by the time the youngsters are ready to dip a toe in the water, the club is no longer playing Premiership rugby.

If the Rugby Football Union had sorted out the English game when it went professional and listened to Fran Cotton — I can't believe I've just said that — then a great deal of money might have been saved or, at least, put to better use. Fran wanted the country's leading players to be contracted to England, whilst playing for regional teams in a British, or European Super League, to provide a better development structure for young English players. The problem I had as director of rugby at Sale was that I had to avoid relegation as a priority. That meant playing average players with experience, often from overseas, rather than bringing on young English qualified players. You simply couldn't afford to get relegated because that spelt financial disaster and the top clubs, collectively, pressed for an end to promotion and relegation for that very reason but ran into opposition from the rest of the game. In any case, the gulf between Premiership clubs and the rest in England is so huge that the euphoria of winning promotion from National One doesn't last long. On recent evidence the promotion spot is almost a poisoned chalice.

At Sale, we were as guilty as the rest when it came to spending money on overseas players but our development set-up was in its infancy and promising players weren't coming through in sufficient numbers. So we were lured into buying in from overseas because we were desperate to hang on to Premiership status but, with hindsight in nearly every case, we could probably have found English players who would have done just as good a job for a lot less money. We ended up with a catalogue of players who simply didn't do it for us.

Janneman Brand was a classic case. The back row came to us straight from the Super 12s and had a big reputation in South Africa. Yet Janneman was a complete disaster and was totally anonymous when it started getting wet, which does tend to happen a good deal in the UK. Dion O'Cuinneagain was another South African who failed to live up to his reputation. We spent a lot of money on Dion but his head-on defence wasn't up to it, yet Ireland, incredibly, made him their captain – until they discovered his deficiencies. What, you might ask, were Ireland doing picking as captain a mild-mannered and very gentlemanly South African in the first place? You can't tell me there wasn't a typically fiery Irishman capable of leading the green hordes into battle.

What we need to ask is whether or not we are being misled by the Super 12s. Is it really the high quality competition it is reputed to be? Is it really better than the Zurich Premiership or, dare one even suggest it, even as good as the Premiership? Could the answer be that the game is refereed very differently Down Under and very well packaged, with the emphasis on spectacle at the expense of rugby's basic ingredients and in contravention of the laws of the game relating to how it is played? I found it very interesting that Janneman Brand came to Sale straight from the Super 12s, was found out to be not good enough for the Zurich Premiership but, immediately he was released by us, was offered another Super 12s contract. He is not on his own either.

The people running rugby union didn't just go overboard about overseas players. As I said at the outset, they suddenly discovered rugby league. England, to be followed inevitably by the Welsh, came up with the idea of "buying" rugby league players and Jason Robinson was meant to be the first in a series of signings to go straight into the national squad. Great message to the union players already there but, quite apart from that, the whole idea was flawed. England were going to pay half of Jason's wages with the balance paid by the Premiership club he signed up for. In Jason's case it was only ever going to be Sale Sharks because, even though he was keen to take on the challenge that rugby union presented, he is such a devoted family man that he wasn't prepared to uproot his wife and children to move to another part of the country.

Not surprisingly, the rest of the Premiership clubs blew their tops when they heard that Jason was joining Sale and that England were planning to pick up half the bill. They immediately threatened to boycott my old club and, in the end, it was owner

Brian Kennedy who was left to foot the entire bill. That was something the canny Scot hadn't bargained for.

The staggering thing is that people at Twickenham, some of whom wouldn't know a Warrior or a Rhino if they fell over them in the street, were suddenly prepared to set aside millions of pounds to buy players unproven in the game. It's no good pointing to the success of Jason Robinson because he is a one-off. He can do things that other players simply can't aspire to, whatever code they play. There aren't any more like him in rugby league.

There are some very talented players but they are two very different games and I can't think of many who could make the switch as smoothly as Jason did. Yet, to some people in rugby union, the mere fact that a person has been involved in a game that was once vilified seems to qualify them for superstar status. Phil Larder suddenly became some sort of defensive coaching Messiah in the England camp and that opened the door to a whole string of retired rugby league players being signed up to teach top rugby union sides how to defend. What a complete load of old bollocks.

Larder's England call brought a few chuckles along the M62 corridor because Phil, even though he once coached Great Britain, hardly covered himself in glory in the other code. He was in charge when the RL version of the Lions toured New Zealand in 1996, which was memorable only for a number of unwanted landmarks, including the worst-ever record by British Lions in Kiwi country: one draw and five defeats in the six tour matches. Which meant, of course, that the GB boys were whitewashed in the three-Test series.

Admittedly, he took Widnes to a Challenge Cup Final when I was there but that was his first season in charge and the club already had some great players that he inherited. "Phyllis", as he was known, was later sacked by both Keighley Cougars and Sheffield Eagles, hardly two of rugby league's big hitters.

Larder had expected to be Britain's coach in 1994 against

Australia but is said to have turned it down because he didn't want an overseas man, New Zealander Graham Lowe, as part of the coaching set up. Interesting, then, that he was apparently perfectly happy to go on the last rugby union Lions tour to Australia as part of Graham Henry's coaching team, his commendable principles clearly thrown out of the window. So what changed Phil?

And what on earth was Ellery Hanley doing in the England camp? Who needs these guys when you've got the likes of Brian Ashton and Andy Robinson coaching England? And don't talk to me about this multitude of coaches – there must be more coaches than players when England train – helping to turn England into the strongest side in the northern hemisphere and into serious World Cup challengers. The reason England look strong at present is not down to all these unnecessary specialist coaches that have been brought in. It is down to the simple fact that England currently has most of the best players in the northern hemisphere, which is galling for me to admit as a Welshman, and a growing strength in depth that must be the envy of most rugby-playing nations.

The Lions even took Dave Alred along on recent tours as kicking coach. A bit excessive, don't you think? After all, Neil Jenkins was a world class goalkicker before he went on any Lions tours and I don't recall Grant Fox, Barry John, Phil Bennett and a host of others needing someone to hold their hands. Jonny Wilkinson is a world class kicker too, hardly surprising with his natural talent and with Rob Andrew as his boss at club level, but he missed the odd one or two in Australia that might have made a difference. Perhaps he hadn't been spending enough time with Mr Alred.

The next thing we know we will have old scrum-halves like Steve Smith going on future tours to make sure Rob Howley, Matt Dawson and Austin Healey know how to put the ball in straight and pass it off either hand from the base of a scrum. I know how to tie bootlaces, so maybe there will be a role for me next time around.

I'm not saying that good coaches can't improve both players and teams but, when you have forwards with the vast experience of Martin Johnson, Lawrence Dallaglio, Jason Leonard, Richard Hill and Neil Back, you wouldn't have to be Einstein to mould them into a formidable unit. A coach is usually only as good as his players and good players have the experience to change tactics during the course of a game when the coach's influence is zero because he's sitting in the stand biting his nails. I know, I've done it – sat in the stand chewing my fingers – and I didn't have players of Johnson's calibre to bail me out, more's the pity!

We had a classic example of the "he's from Rugby League so he must be brilliant" culture at Sale. When Howard Thomas was chief executive there he called me into his office in a state of high excitement to ask what I thought of Barrie-John Mather. He seemed a bit disappointed when I said, "Not a lot," but, despite the reservations of myself and director of rugby John Mitchell, the club went ahead and signed B-J from Castleford for what I considered to be a ridiculous sum. Clive Woodward clearly had the same high opinion of B-J because he picked him to play for England at a time when he couldn't get into our first team. And we were struggling near the foot of the Premiership table at the time so that, perhaps, says it all.

Don't get me wrong, B-J is a great lad and a good player but I never saw anything to suggest he should be playing in the centre for England. He was also even more laid back than me, which is saying something, and used to take everything in his stride. When we told him we were letting him go he didn't throw a tantrum like some of the players. He just nodded sagely and said, "That's cool, speak to my agent."

So good luck to B-J if he has boosted his bank balance with cash that would have paid the combined wages of several players who were making the Sale team ahead of him. I may be barking up the wrong tree but bearing in mind Howard's family links at that time with Steve Smith, Steve's links with Fran Cotton and, in turn, Fran's links with Woodward, one has to wonder whose bright idea it was to lure B-J from league in the first place.

Sale had a perfectly good fitness coach in Lancashire lad Andy Clarke but Jason Robinson was much enamoured of Marty Hulme, an Aussie who was working with Wigan Warriors, and suddenly he was in and Andy was out, even though Kennedy was having to pay the Aussie far, far more than he had paid Andy and considerably more than he was paying me as director of rugby or the coaches, come to that. I suspect that no more than two or three players were on bigger bucks than Smarty Marty. But then he was from rugby league, and an Aussie to boot, so just had to be good, didn't he? Just like Peter Deakin, who was lured from Warrington Wolves to become chief executive. Trouble is that Peter, whose serious rugby playing experience amounted to less than a handful of rugby league games for Oldham, thought he could do my job as well as his own, so I was out on my ear. What did I know, I had only picked up 27 Welsh rugby union caps, won eleven more international caps in rugby league, figured in World Cups in both codes and had played for what was, at the time I was there, the best club side in Europe, Cardiff.

I can't speak for what Cardiff is like these days but it saddens me that they too, like Wales, have turned to the southern hemisphere and ignored the claims of experienced ex-players and coaches. People like Phil Davies and Paul Turner or, for that matter, myself, who at least understand the nature of the beast and have gained experience in what most people accept as the toughest club league in world rugby.

My senior playing career spanned almost two decades and I have seen many changes in that time. In some respects the game has moved away from the people. Corporate hospitality rules at international level and is starting to have more of an influence at senior club level too. That has made it more difficult for the ordinary fan to get international tickets but has, at the same time, enabled entrepreneurs, not to mention club officials, to make a lot of money out of their sale.

The demand for tickets is extraordinary and I have also made a bob or two out of ticket sales over the years. I remember two or three of us applying for tickets at Sale, selling them at a nice profit, and having a splendid weekend away on the proceeds, with not a rugby ball in sight.

There is a certain irony in a situation where the rugby authorities are trying to stop tickets ending up on the black market but in recent years they appear to have done little to help the thousands of junior clubs around the country that have struggled to keep heads above water in a difficult economic climate for amateur sporting clubs. So, what happens? An increasing number of junior clubs sell their allocation and use the money to run their operation. The way it works is that a company will "sponsor" a club and, in return, will receive international tickets. That company will probably have nothing to do with the club concerned and might not even know where it is.

I was offered six tickets by a junior club for each of the England games last season. In return the club wanted £2,500 – plus the face value of the tickets. Deals like that go on all the time and the situation is the same in Wales. Then you have the "entrepreneurs" – no names, no pack drill – who arrive at the bigger clubs waving wads of cash. Those boys will pay serious money. Which probably explains why you can have a holiday in Spain for what it costs to attend an international game with a little hospitality thrown in. Some people clearly have money to burn and, whilst those people exist, there are those who will say, "Thanks very much."

That's just the way it is. And why pretend otherwise? When I embarked on writing my life story, I was determined to be candid, whomever it might upset. I won't name names and land any of the lads in it, but I will tell it how it is. Anyone who pays over their hard-earned money to buy the autobiography of a rugby player – or any sportsman, for that matter – deserves to get the unvarnished truth; not some PR whitewash like so many of these books are.

Above all, to two great games that afforded me opportunities I would have been otherwise denied, may I also say, "Thank you." I have had a somewhat chequered career, with its share of triumphs and disappointments. And, yes, if I had my time all over again I might do some things differently.

But I wouldn't have missed the trip for all the world.

Appendix

HAVING REACHED A crossroads in my rugby career – my playing days were well and truly over and my spell in management had come to an end — I decided to look back over the years and, like a lot of players who reach the autobiographical stage, thought about picking my perfect team. The temptation is to concentrate on finding the best team of an era but I thought it would be more meaningful to pick a team, in each of the two codes in which I played, selecting only players with whom I had taken the field over the years.

My Ideal Rugby Union Team

15 MIKE RAYER A good defensive player and excellent all round footballer, although he never got the recognition he deserved.

14 IEUAN EVANS He was simply electric and could make things happen in games. A tremendous finisher.

13 MARK RING The player I have known longest. "Ringo" read the game well and his natural cockiness was matched only by his versatility.

12 BLEDDYN BOWEN Another outside half who was very similar to "Ringo" in terms of talent. A well balanced player who was great to play outside.

11 DAVID REES Had to bring an Englishman into the side. Reesy is similar to Ieuan – very bubbly, very quick and very strong.

10 JONATHAN DAVIES There shouldn't be any reason to say anything about the little fellow. Another class act from the old Welsh fly-half conveyor belt that has since dried up.

9 TERRY HOLMES A good service and a powerful, committed scrum-half with the ability to play with the effectiveness of a back row when required.

1 JEFF WHITEFOOT My old Cardiff teammate. A big, strong scrummager who wouldn't take crap from anyone. A good bloke to have around, whether on the field or off it.

2 ALAN PHILLIPS "Thumper" was a typical "chopsy" hooker who spent most of his career playing just outside me rather than in the pack!

3 DAI YOUNG First capped in the 1987 World Cup and, at the time of writing, the Welsh captain. Made a difficult but successful move, for a prop, to the other code, largely because he had the skills.

4 JOHN FOWLER Some people may think John a surprise choice but when he was on form he was just the sort of player you wanted in your side. He got around the park, hit rucks hard and won lineout ball. Couldn't ask any more.

5 ROB NORSTER Simply the best second row I have ever played with.

6 ROWLAND PHILLIPS Immensely strong with good hands and tackles like a train. He was also a great nuisance factor.

7 GARETH ROBERTS A typical openside. Gareth was quick, always very fit and would invariably be the first to the breakdown.

8 JOHN SCOTT My old Cardiff skipper had an aura about him. He seemed to do everything at half pace but did it all so very effectively.

My Ideal Rugby League Team

1 IESTYN HARRIS A brilliant all round footballer who could play in several positions in RL. Will be a great loss to the game but should be welcomed in Wales with open arms.

2 GERALD CORDLE Another old Cardiff buddy who made the transition to the 13-a-side code well. Both quick and strong.

3 DARREN WRIGHT My centre at Widnes. Defensively he was superb and, in attack, he was deceptively quick for a big lad.

4 SCOTT GIBBS Big, strong and takes a lot of handling. Again, a great success in both codes.

5 ANTHONY SULLIVAN Apart from Martin Offiah, probably one of the quickest players I have ever seen.

6 JONATHAN DAVIES There was no way I could have left him out of this side either. Quite simply a class act.

7 BOBBY GOULDING Had his problems off the pitch but when on song there was nobody better in the game.

8 ESENE FAIMALO Very quick for a big man and he will run and tackle all day for you.

9 KIERAN CUNNINGHAM Simply the best hooker in Rugby League. Game should be grateful he turned down the code switch.

10 TERRY O'CONNOR Just like Esene, Terry was a big lad who would run all day. A guy who does the hard yards better than most.

11 PAUL MORIARTY Big, quick, hard, good hands. Another rugby union forward who adapted well after switching codes.

12 EMOSI KOLOTO Career ended through injury but he was absolutely awesome when fully fit.

13 LES HOLLIDAY A Widnes teammate. A hard lad who read the game well and he also had a good kicking game.